When I read *Forgiving the Catholic Church*, I was struck by how Bill was so powerfully able to lay bare the trauma he experienced at the hands of a priest, a trauma that negatively rippled through every facet of his life and affected everyone who was connected to him. I was also deeply moved by how Bill was able to use his inner strength coupled with the love and support of others, including most significantly and ironically that of another priest, to eventually forgive the Catholic Church.

During my forty years of working in the mental health field, I have not come across another book that seems so exceptionally capable of serving as both a personal and professional tool for the treatment of trauma victims.

—Richard Keil,
Licensed Clinical Social Worker (Ill)

FORGIVING THE CATHOLIC CHURCH

FINDING JUSTICE FOR THE ABUSED AND ABUSERS

BILL CHRISTMAN
WITH BOB NOONAN

© 2013 by Bill Christman. All rights reserved.

2nd Printing 2014.

Trusted Books is an imprint of Deep River Books. The views expressed or implied in this work are those of the author. To learn more about Deep River Books, go online to www.DeepRiverBooks.com.

No part of this publication may be reproduced, stored in a retrieval system or transmitted in any way by any means—electronic, mechanical, photocopy, recording or otherwise—without the prior permission of the Publisher, except as provided by USA copyright law.

ISBN 13: 978-1-63269-379-2
Library of Congress Catalog Card Number: 2011917176

PROLOGUE

ON MAY 10, 2002, I met my close friend and spiritual mentor Father B, a Catholic priest, in the parking lot of the headquarters of the Catholic Diocese of Davenport. The three-story brick office building was surrounded with rich green lawns dotted with tall, luxuriantly leafed trees, but I was too tense to appreciate the scene. I had asked for this meeting, and I needed Father B with me.

At 36 I had achieved my dream—I owned and operated a successful wildlife damage management business. Yet only two months before, I had attempted suicide. I was hungry for any clues about the torment my life had become, but now I was hesitant. Maybe I sensed what was coming.

"I need a cigarette," I said.

"It's gonna be OK," Father B said. "This is your hour. Do whatever you need to do; say whatever you need to say. Go over the table after the guy if you have to. We're doing this for you."

I ground out the cigarette with my shoe, and we went in. The secretary made a call, and soon after a petite, attractive, middle-aged woman with short brown hair, dressed smartly but not overly professional, came in and greeted us.

"I'm Irene Loftus, the chancellor," she said, smiling. "Bill, you and I talked on the phone. Father Wiebler is in the conference room waiting for us."

When we entered the room, Bishop Franklin, a tall man with thinning gray hair, stood to greet us. He was dressed simply, in black pants and a priest's black shirt and white clerical collar. Whereas Loftus had been open and friendly, he was more formal—a bit distant and almost aloof.

On the other side of a table, sitting facing us, was an older man, probably in his seventies. Although I hadn't seen him in almost 30 years, I recognized him instantly. It was Wiebler. His face wore the detached, examining look it always had.

He was leaning casually back in his chair, one leg crossed over the other knee. He wore a colorful short-sleeved Hawaiian shirt with palm trees on it, short pants and flip-flops on ugly, beat-up looking feet. His shirt was unbuttoned to his belly, exposing sparse white curly chest hair; he looked like an over-the-hill surfer. He was relaxed, unruffled.

I felt the familiar onset of fear: electric trembling in my arms and hands, dry mouth, hammering heart.

Wiebler looked directly at me and smiled. "You're an attractive young man," he said softly, almost coyly. "I'm sure you were an attractive boy."

The comment caught me totally off guard. I couldn't believe what I'd heard. Then, as it often did, my fear changed to rage. *I'm gonna kill you right here in front of everyone,* I thought.

I was in no mental shape to respond rationally; I had lost almost everything of value in my life. I had the strength and the ability to hurt Wiebler badly before anyone was able to stop me. My rages often ended in physical assault. But I couldn't move. I was frozen.

Today, I fully believe that God reached into that room and physically put His hand on me to prevent me from attacking Wiebler. God knew my impulsive nature and the violence I was capable of in my fury. But that day, God decided I would not harm Wiebler, or myself.

PROLOGUE

The room was totally silent. Bishop Franklin's mouth had sagged open, his eyes blank with surprise. Father B was glaring at Wiebler, lips thin in anger.

Wiebler was quiet and composed.

Not a good start, I thought as we sat down.

Loftus sat to my right, Bishop Franklin to my left, and Father B to his left. Wiebler was directly across the table from all of us.

I turned to Bishop Franklin. "Do you mind if I tape-record the meeting?" I asked.

Franklin and Loftus looked at each other. There was a pause, and then Franklin said, "I don't think we need to. Irene will take good notes."

"I'll take good notes," she assured me. She had a yellow legal pad on the table in front of her. As chancellor, she was in charge of diocese reports. I nodded in agreement.

Bishop Franklin cleared his throat. "Well, we're all here to talk about the conversation you and Mr. Christman had over the phone," he said to Wiebler.

Wiebler ignored him. "I'd like to start the meeting with prayer," he said piously, "The Lord's Prayer."

Judging by the expressions, everyone was again caught off guard.

Wiebler bowed his head and began praying out loud. As if we had no choice, we joined him. I felt disoriented. The situation was becoming more surreal by the second.

After the prayer I tried again, as I had on the phone three days before, to describe to Wiebler who I was. I explained that my mother, Mary, my older brother, Jeff, and I had moved to Bettendorf in 1972, when I was five. We had joined Our Lady of Lourdes Church, where he was pastor, and Jeff and I used to hang out at the rectory with him.

"You offered to be a father figure for us," I reminded Wiebler, "a male role model."

He shook his head. "Oh, gosh, I don't remember you."

I went into more detail about some of the things he had done with Jeff and me: pool games, swimming trips to the beach, dinners at the rectory.

He frowned and shook his head. "Sorry, I just don't remember you."

I pressed on. I described my mother, her involvement with the church, her car, my haircut and what I usually wore.

"I don't remember you," he repeated. Then he lifted his left arm and glanced down at his watch.

This means nothing to him, I thought. *He doesn't care.* He knew what this meeting was about.

Angered, I increased my efforts. By now I was repeating myself. I must have gone on for ten minutes. I couldn't seem to let it go; it had become too important to get at least some sort of recognition or acknowledgement from him.

He insisted that he didn't remember me another dozen times and glanced at his watch twice more. There was a maddeningly casual, emotionless tone to his answers, as if I were asking him to recall a minor church social event years ago. He was being polite, but he obviously didn't think it was all that important.

Suddenly, it dawned on me that he could be lying; that the looks at his watch might be theatrics, meant to hurt and distract. He had taken control of the meeting from the beginning, and he was still in charge.

I decided to take back control and confront him directly. It was as if he sensed my decision. He smiled demurely at me. "If only I had a picture of you when you were a small boy. Do you have one I could have?"

"You're not getting one," I snapped. But the comment had the desired effect; it shattered my focus, confused me and again triggered my fear. I started to shake, and my eyes filled with tears. I felt like a helpless child.

I was humiliated at the thought of breaking down in front of everyone. "I ... I need ... I need to take a break," I said, almost stuttering.

Father B led me outside into the parking lot. By then I was a complete mess, sobbing and shaking, unable to speak. Father B consoled me, and I calmed down enough to have a cigarette. Finally, I felt ready to go back inside.

PROLOGUE

Wiebler was still leaning back in his chair. I started questioning him again.

"My mother's a hairdresser," I said, "about five-six, dark hair . . ."

"Yeah," he said, "I remember her now. She was attractive too."

I ground my teeth. *Screw the games.* "Was there any sexual misconduct with my brother or me while we were at the rectory playing pool, or swimming with you at the beach?"

He showed no more reaction than if I'd asked him if we normally took a picnic lunch. He just shrugged. "I went to the beach with a lot of different people."

Didn't he understand the question? What did who he went to the beach with have to do with whether or not he had molested us?

"I have a memory of you molesting me at the rectory and at the beach," I said.

He shrugged again. "I don't recall molesting you."

"That's what you said on the phone!" I was standing now, almost shouting. "You said you didn't recall molesting anyone! What kind of answer is that? How can you not recall something like that? You'd know if you didn't!"

Bishop Franklin and Loftus began asking Wiebler questions. I didn't hear a word. Now I knew.

It had happened.

I had to leave the room again.

When Father B and I returned, Franklin was still questioning Wiebler. I sat and listened for a minute. Franklin was almost imploring; Wiebler was confident and uncooperative. It was obvious who was running the show.

This meeting's going nowhere, I thought. I stood up and interrupted the conversation. "How many kids have you molested during your tenure as a priest?" I demanded. I leaned across the table at Wiebler, my voice rising. "How many other kids did you work over? How many people's lives did you destroy? Two hundred? One hundred? Fifty?"

Wiebler contemplated this in silence for quite a while, frowning. Finally he said, nonchalantly, "Oh, no, no, it wasn't that many. No, no, no. Off the top of my head, about twelve."

"Twelve," I said.

The room became dead quiet. Bishop Franklin put his elbows on the table, dropped his forehead into his hands, and shook his head.

Wiebler broke the silence. "Hey, I'm sorry about what happened to you, Bill."

It was a ludicrous remark, made with absolutely no sincerity. He didn't mean a word of it.

"But I'm glad this came up," he continued. "Actually, I've recognized this is a problem. I've been talking to a friend, a Lutheran priest. I've been addressing it. Now I'll get help."

He spoke of it as if it were a minor, everyday human character defect, like eating too much candy. His tone became querulous. "I've had a rough life," he said. "I'm an old man." He turned to Bishop Franklin. "You remember when this problem came up in the early '80s, when I was going to kill myself. It's in my file."

Franklin gave an expression that clearly said, *Don't say that!* He obviously didn't want Wiebler's file mentioned. I knew as a matter of course that personnel records were kept on all priests. As chancellor, Loftus supervised the diocese archives. I turned to her. "What's in his file?" I asked.

Loftus and Franklin looked guilty, but said nothing. They clearly didn't want to discuss the file.

Wiebler was still talking about how hard his life had been. He described in more detail how he had left the Church in the early 1980s because he was going to kill himself over an abuse-related incident. He told how he had retired formally as a priest, although he still engaged in priestly duties. For example, he said, he'd just returned from being a chaplain on a cruise ship.

"I'm trying to get a handle on this," he assured me calmly, as if that meant everything was fine now.

"By going on a cruise ship?" I asked. "Where there's all kind of children, like some kind of feeding ground? Is that how you're trying to handle it?"

PROLOGUE

"I got counseling," he said. "It's all documented in my file."

"What else is documented about other incidents?" I asked Loftus and Franklin.

After an uncomfortable pause, Franklin said, "We can't discuss Wiebler's file with you."

For the first time I began to suspect they weren't telling me the truth—that they were keeping things from me. "What else is in his file?" I demanded.

"Disturbing things," Bishop Franklin said.

That answer was disturbing. "I'd like to see the file."

"I can't give that to you."

I began to yell at Wiebler. "I can't believe you'd do such a thing and wear that collar. How can you be in the position you're in and do the monstrous things you've done? And then sit there and smirk and be cocky about it?"

"I'm sorry for what happened to you," he said, still leaning back, still unruffled. His gaze was direct, expressionless, almost blank; his eyes empty and soulless. I thought suddenly, *This is not a priest.*

I had to leave the room again. Father B was beside himself with rage. He kept saying, "How could he sit there with no remorse, talking about this as if it were nothing?"

When we came back in the room, Wiebler was gone. Bishop Franklin and Loftus were still there, and a new priest had joined them. He introduced himself as Monsignor Drake Shafer. He was vicar general of the Davenport diocese, second in command behind Franklin.

Shafer put his arm around my shoulder and tightened it, pulling me close against him. "I'm so sorry for what happened to you," he said.

I pulled politely away; I have a difficult time with men touching me, especially when they attempt to be intimate. "Where's Wiebler?" I asked.

"He's gone," Franklin said. "I think we've heard enough."

"Now do you believe me?" I asked. "Is there any question now about what happened?"

"I think you can tell what we think by the look on our faces," Franklin said ruefully.

Franklin and Loftus began talking about some sort of compensation. I was standing beside them, and I assumed they meant payment for counseling, possibly for services in the past as well as in the future. God knows I'd spent enough on therapy.

Instead, they offered me pastoral counseling. I told them I was absolutely not interested. The last time I received "pastoral help," Wiebler had raped me. At that point, I was not thinking in terms of any financial settlement.

We had further discussion about Wiebler. There was great concern about his mental competence, and Franklin and the others concluded that they would not let him leave the Quad City area without a psychological evaluation. Personally, I felt the man had been quite mentally competent; he had manipulated almost the entire meeting.

I told them I thought it would be a good idea for Wiebler to register himself as a pedophile. They agreed. Loftus told me she would be in contact to discuss compensation and to keep me posted on what was happening with Wiebler.

"All I really want is a guarantee that Wiebler can't harm any more children," I said. Then I remembered Wiebler's file; they had known about his pedophilia for a long time. "And an apology from the Church," I added, "for allowing him to harm me."

They assured me they would do these things and that they would be in touch immediately.

I had glanced at Irene Loftus' notepad several times during the meeting. Oddly, she had taken less than half a page of notes. I trusted this group, however. I had turned to them for help because I believed the Catholic Church was a spiritual guide and protector.

That belief would almost be destroyed.

But it would be restored.

CHAPTER ONE

MY CHILDHOOD MEMORIES are jumbled. My earliest is of sitting in Dad's lap while he lounged in a green recliner in the living room. We were eating frozen shrimp, and I could see Mom in the kitchen doing dishes. She wore an apron, and there was a light above the sink. I had a toy dart gun, and Dad and I shot plastic suction-cup darts through the kitchen door at Mom. We all laughed.

I loved cuddling. Dad's lap was secure and strong, and he laughed when he held me. I thought Dad was really something. His name was Wilbur, but Mom called him Bill, and my name was Billy.

My mother's name is Mary. When she held me she felt soft and comforting, and I knew she was happy when I was. She made hot cocoa and buttered toast, and I liked to dip the toast in the cocoa. When we went to Dairy Queen, I always got a chocolate milkshake.

I was a rambunctious little rug rat, and Dad liked the fact that I was into everything. I was always terrorizing the neighborhood, on foot or on my tricycle, and my parents were always chasing after me. A lady on our street had a tall birdbath. I must have decided it looked better on the ground, and I kept running into it with my trike until it fell over and broke. My parents had to pay for it.

My brother, Jeff, is three years older than me. He was a serious kid. He'd spend days putting model cars together, making them perfect. When he wasn't looking, I'd play with them, drive them off the edge of the table so they'd smash on the floor, or crash them together. Dad laughed.

I had a little suitcase full of toy guns. My favorite was a little double-barreled shotgun with corks. When you pushed the corks into the end of the barrels and pulled the trigger, the corks would pop out. I wasn't supposed to take the guns out of the yard, but one day I headed into the neighborhood with the shotgun. My parents took it away from me.

We had a yellow parakeet named Charlie. We all loved him. We left his cage door open, and he flew around the house and then went back in his cage. He'd fly into windows sometimes, thinking he could go outside.

Dad worked for Christman's Small Electric Engine Repair, a family business owned by his mother, Grandma Christman. Dad's brother, my uncle Bud, lived beside Grandma and ran the business. If one of my toys broke, Mom would take me to the shop and Dad would fix it with electrical tape. He'd always get me a small bottle of Coke from the machine. I liked the shop smell of grease and concrete, and I liked going down the narrow spiral stairs into the dim basement, even though I was afraid of the dark. It was cool and damp down there, like a dungeon, and fun to explore.

I remember being scared of the dark at a very early age. Jeff and I slept up in the top attic room, which was dark when the door was closed and the lights were off. I have an early, persistent memory (or fantasy) of a face peeking in the attic window. It was evil, and it wanted me. There was a fire escape ladder from the window to the ground, and I was always scared someone would come up at night and get me.

When I got really scared of the dark, I'd go downstairs to Mom and Dad's bedroom while they were asleep. Dad would be on his back, and I'd climb onto his belly, on my hands and knees. I'd look down on his face, peel back both eyelids, and watch his round white eyes roll around. The rest of his body never moved. I was fascinated

CHAPTER ONE

that his eyes moved while he was asleep, and I went downstairs to watch it a lot. It's a vivid memory. Years later, when Mom told me about his drinking, I realized he had probably been passed out.

Our families got together a lot at Grandma Christman's. Grandma would open the right-hand drawer in the kitchen and take out a Heath bar for me. The grownups drank beer, played cards, laughed, danced and goofed around. Dad got rowdy when he drank. He was the life of the party and made everybody laugh. I thought he was the coolest person in the world. I wanted to be like him when I grew up.

Uncle Bud and Aunt Mimi lived next door to Grandma. Uncle Bud had a pool table and an electric racecar track in his basement. The cars were fun, but I really loved to play pool. When it was nice outside, Jeff and I played in the yard with Duke, their German Shepherd. Duke was huge and almost white. We'd wrestle with him and chase him around the yard. I tried to ride him like a horse, but I always fell off when he started to trot. His shoulders were massive and powerful. We played fetch with a big log I could barely pick up, and Duke carried it around like it was a stick. He was never rough with us, never growled or pretended to bite, and he was always lapping our faces.

My teenage cousin Vicki, Uncle Bud and Aunt Mimi's daughter, used to babysit Jeff and me. She'd line up cushions on the floor against the wall and lay on her back, with her elbows on the floor and her forearms up. We'd climb onto her belly and then up onto her hands until we were standing on them. We'd wobble around and flail our arms until we were standing straight, and then she'd pole vault us across the room onto the pillows.

Vicki had a Camaro, and she took Jeff, Duke and me for fast rides past long, open cornfields in the countryside and through tall green woods. We sat up front. Duke filled the whole back seat. He'd fold his ears back and hang his big head out the window. When we came to a hump in the road, Vicki would stomp on the gas, and we'd rise up over the hump and sort of float back down with a light feeling in our guts. We called it a belly rush. Vicki played the radio loud the whole time. She loved Bonnie Raitt. It was a blast.

In December 1971, right after I turned five, my father died. I was so short I could barely peer over the side of the coffin. When I saw all the white makeup on his face, I knew something was wrong. *Why is he painted like that?* I thought. I still don't like to look in caskets.

Dad had a friend who was a retired police officer. To comfort me, he gave me his police officer hat with a real badge on it. I treasured it for years. I lost it when my drinking got bad.

Charlie died the same day Dad did. Mom heard a thud and found Charlie dead in his cage. I was really confused, because first Dad wasn't coming back, and now Charlie wasn't coming back, all in the same day.

I insisted on burying Charlie. I put him in a shoebox and buried him in the backyard, and then I made a cross and put it in front of his grave. Mom had told me that Dad was going to heaven, so I asked her if Charlie was going too. She said yes.

About a week later, I dug up the shoebox. Charlie was still inside. I was really upset that God hadn't come down to get him and put him with Dad, and I went crying to Mom. "Charlie was supposed to go to heaven with Dad!" I said.

"He will," she assured me. "People go to heaven very quickly, but birds sometimes take three or four weeks."

Consoled, I put Charlie back in his shoebox and reburied him.

CHAPTER TWO
(MARY)

I GAVE BIRTH to Billy on November 6, 1966, in Elkhart, Indiana. A year later my husband, Wilbur, Billy, his three-year-old brother, Jeff, and I moved to Huntington, Indiana. Huntington was a small town of about 15,000 at the time—a one-McDonald's town. It was almost 100 percent white, mostly middle class. It had lots of suburban residential housing; single houses with lawns. There were some small industrial plants, and I think the Christman Electric Motor Repair business did work for them.

A rolling farmland surrounded the town. We were about 25 miles from the city of Fort Wayne, which had a population of almost half a million in the metropolitan area. Our house was a small two-bedroom bungalow, white with black shutters, with an attic dormer that had been finished off. The boys slept in the dormer. A detached two-car garage sat back from the house.

Billy was always an active child, even in my womb. He was an easy baby to be with and care for. He was always smiling, not fussy at all. He ate well, took good naps, went to bed early and slept well. He was a happy baby.

He was also very precocious. He walked at nine months. Once he started to walk and talk, he never stopped. He was a busy kid, on the go constantly. If you didn't keep an eye on him, he would get into something. Just after he started walking, the family went together for a cookout at Grandma Christman's. We were eating outside, and Billy grabbed a hose and sprayed the whole bunch of us. It was the sort of thing his father might do, horsing around.

Billy was stubborn and did not like to be told no. He was constantly pushing the boundaries. When he was three or so, I let him ride his trike outside. The rule was that he was to go no further than the end of the driveway. The second I turned my back he'd be gone, on the loose in the neighborhood. He had no fear of strangers, and he was always in other people's yards. I always had to go find him. He was a born explorer, and very inquisitive.

He was feisty, and sometimes he scrapped with the other neighborhood kids. He wanted to be part of everything they did, even if they were older, and sometimes he did stupid things to join in. If they were playing ball and he got it, he wouldn't give it up. He was a tease, too, like his father, and he didn't know when to stop.

Billy could be an imp and an agitator, but he was very sensitive. He'd stir up some kind of minor trouble and then get upset when people got mad at him. He wasn't a bad kid; he never did anything mean or destructive. He was just mischievous. He was a very attractive child, very cute, with sandy hair and a wonderful smile. It was impossible to stay angry with him for long. He was a charmer, too, just like his father.

Wilbur was good with kids and knew how to play with them. He was a big tease, and the boys liked that. The four of us used to chase each other all through the house with water pistols. We had fun together.

Both boys were very close to Wilbur and me, and very affectionate. Billy loved to sit in our laps and cuddle. Wilbur liked Billy's rambunctious attitude, and Billy idolized his father.

We didn't have a lot of money. For entertainment we went for Sunday afternoon drives through the countryside, and afterward we would stop for hot dogs. Billy always ordered more than he could eat. We finally put our foot down and said he had to eat everything he ordered.

CHAPTER TWO

We lived about two miles from Grandma Christman and Bud, and we were over there frequently. The Christmans got together at least two or three weekends a month, for holidays and birthdays and cookouts and big euchre games. They were great sports watchers, and they bet on everything. There were generally a dozen or more of us.

There was always drinking. Everyone would get a bit loud and rowdy and horse around. They played euchre for money, and sometimes tempers flared. But it passed quickly. The Christmans were friendly, amiable people.

Wilbur, however, was full of rage just under the surface. He was an alcoholic. When he started drinking, he couldn't stop. He could be affectionate and considerate when he was sober, but after only a few drinks he became verbally and physically abusive. It was an instant personality change, like Jekyll and Hyde. He swore and yelled at me, insulted me, threatened me, and sometimes slapped me around.

When he was drinking, I never knew when he'd come home. Sometimes it wasn't until the next day. When he didn't show up at night, I would leave the garage door open for him. Sometimes he'd come in late at night and make me clean the whole house or iron clothes. When he was in a drunken fury, I wouldn't say anything for fear of setting him off further.

He was a bar drinker. One night he got in a bar fight and came home to get a gun to take back. I tried to talk him out of it, but he was so agitated I backed off. I didn't dare wrestle him for the gun. I let him leave, and then I called a close friend of his who was a policeman. He brought Wilbur home.

He was never in trouble with the law. He was a real charmer and could talk his way out of anything. He was well liked, and he was a Christman. Everyone in town knew the Christmans—they were solid, respected citizens.

The abuse usually happened at night, so the kids didn't see much. They were typically in bed when he got home. But I'm sure they heard a lot. They must have heard me crying. One night, Wilbur smashed all the furniture in the basement family room.

He screamed in fury and destroyed everything. I locked the kids and myself in the attic. It was the worst rage I'd seen. Billy doesn't remember any of it.

Wilbur didn't abuse the kids, but he did discipline them harshly at times. He knew Billy was afraid of being alone in the dark, so one time as punishment he moved Billy's bed into the downstairs bedroom and locked him in at night with the lights off. I let Billy out.

Sometimes I had to call Wilbur's brother, Bud, for help. I hated to do it; there was enough tension between them. Wilbur would show up at work drunk, or not show up at all, and Bud would fire him. But he always rehired him. Wilbur was constantly quitting or getting fired and rehired.

I always knew Wilbur's drinking would kill him. One night he didn't come home, and in the morning I went outside to look at the garage door. It was closed. I got a very bad feeling. I knew I needed to get the boys out of there, so I went back in the house and made them breakfast and got them ready for school. Jeff was in third grade, and Billy was going to pre-school. When they left, I worked my courage up and opened the side garage door.

The car was inside. The passenger door was open, and Wilbur was sprawled face-down across the front seat, his right leg hanging out. His left leg was drawn up on the seat, knee forward. His left arm was draped up over the back of the seat, and his right arm was stretched out toward the steering wheel, as if he had been reaching for it.

When I touched his back, I knew instantly that he was dead.

The family thought it was a heart attack. We didn't find out until after the funeral that he had died of carbon monoxide poisoning. Suicide is always a question when carbon monoxide is involved, and Wilbur had just been fired again by Bud. But I feel strongly that it was accidental. Judging from Wilbur's position on the seat, my guess is that he got out of the car on the driver's side, went around to the back to close the garage door, noticed the car was running, opened the passenger door, climbed in and reached for the key, and

CHAPTER TWO

passed out. The car kept running until the carbon monoxide killed him. I told the boys their father had died of a heart attack.

Wilbur was only 36. I was 28. There was no insurance, we had no money, and I had two young boys. The Christmans had always been kind to me, and they were very supportive after Wilbur's death. But I felt there was no future for us in Huntington.

My mother and father and two younger brothers, Roger and Paul, lived in Davenport, Iowa, five and a half hours away. I had always been close to them, so the idea of moving home became very attractive. I was a cosmetologist, and I knew there was a lot more work in the Davenport area. So, in June of 1972, as soon as Jeff was out of school for the year, the boys and I moved to Bettendorf, Iowa, close to my family.

I vividly remember the day we left. I was tremendously sad about Wilbur; he had died too early, and we'd had two beautiful boys together. But something relaxed in me as we drove. It was a sunny day, and it seemed as if I was making a new start. I was excited about our new apartment, and it felt like we were going to something positive. I was independent! I felt like a whole new person. And the boys could finally grow up in safety.

CHAPTER THREE

MY FIRST MEMORY of Bettendorf is of playing with my toy helicopter in our apartment. The apartment had a living room and kitchen on the first floor, and a bathroom and two bedrooms upstairs. Jeff and I slept in the same room.

I started kindergarten that fall, at Hoover Elementary School. I was really proud and excited when I brought my police hat to Show and Tell. I loved playing kickball at recess.

We spent a lot of time at my grandparents. Grandma made us peanut butter or baloney sandwiches, and I loved how she cut the sandwiches diagonally. It made me feel special. She always had a Tupperware container of Cheetos for us. My grandfather had had a stroke and was in a wheelchair. He couldn't talk; he could only make noises that sounded to me like "funawony, funawony, funawony." Jeff and I helped him get around, through doors and into the car. I got so I could understand his noises.

My mother took us to church every Sunday. It was really boring, and it was hard for me to sit still. I wanted to be outside playing. It seemed like they were always passing the plate for collections, and I clearly remember thinking, *Why does God need money?* It bugged me every time we were in church.

CHAPTER THREE

We lived in a U-shaped complex of ten adjacent apartment buildings. There was a wide grassy area in the U and a line of trees and brush at the far side that separated it from the road. There were a ton of kids in the neighborhood, and they played in the grassy area all the time. It was like a big playground.

My best friend, Tony, lived next door in the same apartment building. We met right after I moved in. Tony saw me on the sidewalk with a piece of cardboard on which I'd written "BUTT WEENIE BOOB." I was holding it up to passing vehicles. I'm sure I had no idea at that age why those words had shock value, but I definitely knew they did. Tony thought the sign was hilarious.

We did everything together. He was two years older than me, tall and blond, good-looking and strong. I was small, but he treated me like an equal. We were alike in many ways. Our sense of humor was almost identical, and we were always getting into everything and planning adventures. Tony had also lost his father at a young age.

Tony and I were both physically active. We played kickball and hide-and-seek constantly with the other kids in the neighborhood, and we climbed anything. Each apartment had a front porch roof about ten feet off the ground, and the walls were faced with rough bricks with deep recessed gaps between them. We would get our fingers and toes into the cracks, scramble straight up the wall and clamber onto the roof. Then we would jump off onto the lawn, because it was scary. We were always climbing trees and jumping out from way up over our heads. We never got hurt. We knew how to land on our feet, bend our knees, and roll over.

Tony had a temper. Sometimes, a big kid named Sonny would pick on me at school. One day, I told Tony that Sonny had been mean to me that morning. Just then, Sonny walked by on the other side of the street. Tony instantly charged him, yelling, and knocked him down and beat him up. Sonny never bothered me again.

Tony and I were walking along a sidewalk late one afternoon when we smelled steak cooking. We were starving, and it smelled great. We saw a man grilling out on his lawn, so we hid in the bushes beside his house. When the guy went inside, we ran out and grabbed the steaks off the grill. We were eating them in the bushes when the guy came back out. He started swearing like mad; he couldn't believe his steaks had disappeared. Tony and I burst out laughing, which allowed him to zero in on us. He chased us down the street but never got close enough to identify us.

Seeing the guy's reaction was more fun than eating the steaks, so we raided more grills. We'd laugh and laugh at how we imagined the people would act and what they'd say when they found their supper gone right out from under their noses. We never got caught, but it got so people in our neighborhood wouldn't leave their grills unattended.

The apartment buildings in our U-shaped complex were linked, all in one long building. One time, Tony and I went up into my attic and discovered that all the apartment attics were connected. We walked along the bottom chords of the rafters, over every apartment. It was one big, long room up there, dark and hot above the insulation, with just a few chinks of light coming through the vents. Each apartment had an attic door like ours that led down into the apartment.

One day, we were outside when we smelled apple pie through one of the open apartment windows. We counted down from my apartment to find out which one it was, went up into my attic, walked through the rafters until we came to the right apartment, and went down through the attic door. No one was home, so we went into the kitchen. Our hearts were pounding, because we were sure we'd go to jail if we got caught.

The pie was on the kitchen counter. We ate half of it and then went back up into the attic and down into my apartment. We killed ourselves laughing about what the people would say and do when they discovered half the pie gone. We actually stood on the sidewalk outside the apartment, hoping someone would run out screaming about their pie being half gone. We wanted to see the look on their faces.

We went into other apartments for food a couple more times, but we eventually gave it up out of fear of getting caught. We entertained ourselves for hours imagining peoples' shock and disbelief

CHAPTER THREE

when they discovered their food had disappeared from their grills or apartments, and they couldn't explain how it happened.

There was a big coffee and doughnut shop named Donutland right near the apartments, and Tony and I liked to hang out there. It was a brick building with big front windows. The girls running it were in high school, and they were nice to us and gave us free donuts and hot chocolate. They knew we were poor kids from the project. They'd tell us they thought we were cute. They all looked pretty to us, and we had crushes on them. We'd sit at the tables by the front windows watching the traffic go by on 18th Street and horse around, plan adventures and yell across to the girls behind the counter. When we got too rowdy, they made us sit at the back tables so we didn't aggravate the customers. On rainy days we spent hours there.

There was a manmade pond about a mile from the apartments. It was a favorite kid hangout. Everyone called it the lagoon. There was a small wooded island in the middle of the pond. The water was shallow in most places, and Tony and I would wade out, allowing the cool bottom mud to squish between our toes. We'd go out to our knees, sometimes to our waists, but we didn't dare go all the way out to the island because of the snapping turtles. Their thick, blunt heads would surface unexpectedly, peer about ominously, and then submerge. Tony was always telling me a big one could rip a leg off. When a head popped up near me, I'd freak out, yell, and splash as I headed for the bank.

The belief among us kids was that a snapper could break a broomstick with one bite, so toes were obviously an easily detachable snack. At any minute while you were wading, a submerged snapper, invisible in the murky water, could be opening its huge sharp beak right beside your toes. Nobody ever got bit, but the suspense increased with the depth of the water. I was always afraid a monster turtle would grab me by the leg and pull me under. Tony teased me relentlessly about snappers. He said they loved to hold kids underwater until they drowned. I was terrified of them.

Tony loved to fish, and he got me into it. The little kids fished for bluegills, but we went for carp. I considered myself a big kid because Tony was, and we were equals.

We baited our hooks with a single kernel of corn, and when we hooked a carp on our small poles the battle was absolutely stupendous. The pole bent double and almost jerked out of our clutching hands. The water boiled, and it was all we could do to get the line back onto the squealing, protesting reel. We lost most of the carp we hooked; they were simply too big for us. But we got some up onto the bank. One shimmering, flopping, 10-pound carp with a bulging, muscular back, its sides covered with a diamond pattern of wide gold scales, was pure beauty and huge excitement. This was big game indeed for two young boys. We were kings of the world carrying one home.

Sometimes we hooked, and managed to land, a snapping turtle. These prehistoric monsters, dark and massive, came reluctantly out of the deep with slow, stubborn, rugged resistance. Once on the bank, they lumbered toward us, jaws gaping. We'd reach a long stick out, and the beak would slam shut on it. When we cut the line, the beast would plod back into the lagoon and submerge. They scared me spitless.

We hunted bullfrogs in the cattails along the edge of the lagoon. I was great at sneaking up on them on my belly in the muck and weeds and grabbing them. But our main activity was exploring. Tall woods with thick underbrush higher than our heads surrounded the lagoon. We crawled and pushed through, followed foot paths and animal trails, walked on logs, climbed trees and jumped out, and checked out everything. Older kids had built brush forts in the woods, and we went in and played with their stuff. When they found out what we were doing they chased us, but Tony and I could weave, duck, jump and run faster than anybody through the brush, and they never caught us. We would laugh uproariously when we lost them.

The woods were interspersed with big overgrown fields, and I loved wading through the waist-high grass and weeds. In one field, we discovered a huge pile of tree-length logs. There were animal holes in and around it. This woodpile became a favorite hangout, and we climbed it all the time.

CHAPTER THREE

We were in the water constantly. The lagoon was drained by Duck Creek, which went all the way to the Mississippi River, three or four miles away through the woods. The creek was about knee deep in summer, and we waded barefoot along its rocky bottom. The cool, clear water would caress our legs as we flipped rocks over with our feet, hunting crawdads. We'd peer into holes in the bank and poke sticks in to see if anything would charge out. We lifted rocks and logs and found snakes, salamanders and worms.

I fell in love with the outdoors those first two summers. The woods, fields, lagoon and creek were a captivating, seemingly infinite wilderness full of adventure, physical challenges, interesting animals and bugs and dangerous beasts like snapping turtles. It begged for exploration. I was fully alive in it.

There were only a few gloomy spots in my life. I was still afraid of the dark, but Mom cracked our bedroom door to let in a slice of the hall light. I wet my bed almost every night until I was about eight. I'd wake up wet and start crying, humiliated. Mom was very patient. She'd come in and console me and put a towel down on the wet place while I changed into dry pajamas. The next day she'd change the sheets. She never got mad at me about it.

Another thing I didn't like was loud verbal fighting between adults. It wasn't all family love and light in our apartment complex, and sometimes the shouts of arguing grownups would blast out through a window. I'd stop playing, and my heart would pound.

I also didn't like it when Mom got mad at me. She didn't get angry very often, or for long; it wasn't her nature. But sometimes I pushed her too far, and then I'd get the stern look. It scared me, because I thought she didn't like me anymore. I'd tell her I was sorry and beg for a hug. If she didn't soften instantly, I'd start sobbing, and she always ended up wrapping her arms around me and holding me close.

But life was good. When morning light woke me, I dressed and went downstairs fast, wolfed down breakfast, and charged out the door. I couldn't wait for the day.

I was happy in Bettendorf that first year and a half.

CHAPTER FOUR
(MARY)

BETTENDORF WAS BASICALLY a bedroom community for local industry and several colleges, with many apartment houses and single-family dwellings. Our apartment had two stories, a basement and a postage-stamp lawn. It was new, and very nice. The neighborhood was friendly and full of children. I loved it.

My parents lived 20 minutes away. We'd go over for supper and barbeques, and we often spent the night. My mother babysat the boys while I took courses to get my Iowa cosmetologist license, and then later when I started working.

In September 1972, Billy started kindergarten and Jeff started fourth grade. Both boys seemed to make the adjustment smoothly. Bettendorf had a good school system, and I decided to stay. I felt it was important for the boys to remain in the same system until they graduated from high school.

The Christmans were Catholic, and Jeff and Billy had been baptized. Wilbur and I hadn't gone to church much back in Indiana, but now that I was a single mother I felt the boys needed more structure. So we joined Our Lady of Lourdes Church in Bettendorf and went to Mass almost every Sunday.

The boys seemed happy, although Billy was still a handful. He never got into anything serious or destructive; just the usual

CHAPTER FOUR

mischievousness, always testing his boundaries. As I mentioned, he was an attractive, appealing boy, and people quickly forgave his minor misbehaviors. His friend Tony was a good kid, and I was happy to see them together. When they didn't have school, Tony would knock on the door early in the morning looking for Billy, and off they'd go for the day. They were inseparable all summer.

The neighborhood kids ran unsupervised all over Bettendorf in those days. Nobody worried about sexual predators. Like most parents, I told my boys to be home for lunch and dinner, and I didn't worry about them.

Billy's interest in the outdoors started when Tony introduced him to the lagoon. They spent most of their time there. It was a healthy, safe place to play, and I was delighted they were there so much.

Although Billy's behavior didn't change radically after his father's death, he missed his dad terribly. Shortly after we moved to Bettendorf, he looked up at my mother and, with little boy seriousness, told her, "I don't have a daddy anymore." It broke her heart.

Billy was always looking for a father figure, and Jeff needed one too. I gave it a lot of thought, but I didn't know what to do. I definitely wasn't ready to start dating yet.

About a year after we moved to Bettendorf, I was at an outdoor carnival/baked goods church fundraiser when our parish priest, Father William Wiebler, sat down beside me in a lawn chair to get acquainted. I told him I was a widow with two boys. Their need for a father figure came up, and I was thrilled when Father Wiebler said he'd be glad to help. He had a pool table at the rectory, and he said they were welcome to visit. He offered to take them fishing, too. I felt it was a good match. Both Jeff and Billy liked pool, and Billy loved fishing.

I thought it was wonderful that Father Wiebler offered to spend time with my sons. I felt he would be a good adult male role model for Jeff and Billy. I was grateful, and relieved.

CHAPTER FIVE

MOM TOLD JEFF and me that Father Wiebler was going to spend time with us. She said he had a pool table at the rectory and that he was going to take us fishing too. It sounded great, although I thought Father Wiebler was kind of scary. At Mass he wore long white robes and walked around up front by the altar, making slow, sweeping motions with his arms and talking in a loud, serious tone. He was obviously in charge.

My understanding of God was that He could do anything and knew everything. Basically, He ran the whole world. I knew the church was God's house, so it made sense that because Father Wiebler was boss of the Mass and hung out at the church, he might be God! But Father Wiebler had a green Mustang. That was cool, but strange. Why would God drive a Mustang?

Mom drove us to Father Wiebler's. Close up, he was still scary looking. He was tall, and balding with scattered hair around the edges, and had a hooked nose. But he was friendly.

Although he was supposed to spend time with us as a kind of father, I don't remember him saying much to us. He didn't talk about serious things or give advice, and he didn't tease us or joke around with us like Dad did. What I do remember is that he was always looking at us while we did things.

CHAPTER FIVE

The pool table was in a big, dark, study-type room. Father Wiebler played pool with us sometimes, but usually he sat and watched silently while Jeff and I shot pool and laughed and horsed around. I'd look up, and Father Wiebler would be leaning back in his chair scrutinizing me. I felt as if he were examining me. One time when Jeff and I ate dinner with him at the rectory, throughout the meal he kept looking directly at me. It made me really nervous. I didn't look back at him.

At least a of couple times he took Jeff and me to Buffalo Beach, on the Mississippi, so we could swim. He didn't swim with us. He just stayed on the beach and watched.

For a while Jeff and I hung out at the rectory a lot. It was fun at first, but Father Wiebler made me increasingly uneasy. One night, Jeff and I were having dinner at the rectory. Father Wiebler was sitting at the head of the table, and for some reason I was so scared I couldn't eat. I was paralyzed. I didn't dare move. I didn't dare look at him.

Some time after that, we stopped visiting him. About that time my attitude toward church began to change radically. Before, church had just bored me; now it frightened me. I became extremely nervous as soon as I entered the church, and when I saw Father Wiebler looking in my direction, I was sure he was staring at me. A feeling would sweep through me that for some reason I was so bad I didn't belong in church, and I would become rigid with fear.

CHAPTER SIX
(MARY)

BILLY BEGAN TO change when he was in first grade. He had always done things that were on the edge of serious misbehavior, but nothing really bad. He was impulsive and often acted without thinking the consequences through, but afterward he'd feel guilty. He'd usually come to me and tell me about it to get it off his chest. He wanted instant forgiveness. He'd do something to tick you off and then be remorseful, almost crushed, and insist on immediate absolution. His repentance was so sincere, and he was such an appealing boy, that it was almost impossible not to forgive him.

Then I got a call from the school principal. He said there had been a problem, and he wanted to see me. I could understand a teacher having some minor difficulty getting Billy to sit still or follow an order, but this sounded more serious. I was nervous about going to the meeting.

The principal said Billy had refused to do something the teacher had told him to do, and when reprimanded he had said to the teacher, "I'll be nice to you if you be nice to me." Billy's tone had been angry, and the teacher felt he had been defiant and disrespectful. I cried during the meeting. I was young and insecure and very naïve. I felt like I was a failure as a mother. I left the meeting frightened that Billy had crossed a line of some sort.

CHAPTER SIX

I got more calls from the school. Then I was told that Billy had yelled at his teacher, tipped his desk over, and run out of the room. That was just the beginning. Before long, he was considered a behavior problem.

At home, Billy gradually became more disrespectful. Until then he had been a typical boy. If I said, "You're not cleaning your room like you should," I'd get the usual frowns and sometimes even stomping off upstairs to his room. But he always did what I asked, even if unwillingly.

Now he began to be increasingly defiant and talk back to me. And he no longer wanted to cuddle. He'd always been physically affectionate; now he shrank from being touched. I thought it was because of the loss of his father.

CHAPTER SEVEN

I DON'T KNOW exactly when it started, but by the beginning of first grade I was afraid all the time. I don't remember any gradual transition. It felt like one day I was a happy kid, and then the next I was afraid all the time.

Every morning I woke up anxious, my stomach a tight fist and my mind filled with a single thought: *Something bad is going to happen today*. It wasn't a fear of anything specific, like snapping turtles; I was only scared of them when I was wading, and I didn't think about them much otherwise. This new fear was a sense that some unnamable doom was going to descend without warning, and it stayed with me all day. It was mostly in the background, but it sometimes would flare up unexpectedly into pure panic, like a chronic low-grade infection erupts into a boil.

I was sure the bad thing would happen when I didn't expect it, so I stayed on guard. I'd forget about it for a minute and then remember with a jolt, and panic would fill me. I hadn't been watching! It could have happened then! I'd shake from the close call. I couldn't let my guard down!

About the same time the anxiety started, I came to believe I was a bad person. I couldn't think of anything really wrong I'd done,

CHAPTER SEVEN

but I knew I was somehow bad. Tony and I raised hell, but I knew it was kid stuff, and most grownups even got a kick out of it.

Although I couldn't figure out what this new sense of being bad came from, it was so real that I knew it was true. I knew I was somehow defective. I was different than everyone else, and I was ashamed of it. I knew that if people knew how bad I was, they'd be disgusted with me. They wouldn't want to be around me. They'd make me go away.

I'd never felt this way before. It didn't make sense, because there really wasn't anyone in my life who didn't like me. My Mom, my grandparents, my uncles and my brother all really liked me, and I had a lot of friends, plus a best friend. But I knew I was bad.

I was sure people could tell my true nature just by looking at me, especially when they looked into my eyes. So I avoided direct eye-to-eye contact. When I caught people looking at me, I looked away or walked off. I hated being stared at, especially by adults. I figured it was easy for them to see whether people were bad, because they had authority and were smarter than kids.

I became sensitive to the slightest facial hint of disapproval. Every kid knows "The Look," that stern adult stare of disapproval and suspicion. I'd gotten it plenty of times, and until now my reaction had usually been to become cautious and plan excuses in case I was actually accused of something. I'd always considered The Look just a warning sign, an alert. But now it filled me with shame. It meant my secret was out; people could see how bad I was, and how much of a disappointment.

I knew my mother loved me, but now when she gave me The Look, I panicked. I was terrified she didn't love me anymore. I'd demand a hug. If she didn't give in instantly, I'd start whining and pleading. If that didn't work, I'd throw a fit and work myself into a sobbing fury. I'd stomp off to my room and throw myself onto the bed, making sure the door was open so she could hear me bawling. Sooner or later she'd come in and sit beside me.

I'd always had a temper when I didn't get what I wanted, and when my mother was upset with me, I wanted her approval above all else. Right now. My tantrums were part deliberate manipulation, because I knew they wore her down and shattered her composure. But now there was an element of pure fear in them; maybe she'd stopped loving me because she realized how bad I was. That was unthinkable.

Looking back over years of violence, I can now clearly see that fear often preceded my rages. Back then I only knew that my childish outbursts were effective and cathartic. I felt better, plus got what I wanted. I had no idea how destructive that behavior would become. I was just a child.

I knew something was seriously wrong, but I didn't tell anyone, not even Tony or my mother. I had a strong sense that it was something I should hide. I didn't know how to describe the feelings anyway. How does a child verbalize such things?

When we first moved to Bettendorf, I fit in fast with the neighborhood kids. There was usually a game of tag, Hide-and-seek or kickball going on, and I was always in it. I loved being part of the group. But after the fear entered my life, I was filled with anxiety whenever I was asked to play. I was sure I'd mess up somehow in front of everyone and they'd all be disgusted with me. I worried that they would laugh at me and I wouldn't be picked anymore.

I was always one of the first ones picked to play kickball. Kickball is a version of baseball, where the pitcher rolls an inflated rubber ball about the size of a basketball to the "batter," who kicks it and tears around the bases. Meanwhile, everybody on the other team goes nuts trying to kick, carry or throw the ball back infield and clobber the batter with it before he gets home. There was lots of frenzied running, dodging, falling, sliding into bases, bodies slamming together and yelling. I loved it.

Now, my stomach cramped when I was asked to play.

When the frantic action started, my fear disappeared. Being at bat was best. There was no room in my mind for anything but that ball rolling toward me, and when it crossed that invisible line right in front of me, my right leg automatically swung forward. The impact would jar with gut-thudding satisfaction. The ball would fly off, and I'd be running instantly.

CHAPTER SEVEN

No one could catch me from behind, and not many could from the side. I had absolutely no fear of getting hit with the ball or being knocked down. All that mattered was my explosive, powerful charge. My feet gouged dirt and thrust me forward, fists clenched and arms swinging, and I flew along the base line with teeth gritted in a savage, gleeful grin. If someone was waiting at a base with the ball, I ran right at him. I didn't care if I was already out; the collision was a reward in itself. Sometimes the person jumped back out of my way. He was afraid of me! Nothing could stop me!

But eventually I'd be waiting on base or in the outfield, and as my heart slowed and the action paused for me, a cold, clear thought would rise.

I'm having fun.

With that realization my exhilaration would evaporate, and the fear would return with a vengeance. I was different from the other kids. I wasn't part of the game. I was bad. Defective.

It was ludicrous, really. I might have just put someone out or gotten to base or even made a home run, but the conviction that I was a failure would overwhelm me. A vast gray gulf would open between me and the other kids. I was over here, flawed and alone; they were over there, happy and together.

I'd stand there dazed. I couldn't think. The game would continue, but I couldn't play. I couldn't move.

It wouldn't take long for the other kids to notice something was up, and faces would swing my way. "Hey, Billy, what are you doing?" I heard concern, but I heard impatience too. I was messing up the game. Dread would fill me. I knew I'd screw up.

Kids would gather around me, puzzled. "What's wrong Billy?" I had no idea, so I'd stand there silent. Eventually they'd just get mad at me.

"Why don't you play?"

"What's the matter with you?"

"You're ruining the game!"

I literally could not speak. Their frustration and voices would rise, and finally my fear and confusion would explode into anger. I'd yell, "Leave me alone! Leave me alone!"

I didn't want them to leave me alone. I wanted them to tell me they didn't care if I was acting weird—that they still liked me and wanted to play with me. But a bizarre thing happened. The more I wanted them to include me, and the more they tried to do so, the harder I pushed them away. When they pleaded, "C'mon, Billy, let's play. How come you won't?" I'd work myself into a frenzy. Face contorted, lips peeled back and eyes bulging, I'd scream, "Leave me alone!"

Finally, they'd do exactly what I demanded. I'd watch them walk off shaking their heads, talking low to each other. I was sure I knew what they were saying.

"Billy's messed up."

"He's stupid."

"I don't like him."

I'd created my own proof. I was a failure. I was bad.

Maybe I was mad at the other kids because I wanted them to like me even though I was bad. Maybe I was simply so furious and frustrated at my turmoil that I was lashing out at whoever was the closest and most available.

I knew I was punishing mostly myself, but I also felt a cathartic surge of relief from my fear. It was like lancing a boil. Years later, I heard an alcoholic with the wisdom of years of recovery say that for something to be truly addictive, it had to be both very painful and very pleasurable. When he said that, I remembered my childhood ranting at my friends, and I had a glimpse of how that behavior came to dominate my life—how I came to seek out rage and nurture it.

Those were my first conscious experiences of the perverse human impulse to destroy the very thing I wanted the most. I was only seven, but I was losing my innocence. I was toying with one of mankind's most ancient destructive urges. The act of biting the hand that reaches out to you is biblical in its antiquity—and self-destructive. I was taking my first tentative steps toward suicidal behavior. Of course, I didn't understand that at the time. I was just a child.

CHAPTER SEVEN

Driving away the other kids had another, unintended effect on me. Because I really wanted them to like me, I hated myself for repulsing them, which fed the belief that I had to be really messed up. After all, why did I do that? Who would do such a thing?

When these encounters happened, or when the fear became intense, I sought desperately to be alone. I'd leave the game and hide in the trees and bushes along the far side of our apartment play area and secretly watch the kids go on playing. I became a sad observer of childhood, a yearning voyeur of the innocence that had in some inexplicable way been ripped from me.

I longed to be part of the crowd, and I feared being part of the crowd.

I was uncomfortable when kids stared at me. A bunch of us would be talking and laughing about something, but I couldn't join in completely because part of me was on guard. They'd laugh so I'd laugh, pretending to be one of them. But I'd be watching.

Sometimes I'd catch one of them looking at me directly, without speaking. It filled me with anxiety. Maybe they knew I was messed up! Then I'd get mad. I'd stare back at them until they looked down. Sometimes I'd lose it and yell, "Don't look at me!" and everyone would jump.

That sure put a damper on the camaraderie. But it also gave me a feeling of power. I perfected the clenched-jaw, tight-lipped, furrowed-brow glare, and I came to relish the flash of fear on the other kids' faces when they looked away.

It made them edgy and nervous to be around me. They couldn't understand the intensity of my reaction, or even why I had reacted. I'd walk up to a group of kids, and they'd get quiet and look at me. I would interpret that as them seeing something wrong with me, which only served to increase my apprehension and make me more likely to react. It was a downward spiral.

Kids started to avoid me. But I was beginning to enjoy their fear of me. I got a perverse satisfaction out of seeing kids move away when I approached.

I spent a lot of time wondering what was wrong with me. All the other kids seemed to have fun all the time. Why was everybody else OK when I wasn't?

Bedtime was bad. In the darkened room the day's bright images faded, and with nothing sensory to distract me, the fear would rise almost to panic. There was no relief that I'd made it through the day; only dread of tomorrow. Sooner or later, I knew something bad was going to happen, and the longer it took to get there, the closer it had to be. The hall light through the wide open door didn't help. I'd lay curled on my side, knees drawn up, eyes squeezed shut, heart thudding, mouth open for short quick breaths.

I could hear my brother, Jeff, breathing softly, asleep in his bed across the room. It comforted me tremendously.

There were places I could go and people I could be with that made me feel safe. I was at peace at the lagoon, in the woods, along Duck Creek, and climbing the woodpile. During the summer we wore just T-shirts, shorts and sneakers, and when the tall grass of the fields brushed my bare legs, everything was all right. I'd sit on a rock in the woods, and with leaves rustling softly overhead, the fear seemed like a dream I couldn't quite recall. It was like coming out from under a cloud. I could let my guard down.

Tony and I stayed best friends. It didn't seem to matter to him that I acted weird sometimes; he simply accepted me. He always thought I was neat. Although I never lost my temper at Tony, my growing anger must have been obvious. But he never mentioned it. I'm sure he understood. Maybe he even approved; he had a temper himself. We were both different than other kids, in similar ways. Not only had his own dad died when he was young, but two of the fathers of his half-siblings had died as well.

Tony and I played with a few kids his age sometimes. They accepted me, and I felt protected by them. I looked up to them, and I liked that hanging out with older boys added to my tough image. They were misfits of a sort themselves, so I felt normal around them.

CHAPTER SEVEN

Donutland was another sanctuary. When I walked into the bright, open room filled with the smell of fresh pastries and coffee, and the girls behind the counter all smiled at me, I was happy. It was the large groups of kids that unnerved me, the mob playing around our apartments. The more people that were around me, the more on guard I had to be.

One evening at dusk, some kids and I were playing tag when I got scared and hid in the bushes. One of the kid's dads must have been watching us, because he came over and asked if I was OK.

I wanted to tell him I wasn't. I wanted to tell him I felt horrible all the time and that I didn't know why. I wanted him to console me, maybe even fix things. But I screamed, "Leave me alone! Leave me alone!" until he walked off shaking his head.

I cried bitterly after he left.

CHAPTER EIGHT

WITH MY FEAR came trouble in school. I'd never liked being told that I couldn't do what I wanted to do, but when I started kindergarten, I understood clearly that my teacher was the boss. I knew I had to do what she said. I behaved better for her than I did for my mother. I knew exactly how far I could push Mom, but I never tried that with my teacher. Besides, school could be fun. I always had trouble sitting still, but I could depend on school to produce more interesting activities and commotion than seat-squirming boredom.

That changed in the first grade.

One day early in the year, for no reason I can recall, the familiar panic overwhelmed me while I was in class. I simply stood up from my desk and walked toward the door. All I could think of was that I had to get away from everybody.

The teacher was standing at the front of the class. She called my name, and I stopped, my back to her. She asked me what was happening. I didn't answer; I had absolutely no idea, and I couldn't speak anyway.

She walked over and stood in front of me. She must have seen fear in my face, because she asked me with concern what was wrong.

CHAPTER EIGHT

I didn't respond.

She told me to sit back down.

At that, I found my voice. "No," I said.

She told me again, this time firmly.

When I saw her expression become stern and heard her order me to do the opposite of what I wanted to do, my fear transformed instantly into anger. I don't remember exactly what happened next, but I got sent to the principal's office.

I was upset all day. I knew I'd behaved badly, and that night I told my mother what happened. I was desperate for forgiveness. She held me until I stopped sobbing.

It was the first time I remember actively defying an adult. Before then I wouldn't have dared. But something about that particular situation pushed me over the edge. I think it was a combination of my pressing need to get out of the room and being forced to do something against my will.

My mother got called in to see the principal. I felt awful remorse; in my child's mind that was as bad as getting in trouble with the police. But it happened again, and then again. Anxiety would rise and peak without warning. I'd sit rigid for a minute, and then the compulsion to leave the room would wipe out any thought of consequences. Each time, I ended up in the principal's office.

One day, the teacher stood in front of me and ordered me to sit back down. I consciously thought, *Screw her!* and walked around her toward the door. She took my arm to stop me, a natural enough thing to do with a stubborn child.

The result, I'm sure, astonished both of us. I went completely ballistic.

I started yelling at her to let go. I yanked free of her hand, grabbed the nearest desk and threw it over on its side. I pushed over a couple more desks, screaming with rage, and ran out of the room bawling.

Of course, I ended up in the principal's office again, and my mother got yet another call.

By now I was an acknowledged problem child. When I got thrown out of class, I had to sit alone in a room off the school secretary's office. I could see her through the door, and sometimes we'd chitchat. I had to stay there for an hour or so. The room was cold and eventually I'd get bored, so I was always ready to go back to class. I'd behave for the rest of the day. The explosion of rage seemed to have purged the intense fear.

There were never any other consequences besides being sent to that room, and it didn't take long for me to realize that I'd gotten exactly what I wanted—out of the classroom. Before long I lost all fear of the principal. He'd basically stepped out of the whole dance anyway. When I got in trouble, I was just sent to the room by the office.

I had discovered new power: over my teacher, over the principal, and, most importantly, over my fear. When I blew my stack and fought the authorities, I won.

Until then, I had respected the right of grownups to run the world. Now I began to think maybe I could ignore the rules. Maybe I could do whatever I wanted. Maybe my anger made me more powerful than authority.

After that, I was always in trouble. I'd create a scene to get out of class whenever I felt like it, even when I wasn't afraid. I'd just get up and start walking around the room. The teacher would do her thing, and I'd end up in the time-out room. Predictable as clockwork. If I wanted to go to the bathroom I didn't raise my hand and ask; I just got up and went.

Some of what I did was to get out of class, but part of it was to let those in authority know they couldn't make me do anything I didn't want to do. I wanted to challenge my teacher and show her she had no power over me. Her last resource was to kick me out of class, which was fine with me. I'd won again.

I feared any control over me. I was angry and disturbed by anyone who tried to force me to do anything against my will—particularly if he or she touched me. That was the one thing I could not stand above all else. Even a hand on my shoulder to gently steer me into line with the other kids would set me off. I simply could not tolerate anyone physically trying to control me. It infuriated me, and I wanted to kill the person. If my teacher touched me to

CHAPTER EIGHT

restrain me from doing something, I'd push her, hit her and scream, "Get your hands off me!" I'd shiver with shock and with power.

I had no idea why I reacted so strongly. I remember seeing a psychologist at school. He showed me what seemed to be inkblots and asked me what I thought they were. Of course I didn't understand what was going on. But I comprehended one thing very clearly: here was more proof that I was defective and different than the other kids.

Losing my temper and acting out at school made a real impression on the other students. I talked back to the teacher and did what I wanted and even swore—and I got away with it! The kids avoided me more, and to me that was proof they were afraid of me. I was a tough guy. I gloried in it. I strutted around like I was king of the classroom. It was ridiculous, really. I was just a skinny little punk. The only muscle I had—the only power—was my rage.

At home, I didn't want to sit with Mom anymore. I no longer liked being hugged. I became more defiant, and I fought back against anything she asked me to do. I talked back to her. I said hurtful things and then watched for the flicker of pain on her face. I felt powerful and remorseful at the same time.

I punished her, and then cried quietly in my room. Why had I hurt someone I loved? I must really be bad.

CHAPTER NINE

BY THE TIME school let out for the summer, I was well aware that the worst fear attacks came when I was in social situations with kids I thought were normal. Before, whenever I saw kids clustered together, I would hustle over, curious about what was going on and anxious to join. Now I turned away if I saw more than a few kids together.

I spent more and more time with Tony. There was plenty of fun stuff to do. We hunted for golf balls in the pond at Palmer Hills Golf Course, about a mile from town. We knew the hot spots where most of the balls rolled off the green into the water. We wore just shorts and felt for them in the cool muck with our bare feet. We waded around the edges first and then worked our way out until the water was up to our necks, our arms floating on the surface for balance. We ducked under for any balls we felt. The bottom dropped off fast; it was ten feet deep in the middle. I was sure there was real treasure down there. When it got too deep to reach bottom with our feet, we dove and groped the mud with our hands.

I freaked when I hit weeds; I was convinced snapping turtles were hiding in them. The weeds felt like netting, and when my hand poked into them I quickly headed for the surface and the shore. Tony was always telling me the turtles would rip my leg off

CHAPTER NINE

or pull me under and drown me, and I believed him, even though he stayed out there diving into the weeds and never got bit. I always made him wade in first. He covered more area than I did and dove deeper, almost to the center.

The groundskeepers were always chasing us off, but they never caught us; we were too fast. We laughed and yelled at them while we ran. It was fun getting chased—an adventure—and I was getting to like mocking authority. I was also beginning to realize that adults couldn't really do anything to me. It made me feel even more powerful.

We saved the balls in an old pillowcase, and when we had a bunch we'd sit at the tee box and sell the balls to golfers for fifty cents apiece.

If I couldn't avoid other kids, I acted mean to them. I was convinced that any new friendship would go bad, so I didn't let anyone get too close. There is at least some conflict when kids play together, but I was so sensitive that I thought the slightest criticism or hint of disapproval meant the other kids didn't like me. I was surprised when someone acted like he might like me—that he actually wanted to play with me—and I clung to him at first. But sooner or later he'd disagree about whose turn it was or why he didn't want to go somewhere. All it took was for a new friend to not want to play the same games as me, or to play them the same way, and I fled.

I came to trust no one. Every time I liked someone or thought he was one way, I found out he was different than what I thought, and I freaked out. I couldn't trust people to be what I first thought them to be, so I watched until I saw some sign they didn't like me, and then I avoided them. I thought everyone was right to not like me. I became progressively more isolated.

Why wasn't I like the other kids? The answer never came, and I lost hope waiting for it and became angrier. It wasn't fair. With that growing resentment gradually came a resolution: someone would pay. And with that decision came power and a need to punish someone.

The power was seductive. I dwelled on it, and in the process I unknowingly participated in the courtship between my fear and my anger. Eventually, their unholy marriage would produce depraved offspring: violence. But I didn't know that. I was just a child.

My second-grade teacher was a woman. I gave women teachers a particularly hard time—I don't know why. My gym teacher from kindergarten to third grade was a man, and I behaved for him. I liked gym, anyway; I didn't have to sit still.

The fear attacks became paralyzing and now happened at least three or four times a week, usually in school. There was no escape in school; I had to behave, sit still and fit in with normal kids.

I'd be listening to the teacher drone on when the familiar wave of jagged electricity would rip through me. I'd go physically rigid and my mind would stop and lock up. Mental and physical rigor mortis. I could hear the teacher, even recognize individual words, but they didn't make sense. I was on another planet.

At the onset I always tried to control it and hide it. I stifled the short, shallow breaths with tight lips, my clammy hands clenched under my desk. But the paralysis terrified me, and the only way I could break free was to force myself to move. So I'd stand up, and the teacher's eyes would zero in on me, and off we'd go on another round of confrontation and class disruption.

By now, I regularly talked back to my teacher and any school authority. I was on the offense. I wanted to hurt them. I acted out almost daily, leaving the room without asking, going the bathroom and not coming back, wandering the halls, sometimes going into other classrooms. It got me a lot of attention and prestige with the other kids. The whole room would stare at me big-eyed and quiet while I strutted around, and I ate it up. But they also drew back from me. Hardly anyone asked me to play with him or her anymore.

The Catholic Church defines the "age of reason" as the time when children become morally responsible. At this point, they are able to distinguish right from wrong and choose between the

CHAPTER NINE

two—they are able to sin. The Church puts this age at about seven. I turned eight in second grade.

Until now, my transition from fear to anger had been unconscious, and my anger didn't always result in losing my temper. But some time early in the second grade, I became fully aware of the fact that when I was angry, my fear temporarily faded into the background. Once I became conscious of the connection, I learned I could feed my anger. I poked at it like a tongue probes a canker, keeping it irritated and alive. In my mind I went over past scenes with teachers, exaggerating their attacks on me until my teeth clenched.

Rage gave me the biggest payoff. When I exploded, the fear evaporated completely and stayed gone, sometimes for hours. I swelled with power.

My feeling of helplessness was so extreme that the slightest feeling of power was intoxicating. Until now it had taken someone else to trigger my fury, but once I became fully aware of its rewards, I deliberately whipped myself into ferocity. And the more I did it, the more adept and faster I became at it. I could rage at will. It was a primordial, seductive human alchemy: fear birthed anger, anger birthed fury, fury obliterated fear. I still had no idea what created the fear, but that no longer mattered. I had a tool now.

Anger can be beneficial. When Christ was infuriated at the moneylenders in the Temple, His actions and words were constructive and instructive. But rage, deliberately fed, can become a virulent disease that sickens both the victim and the perpetrator. My wrath was a false solution, a temporary escape that only increased my misery. It made my anger chronic and created more fear. It also proved that I was bad. But I didn't understand that. I was just a child. So I nurtured my rage, and it dug its talons deeper into my soul.

It didn't matter who I attacked; he or she didn't have to deserve it for the fear to be vanquished. And here I sinned further. Because I'd do anything to escape, it no longer mattered to me who my victims were. I began to not care who I hurt as long as it made me feel better—a universal human sin as ancient as the soul itself. I was willingly participating now in my own corruption. I had crossed a line; a victim myself, I created more victims. Once a loving child, I became cruel, and enjoyed it.

I was dancing with the devil. He would provide more partners. Some would force themselves on me, others I would choose.

That winter I started going to Confraternity of Christian Doctrine (CCD) classes at church in preparation for First Communion the following Easter. The Catholic Church encourages First Communion at the age of reason, because children are now supposedly capable of understanding and participating in the sacraments. About all I remember from the CCD classes is that I got in some kind of trouble with the teacher and had to sit in the "blue room," whatever that was.

For First Communion, we had to march slowly up the aisle to the altar, in line, with the palms of our hands pressed together in prayer, our thumbs against our chests and our fingertips almost touching our chins. I got about halfway to the altar, and looked up. Father Wiebler was standing up there, with his long white robes and direct stare. He looked giant and accusing.

I stopped walking; my legs wouldn't move. The kids in line behind me stopped, and the back of the kid ahead of me moved away. My heart pounded, and I couldn't breathe. Then my legs came back to life and I ran out of the church and hid in my mother's car.

Communion has been described as spiritual food for the soul, strengthening it against evil. Wiebler blocked my path to it. I couldn't face him.

The more I challenged adult authority, the more I discovered they weren't really going to do anything to me that hurt. They had no real power over me.

There was a cigarette machine at Donutland. Mom would give me money for cigarettes and a note saying it was all right for me to buy them for her. It was an old machine, with a slot at the bottom. I'd get on my knees and stick my skinny arm up in the slot, and

CHAPTER NINE

with my middle finger I'd flick the edge of a pack of Salems until it dropped and popped out of the slot. Then I spent the money on donuts.

The cigarette machine was across from the counter. The girls must have known what I was doing, but they never said anything. Somebody must have noticed they were missing a boatload of Salems and that the money wasn't there, but no one ever said anything about that, either. That increased my contempt for the law. I became bolder at breaking it.

CHAPTER TEN

GOOD PEOPLE WERE placed in my path, too. The summer between second and third grade I went to Camp Abe Lincoln, a YMCA recreational camp. I was about eight. I went for a week each summer until I was 13.

It was a big place, about 300 acres, mostly wooded. There was a big log cabin lodge where we ate and a lot of little log cabins with bunk beds we slept in, about ten kids per cabin, with one adult counselor who had a bed by the front door. The girls were on one side of the camp and the boys were on the other. The cabins were old, dim and musty inside. They were made from real logs, with wood floors and shake roofs. I thought that was very cool.

We did all kinds of stuff at camp: played games and sports, hiked, rode horseback, canoed and fished in the pond, sang around the campfire, and learned how to shoot a bow and a .22 rifle. It was a fun place. I was too busy to feel much fear, and for the most part I was happy. The week was too short.

Happy Joe's Pizza was three blocks from our apartment. It was a square building with double doors in front and parking all the way around the building. Tony and I bought pop there and hung out inside. The staff, all young adults, always acted glad to see us, and

CHAPTER TEN

we were all on a first-name basis. The dining room was warm and cozy, with a pretty brick fireplace. I felt safe there and accepted.

One day I saw Terry, the manager, picking up trash in the parking lot. He was a tall, slender, balding guy with a moustache.

"I'll do that if you pay me," I said. "So I can buy pop and pizza from Happy Joe's," I clarified, to seal the deal.

He handed me the trash bag. "Finish up and I'll give you a pop."

I went over the driveway about a dozen times and bagged every speck of trash I could find. I insisted that Terry inspect the job.

"Fantastic!" he said. I felt he was greatly impressed. "You want the job? You have to promise to keep it clean. I don't want trash building up."

I was the official driveway trash guy! I was so high on Terry's approval and confidence in me that I pored over the driveway daily, snatching fragments of litter like a chicken pecking microscopic bugs, until Terry told me that once or twice a week was enough. I strutted around the staff. I was no longer a mere customer—I was a member of the crew. An equal! The waitresses slipped me slices of pizza, and my belly was always round with pop.

I stuffed the trash in a plastic trash bag and put the bag in a dumpster out back. There was a farm out behind the restaurant and a wood fence with a pasture on the other side, with horses in it. I really wanted to ride those horses.

Like Donutland and the outdoors, Happy Joe's was a sanctuary.

Until then, I'd only tried to scare other kids. That summer, I started bullying them. I hated my fear, and I hated myself for feeling it, and when I saw fear in other kids, by some perverse twist I hated them for having it. I started to attack them for it.

I was so obsessed about my own defects—so sensitive to supposed insults and hints about my own failings—that I developed an absolute gift for spotting insecurities in others. It was like a superpower. I could glance at a sea of faces and catch a flicker of eyes turning aside in avoidance or going down in shame. I could see a kid shrinking into himself, or a gaze going blank in the search for invisibility, and somehow I'd know why and attack.

"How come you're so short? No wonder no one likes you."

"That's a stupid shirt! You always wear stupid clothes?"

I knew the instant I hit a sore spot, and then I was merciless. Teasing had been a Christman family activity in Indiana, but I nurtured it into a vicious art. Verbal torture became my trademark.

The kids I tormented always backed down. Sometimes they cried. Afterward, I always felt powerful, and yet sad at the same time. The perverse, contradictory human passion of a frightened soul purposely destroying the thing it wants most. Somewhere inside me I still wanted to be friendly and fit in. But the negative was simply too seductive. I was powerless to resist the urge to destroy and the power it gave. I didn't understand why I did it. To me, it was just more proof that I was defective.

My attacks were still verbal. I hadn't started hitting yet. I didn't attack often—usually only when I couldn't avoid groups or found myself cornered. And I only bullied boys. I didn't pick on girls until I got interested in them in junior high.

We still spent a lot of time at my grandparents' house. Jeff and I pushed Grandpa's wheelchair around and talked to him. For years we helped him get in and out of the van to go to the hospital, to his treatments and to his doctors. But Grandpa and I gradually became enemies in my mind. Sometimes he was irritable, and when he was gruff with me I thought he didn't like me, and I got even.

He'd say, "Funawonay, funawonay, funawonay," and I'd nod like I understood and say, "Funawonay, funawonay, funawonay." It ticked him off; he knew I was mocking him. But I'd act like I was puzzled. "What's wrong, Grandpa? Funawonay, funawonay?" It made him more irritable with me, which made me torment him more.

Uncle Roger lived with my grandparents. My grandfather had his stroke when Roger was 15, and he stayed there to take care of his father—he never got married. Uncle Roger was great and I looked up to him. He was always happy to see me, and he'd kid around

CHAPTER TEN

with me and treat me with respect. I knew he liked me. He'd give me projects to do to make money. He owned a school bus business. He had seven vans, and he subcontracted to the Davenport school district to pick up kids on the city outskirts. He'd have me clean up the vans and stuff, and he paid me.

Roger taught me to work hard and do a good job. He could be fussy and strict, and if I didn't do the work right (which was the norm), he'd make me redo it. "Come on, Bill!" Then he'd catch himself and say, "But you're almost doing a good job, now let's redo it." He knew my feelings were easily hurt, so he'd change his tone.

I resisted him and made him pay at times for his refusal to let me do a sloppy job, but it helped me to be successful in business later in life.

I always felt at home and at peace when I was at my grandparent's. They knew I was a handful at home and in school, but I acted better with them because I valued their approval.

That, too, would change.

CHAPTER ELEVEN

MY THIRD-GRADE TEACHER was another woman. By then I was an acknowledged behavior problem, and the authorities and I had settled into a well-oiled routine. I'd do the same disruptive behaviors, get thrown out of class, return, be quiet for a time, and then act out again.

Mom started dating occasionally. I don't remember much about the guys. I wanted her to marry a rich guy. We didn't have much, and I wanted what other kids had. I couldn't believe what some of the parents bought their kids: mopeds, sports equipment, all that stuff. We were poor. I didn't resent Mom for it; I knew she worked hard to support us. But I wanted stuff.

Mom dated one guy who I thought was rich because he drove a Cadillac. He took us all out to eat and told Jeff and me that we could order anything we wanted. I figured he was trying to impress Mom, so I ordered lobster to make him pay for dating her. It cost $50, and he was fuming. So was Mom; she knew why I had done it.

I did try to make friends. For a while I hung out with two neighborhood kids named Dean and Marlin. Like my mother, Dean's mom was a hairdresser. She had her own horse. She was a great rider, and she'd take Dean and me to the stables and teach us how to ride.

CHAPTER ELEVEN

I had a crush on her; I thought she was really pretty. She treated me really nice. Her horse was trained to come out of the chute to rope cattle. When you got on that horse, all you had to do was nod your head and it would just take off, or turn. It could feel you nodding. I was amazed. I felt powerful and dominant on top of that huge, strong animal that responded to my slightest movement. I really wanted to ride the horses behind Happy Joe's.

But Dean and Marlin were better friends with each other than they were with me, and I felt like an outsider. I couldn't take even the hint of that possibility, so I just stopped coming around.

Years later, when I was homeless, Dean let me stay in his basement for a while. That's where I was almost killed by a SWAT team.

A kid named Robby lived next door to my grandparents, and he and I played in the big woods behind the houses. We made little camps and cooked cans of beans over campfires and pretended we were living in the wilderness.

Robby's dad was crippled. He and I got along well. He was a dispatcher for barges on the Mississippi, and one day he got approval to take Robby and me for an overnight run on a tugboat named "Grandpa Shorty." It was in the middle of a terrific storm. The wind drove drenching rain sideways and whipped the river into raging whitecaps. I stood outside on the heaving, slippery deck holding onto the rails, looking down at the waves. I knew I was dead if I fell in, but I felt invincible. The entire universe was alive, powerful and exuberant, and I was part of it. I loved it.

The captain was up top in his cabin, nonchalantly looking at girlie magazines while he drove the boat and pushed a huge barge down the river. He wasn't even remotely concerned about the storm, which I thought was enormously cool of him. I felt a kinship; he and I were fearless, heroic. We were warriors.

The two other crewmembers were friendly too, and Robby and I had full run of the whole ship. We flipped through the girlie magazines, ran around, checked out stuff and ate in the galley. We stayed up all night.

Robby's mom acted like she liked me, but in my paranoia I suspected she was faking it. I worried that she thought I was a bad influence on Robby. I was sure she could see that inside I was really a bad kid.

CHAPTER TWELVE

THAT SUMMER AT Camp Abe Lincoln I caused trouble and annoyed the staff without mercy, but I had fun. I still cleaned Happy Joe's parking lot every weekend, and they started giving me a few jobs inside. I cleaned out the fireplace, set up tables with placemats, plates and silver, and cleaned the grease trap. They paid me with pizza and pop.

One night, a karate teacher came into Happy Joe's with his wife and kids. He and I got talking while I bussed his table, and he invited me to observe one of his classes.

He taught in his basement. I stood back against a wall and watched young guys pair off in the ring and dance toward and around each other, whirling and delivering these wild, impossible, graceful arm and leg punches. I was hypnotized, especially by the lofty, arcing kicks higher than their heads. They literally left the ground at times.

I'd seen plenty of fist fights in movies and on TV, but this was like no combat I'd ever witnessed. It was real, not staged, and the combination of raw power and elegant, rapid movement blew me away. I understood instinctively that the graceful, seemingly effortless moves required discipline, strength and practice. These were trained warriors!

I couldn't take my eyes off the action, and the karate teacher knew he had a live one. At the end of the class he came up to me. "You want to take lessons, Billy?"

Too shy to speak, I nodded.

"Don't worry about the cost right now," he said. "We'll work something out. Think it over. Let me know when you want to start."

I went home a changed man. I fantasized endlessly that I was a karate expert. My specialty was to spin completely around and kick a gun out of a criminal's hand, or kick him smack in the face and flip him over backward.

By coincidence, around this time I saw the groundbreaking martial arts film *Return of the Dragon*, starring Bruce Lee and Chuck Norris. It was gasoline on my fire. In the movie, Bruce Lee single handedly defeats armed mafia thugs who are harassing his friends, and then he defeats foreign martial artists sent to kill him. In the final duel, Lee kills the best of the foreign martial artists, Chuck Norris. It's a classic story of a single warrior defeating the forces of evil, and it pumped me up tremendously. I decided I would be a kickboxing martial arts hero. I would interrupt crimes, defend the helpless, and triumph over evil. I throbbed with nobility and power.

My fear disappeared completely during these fantasies, and I sensed I was seeing a way out of hell. I knew I could do this; it was within my reach, and I was positive that once I was a kickboxing expert no one would ever again be able to hurt me.

It was the first real glimmer of what it meant to be a warrior. I'd been a victim for so long, blindly attacking anyone within reach, that I no longer had any idea that it was possible to battle effectively with what was hurting me. But now I saw, for the first time, that I might be able to control my destiny. I was too young to be aware of the significance of that shift from victim to potential victor, but that karate teacher, and Bruce Lee, gave me a gift. They showed me what a warrior was and that I could be one.

But I never called the karate teacher. I was terrified I'd fail.

CHAPTER TWELVE

It was awful. I'd imagine beating up opponents and bathe in a wave of confidence, and then the image of the karate teacher would appear, and he'd frown and shake his head. "I'm sorry, Billy, you're just not good enough. You don't have what it takes." My shoulders would slump, and the fear would roar back and paralyze me.

Weeks went by on my emotional rollercoaster, and I knew my chance was slipping away. Then one night, the karate teacher and his family again came to Happy Joe's. I hid in the kitchen, my heart pounding. I was terrified that he'd ask me why I hadn't called him and that I'd have to tell him I was afraid. I was ashamed.

I hid every time he came into the restaurant. I imagined him seeing me and being disgusted. "There's that kid who doesn't have what it takes."

I hated myself.

I would fall far from that first hopeful glimpse of freedom. But I never lost the desire to be a warrior.

CHAPTER THIRTEEN

IN SEPTEMBER 1976, when I started fourth grade, we moved into a split-level, single-family house on Manchester Drive. We shared it with a friend of Mom's also named Mary, who had a daughter. It was a big house with four bedrooms, and Jeff and I shared a bedroom in the basement. I started going to Armstrong School. I had to take a bus because it was on the other side of town.

That September, my mother started dating Wally Warren. He was a retired military guy, and he sometimes wore his uniform when he visited us. He'd been a captain in Vietnam.

He and I butted heads instantly.

I always argued with my mother when she asked me to do chores. The first time I did it in front of Wally, he flipped out. "You don't talk to your mother like that!"

Is that right? I thought. *Nobody tells me what I can't do!*

It was war from the get-go. He decided I needed discipline, so he started bossing me around. I hated that. It was no secret I was trouble in school, so he decided it was his job to lecture me on how to respect authority. We couldn't have been a worse fit; a man whose life was based on structure, obedience and authority and a willful, cruel boy who was instantly enraged by the slightest attempt to control him.

CHAPTER THIRTEEN

I decided I'd have to run Wally off. As far as I was concerned, she was my mother first and his girlfriend second, and he needed my approval, not hers.

I still raised hell in school, made excuses to go to the bathroom, and didn't come back to class for 20 minutes—the usual. I hated sitting still. But this year, I discovered the joys of being a class clown.

I started picking on people out loud in class. It aggravated the teacher, and I got detention, which I hated because it was so boring. But I got laughs, which I loved. All of a sudden, I was cool. It was a big deal for me, a revelation. I could get approval for being a pain. It was well worth detention.

I was getting really good at teasing. I mainly persecuted the nerds, because they were already low on the food chain and their failings were obvious and well known. Plus they never fought back. Guaranteed laughs with no danger.

My fourth-grade teacher was Mr. Fisher, my first male teacher. He was tall, with an athletic build, and had dark hair and a moustache. One day, we were doing fractions and decimals in math, which I hated. He had asked some nerd to convert some number or something, and before the kid could answer I had chimed in.

"He can't answer that," I said. "He's a retard. You're just embarrassing him."

The class snickered. "That's enough, Billy," Fisher said.

"But I'm trying to help him. Retards need help."

More laughter, and instant detention. Fisher didn't tolerate that behavior.

He got my number fast; he knew that if he tried to reason with me, it would just give me more audience time. So he nipped it in the bud. He knew how to handle me. When I mouthed off, he'd say, "All right, Billy, let's be quiet and do the work. If you finish without causing any more trouble, I'll let you draw tugboats." I loved drawing tugboats. And I knew the other option was detention. Fisher and I had a deal; I'd make a wisecrack and get some laughs, he'd cut me off, and I'd shut up. I didn't push it, and neither did he. Mutual respect.

He treated me like a real person, not like a little kid. I respected him for that, so I didn't want to cause him too much trouble.

During breaks, a buddy of mine and I pitched half dollars against the wall in the hallway outside the classroom. Whoever's coin ended up closest to the wall won the other guy's coin. My buddy stole his to play. If we worked hard in class and got our work done, Fisher sometimes let us go out in the hall just before class ended and we always pitched coins.

My brother, Jeff, seemed fine, happy and normal. He was better in school than I was, too. But I didn't resent him for it. I admired him for not being deficient like me. I felt inferior to him.

I overheard the mother of one of my friends say, "I don't want Billy over here anymore." The kid asked why, and his mother said, "He always looks like he's up to something." More proof that grownups could see that I was bad.

During the school year, I cleaned Happy Joe's parking lot on weekends and worked a few evenings after school. I got to know the employees really well. There were eight or nine of them: the manager and a couple assistant managers, two or three cooks, and some waitresses. They were mostly in their twenties. I looked up to them, and they really took to me. They knew that I didn't have a dad, and they stepped up to the plate. That November, Terry, the manager, made a big deal of my birthday. He threw a staff party and even hired a banjo player. I felt special; they really cared about me.

One of the assistant managers was assigned to another store, and when he left he gave me a two-foot long F16 fighter plane model. It reminded me of my uncle Phil, a decorated top gun pilot during the Vietnam War. I was always touched when someone gave something to me and tried to cherish it. When I lost the model during my drinking days, I was ashamed.

I started having trouble at Happy Joe's. I hated cleaning the grease trap and washing dishes, so I'd do a lousy job. Sometimes

CHAPTER THIRTEEN

I'd even quit. They were real patient with me, but a few times I got fired. Then I'd feel bad. I missed them. I'd realize I'd been stupid, and I'd come back and apologize, and they always rehired me. I was basically dependable, though, until my drinking got bad.

At that age, alcohol didn't do a thing for me. At family parties I'd grab a glass of Mom's beer and steal a quick sip before she could grab it back. I loved the taste, and I'd sneak one sometimes from the frig, but I never got a buzz or anything. I just did it because I thought it was cool.

If my mother wouldn't let me do something, I'd argue with her, badger her incessantly to wear her down, pretend to be more upset than I was, and work myself into a frenzy. Sometimes she gave in, but not always. When she didn't it infuriated me, and the temptation to hurt her was irresistible. I'd say harsh, cruel things, and pain would flicker across her face. *Take that!* I'd exult. Then, alone, I'd grieve. I loved my mother. She had never been anything but nurturing to me.

One afternoon, I heard her upstairs talking to her friend Mary. Mom was sobbing quietly. I panicked. I ran outside and waited beside the road until a cop drove by, and then I flagged him down and said frantically, "There's something wrong with my mom!"

He went into the house to check, but everything was OK.

Mom kept dating Wally. I couldn't stand him. She was sympathetic, but she was not about to be pushed around on this point. "He cares about me, Billy," she said. "He respects me. He likes me for who I am."

I had no idea what she meant, and I didn't care. I just wanted him gone!

At my grandparent's I started acting up more. Roger would catch me smoking cigarettes, and he'd lecture me. I took it from him because I respected him. But I argued more and more with my grandfather. He always followed me around watching me while I did chores, and when I did the job halfway (which was often), he'd get upset and rag at me about it. My hair was getting longer, and he was always pointing to it and trying to tell me it was too long. I felt like he rode me all the time, which to me meant he didn't like me, which meant I didn't like him, which meant I made him pay.

I was a master at irritating him. When no one was around I'd say, "Funawonay, funawonay, funawonay!" roll my eyes around, gape my mouth and flop my tongue out. His face would contort and turn red, and he'd start shouting, "Funawonay, funawonay!" When he got loud enough, my grandmother would come in the room. It was easy to get her on my side. I'd frown with concern and say, "I don't know why he's upset." She'd lecture him. "He's your grandson. He's trying to be nice to you, so stop treating him like that." That really wound him up, and I'd smirk at him from behind her.

I was a sadistic little jerk.

I made friends with a neighbor kid whose parents were religious, and I started going to his house. His parents constantly talked to me about Jesus and being saved. They were very nice to me, and eventually I felt comfortable enough to tell them about my father, including how he used to be mean to my mother. They were sympathetic, especially about his death.

Then I asked my friend's father, "Is my dad in heaven?"

"No," he said matter-of-factly, as if he were talking about something as obvious, and as trivial, as whether or not pigs flew. "Your father went to hell."

I never went back.

That callous judgment, uttered with complete conviction, filled me with fear of God. I loved my father. And on some level, I knew I was like him. I was damned, too.

CHAPTER FOURTEEN

SUMMER CAME, AND my mother was still dating Wally. I settled into a sullen resentment.

Happy Joe's started giving me some cash, and I was now considered a regular employee. I swaggered around the restaurant with importance, and I worked hard. They respected me.

Tony and I would lean against the fence behind Happy Joe's and let the horses eat apples out of our hands. They were the scraggly barnyard kind, not the ones you see at a racetrack. One was white, one was black, and one was multi-colored.

One day, I was sitting on the fence feeding the white one and petting him, and when he turned sideways against the fence I jumped onto his back. He took off bucking and threw me off. I was unhurt, and the horses all just stood there looking at me. I climbed back over the fence, and they came in for another snack. This time Tony jumped on one. He got bucked off too. It became a game. The horses didn't seem to mind; maybe they liked bucking us off. We were never able to stay on, but we never got hurt, so we kept trying.

School was out, I had what was to me was a prestigious job (and money), and my best friend and I hung out constantly. Wally was a pain I could deal with; I was sure I had him on the run. And

I was going to Camp Abe Lincoln soon. For the first time since I could remember, I was more happy than fearful.

Then I was introduced to alcoholic drinking, by a camp counselor and teacher, in Moline. This man was the counselor in my cabin at Camp Abe Lincoln. He was about average height, thin, with dark hair and a prominent nose. He paid attention to me, told me what good kid I was, and sympathized about my father's death. He was really nice. He listened to me and made me feel like a real person with something meaningful to say.

One day, the counselor got a buddy and me out of some camp function and took us to our cabin. He told us he had some stuff in his trunk that tasted good and took out some bottles of Cold Duck wine, one for each of us. We didn't know what it was—we thought it was pop. We had no idea it was alcohol. It was bubbly, and it tasted and felt like grape pop. It was delicious. It went down real easy, and I drank the whole bottle in big swallows.

I have no idea how that first drinking session ended, because I blacked out. I remember getting a buzz in the cabin, and then my memory is a complete blank. Evidently I took off, because they had to form a search party for me. They found me in the woods, curled up next to a tree.

The other kid and I wouldn't tell where we got the alcohol. They were going to kick us out of camp, but the counselor covered for us. He said we had gotten into his personal wine supply without his knowledge and drank too much because we thought it was pop; we hadn't gotten drunk on purpose. He got reprimanded for having wine in the cabin, and we got off with lectures.

I'd never really felt anything from drinking Mom or Wally's beers, but this time it was different. The fear had evaporated as soon as the buzz arrived, and I felt wonderful—relaxed, happy, numb, then blackness. It was the first time I knew that alcohol could do something for me. I decided immediately to drink every chance I got.

The next time was with Beck at his house. He began to pick me up at home and take me to his apartment to watch TV for the evening. Mom thought it was all right because he was a counselor

CHAPTER FOURTEEN

and a schoolteacher, and she was probably happy to keep Wally and me apart.

On one visit, he asked me if I wanted to drink. I told him I liked beer, so he got some. I guzzled it because I knew what was coming, and sure enough, about halfway through the first bottle, the buzz reappeared. By the second bottle I felt strong, confident, happy. A different person. Alcohol was the answer I'd been searching for.

After that, he had beer for me each time I visited.

I was a blackout drinker from the beginning. I drank steadily until I was drunk and had no memory of what happened afterward. It was to be my basic drinking pattern.

One night, I was sitting on the floor and the counselor was sitting on the bed. We were watching TV and drinking Red, White & Blue beer. I'd guzzled a few and I was pretty buzzed. He came down off the bed and sat beside me, and something happened. I don't remember what except that it startled me, and I sort of blacked out.

A short time later I was in a store when he came in. He stopped short when he saw me.

"Hi!" I said, glad to see him.

A look of fear came over his face, and he turned and left the store quickly. I was puzzled and hurt. I thought he was a friend. And I wanted to ask him what had happened that night. Something about it seemed odd. It bothered me for some reason.

I never heard from him again. I ran into him occasionally in public, and whenever he saw me he'd look at me with panic and leave, fast. I always tried to approach him and ask why I didn't hear from him again, but he'd do everything he could to get away from me.

The counselor was arrested in 2000 for aggravated criminal sexual abuse and spent time in prison. For years he had invited adolescent boys to his home to drink, and then seduced them. It was his basic approach. He was caught when two boys told their school superintendent he had sexually abused them.

The counselor is registered in Illinois as a sexual predator. He lives near me, and I've often thought about knocking on his door and asking him what happened that night. I think he ran when he saw me because he was afraid I would confront him.

I can't be sure he molested me. But he definitely launched my drinking career.

After the counselor disappeared, Wally was my only source of alcohol. I stole enough of his Stroh's to get a buzz. I could only take so much without getting caught, so I had to control it.

My behavior at home got worse. I became particularly abusive to my mother. There were some kids whom she didn't want me to hang around. I'd ask her if I could go see them, and when she said no, I'd give her a hard time. I'd wait until she was at work, and then I'd call her and ask again. She'd say no again, and I'd get abusive. Finally she'd hang up on me. I'd call right back and yell, "Don't you hang up on me!" Then I'd start in again. I'd wear her down until she gave in. I was relentless.

She didn't always give in. Then I made her really pay.

That summer I stayed away from home as much as possible during the day, because Wally was there and Mom was at work. He was worse when Mom wasn't around. He toned it down when she was with us. Then one day, the bomb dropped. My mom asked Jeff and me what we thought about her and Wally getting married.

"No, Mom!" I yelled. "I don't like him! Don't do it! It's not going to be good, Mom."

She did it anyway. And she paid for it. I made her pay for it.

Just before school started, we moved into a small house on Brookside, across the road from Bettendorf High School. On September 24, 1977, my mother married Wally.

He promptly called Jeff and me in for an official fatherly talk. What I remember him saying was probably distorted by my resentment at the time, but what I heard essentially was, "I'm not here to be your friend or your pal. I've married your mother, so you guys are my responsibility now. I'm here to teach you."

To me it seemed like a stupid thing to say to a couple of kids. He thought he now had the right to give us orders, and he thought

CHAPTER FOURTEEN

we'd follow them. I thought, *You don't know what you're in for. I hope you really like Mom, because its not gonna be fun around here. I'm going to make your life hell.*

The conflict between Wally and I ramped up immediately. I had assigned tasks at home: do dishes, clean up dog poop, mow the lawn. I didn't want to do any of it, so I didn't put much effort into it.

"Do it again," Wally would say. "You're gonna do it right."

"I did it right, and I'm not doing it again."

"Yes, you are."

"No, I'm not."

And so on.

Jeff was more agreeable. But Wally would pick on him too, and that would irritate me and then I'd take Wally on. I was very protective of Jeff. I'd get the attention off my brother and take the heat.

I'd yell at Wally and then say, "You yell at me, but you leave him alone. He's off limits. If you want to mess with someone, you mess with me." He never hit me, but we sure had some shouting matches.

I did all kinds of things to make him crazy. I used his tools without permission and didn't put them back. I stole some of the dollar coins he saved in a jar down in the basement. I stole cans of his Stroh's beer out of the frig. I loved thinking about him being puzzled when he ran out of beer before he thought he should have.

He hated that I was a behavior problem at school, and I hated his lectures on respecting authority. I was proud of my contempt for authorities. In my opinion they were all jerks, him included.

I was angry with my mother for marrying him, and I punished her viciously for it. I argued, yelled and terrorized her. When she stood firm or sided with Wally, I got back at her. She loved plants—the house was full of them—and after one fight with her I sprayed every one in the house with her hairspray. I wanted to kill them all. I was infuriated when nothing died.

That winter, I lashed out at everyone. At school I was defiant and insulting to any authority figure, and at home I made life miserable for my mother and Wally. My only escape was the infrequent booze I could steal, and Happy Joe's. I worked there some days after school and stayed as long as I could at night. I didn't want to go home, because Wally was there permanently now.

Life sucked, and I made everybody pay.

Things didn't get better when school ended for the year. That summer was my last at Camp Abe Lincoln.

I was 12, which made me eligible to be an assistant counselor in one of the little kids' cabins. I really wanted to do it. I was officially made a Counselor in Training, a CIT, and I felt pretty important.

As part of our training, a group of us CITs went on a week-long canoe trip down a river, camping out along the way. I clashed immediately with another CIT, a guy about 20. I did something to make him mad; I probably left camp to go exploring without permission or something. I'm sure I teased him about it. He lost it and started choking me. He was a big guy and nearly killed me before another CIT pulled him off. It was reported, and they threw him out of camp.

They knew I'd played a part in it too, and they said I wasn't allowed to be a counselor that year. So I quit. I left camp early and never went back. I loved Camp Abraham Lincoln, but I threw it away. I saw it as punishing them, but I knew I was the one being punished. More proof that I was messed up.

That summer I had my first conscious sexual experience. Of a sort.

A couple of kids and I were on a bowling team, some kind of kid's league. An older guy, probably in his forties, was the janitor at the bowling alley. He was a short man, bald, with a belly, and he wore glasses. He gave us pointers on bowling, so we considered him our bowling coach.

He asked us if we wanted to make some money helping him clean the alley after it was closed at night. When a kid worked for him, he or she spent the night at his house, and he took the kid home in the morning.

CHAPTER FOURTEEN

One night, a friend of mine and I both worked at the alley and stayed overnight at the bowling coach's afterward. Mom must have agreed to it. I probably gave her a snow job about how the guy was a great bowling coach and good to kids.

The guy's apartment was small. His double bed was in the same room you entered when you came through the door, on the left side, and there was a couch against the right wall, where visiting kids slept. That night my friend got the couch, and I had to sleep in the bed with the coach.

I was on the left side of the bed, lying on my right side, facing the couch across the room. I was covered with an Afghan-like blanket. The coach was on the other side of the bed, against the wall.

Sometime during the night, the guy grabbed me and wrapped his arms and legs around the blanket and me in a tight bear hug. He started humping me, over and over, very fast. I woke up instantly in a panic. He had total physical control over me—the one thing I feared most.

I didn't know that much about sex, just the usual stuff I'd picked up from other kids and skin magazines, but I knew this guy was somehow having sex with me. It completely freaked me out. I knew what was happening was wrong, but I was paralyzed with fear. I couldn't move. I tried once to scream, but I couldn't make a sound. That terrified me even more. Finally, he let me go and rolled over away from me. I could feel sticky stuff through the afghan.

My friend slept through the whole thing. I wanted to leave, but I couldn't move. I couldn't even get out of bed. I spent the rest of the night unmoving, with my eyes open, consumed with shame and paralyzed with fear.

The man said nothing the next morning, and neither did I. To anybody. I got out of there as fast as I could. I have no memory of ever seeing him again.

The fear, and the panic attacks, returned with a vengeance.

CHAPTER FIFTEEN

AROUND THIS TIME, I started sixth grade at Bettendorf Middle School. It was about a mile from home, and I walked there. It was kind of an adventure following the creek and cutting through people's yards to get there each morning. I liked walking through the brush and weeds and sneaking through people's property without their knowledge.

A couple of the older guys working at Happy Joe's shared an apartment, and they let me come over sometimes. We'd work on model planes or just hang out. I loved it when older guys paid attention to me. I never stopped looking for a father. I'd bug them at the apartment and demand their attention until they got tired of me and ran me off.

That November I turned 12, and the guys started taking me duck and pheasant hunting. I was in heaven. I didn't hunt; I just tagged along. I usually went with Terry, the manager. He was cool; he played rock and roll, he drove a Jeep, and he had a wonderful black lab named Gertie. She could find anything, and I thought she was the best field dog in the world. She and I were buddies. She rode beside me in the Jeep, and I helped her retrieve the pheasants Terry shot.

The pheasants would scare me when they exploded up out of the weeds in front of us. I carried the ones Terry shot. They were big

CHAPTER FIFTEEN

and heavy in my hands and elegantly beautiful: long, light brown, black-barred tail feathers; striped wings; black-spotted golden sides and back; iridescent green head; vivid white neck ring.

Terry taught me the basics of how to hunt and about hunter safety: never point a gun at anybody, unload it before going over a fence, and always keep the safety on. He gave me books about safety and hunting.

We were duck hunting the first time he let me use his 20-gauge shotgun. He sat on my right in the blind. Some ducks flew in from the left, and I stood up and swung on them, following them to the right toward Terry. I shot, but I missed.

Terry took the gun away from me. He said I'd swung too close to him because I wasn't paying attention, which was how accidents happened. He'd been sitting and was in no real danger, but he wanted to teach me a lesson. I was horrified that I might have hurt someone I loved. To this day I'm extremely careful with guns.

I loved following the guys through the brush and tall grass, sitting in the duck blind, carrying birds and playing with Gertie. Terry took me hunting until my drinking interfered. Eventually he got married, and by then I was drinking more and more. I lost touch with him. But I'll never forget the time he took with me.

By now, my hair had grown down to my shoulders. It was frizzy, like an Afro. Wally hated it. So did my grandfather. He wanted me to have a crew cut. I'd flip my hair at him just to get his goat, and he'd go nuts and start yelling "funawony, funawony, funawony!" and chase me in his wheelchair. There was no way he could catch me. I'd let him get close, and then I'd run downstairs to Roger's office and laugh up the stairs at him while he sat at the top yelling.

Grandma would tell him, "Now, you stop it, that's your grandson." Once again I'd stand behind her making goofy faces and flip my hair at him. It drove him nuts with rage.

When I was mowing the lawn, he'd wheel his wheelchair up and down the sidewalk, watching me. He'd point back and forth at me and the grass, and yell, "Funawonay, funawonay, funawonay!" He was trying to tell me to keep the lines straight. I'd point back at him and yell, "Funawonay, funawonay!" Then I'd weave around with the lawnmower—cutting looping, crisscrossing lines in the grass—make faces at him and act like a crazy man. It infuriated him.

There was a black kid at school named Henry. He was a troublemaker like me, and we became instant friends. We teased each other constantly and always tried to get each other in trouble. We kept the class in a constant uproar.

The whole class would be quietly reading and I'd say loudly, "Henry, too bad you're too stupid to understand this."

"You know all about stupid," he'd say.

The teacher, Mr. Winters, would step in, but we'd ignore him and pretend to have this huge verbal fight.

"Both you boys be quiet NOW!" Mr. Winters would roar.

"But he called me stupid!" I'd protest, looking hurt and wounded. We would both shout at each other in feigned indignation, call each other names, and then off to the principal we'd go.

The class loved it.

Detention was a real pain. They made us write stuff over and over. "I will not disrupt the class." I hated it. *You idiots think writing this 400 times will make me a good kid? How stupid are you? Where did you get your degree?* It was lame, and it just made me want to do more bad things. So I acted up in detention as well, because they were forcing me to do something against my will. Naturally, that produced more detention.

Mr. Winters, my homeroom teacher and history teacher, didn't put up with anything and sent me to the principal the second I got out of hand. But he never acted as if I were worthless. He understood me. He ran a tight ship, but I could sense that he respected me. Just like Mr. Fisher had. I was glad Mr. Winters was my teacher.

I continued to drink when I could get alcohol, which wasn't often. Although Wally couldn't prove it, he knew where his beer was going, and he kept a close watch on me, so I had to be careful. I thought about drinking all the time.

CHAPTER SIXTEEN

MY DRINKING PICKED up when school ended. It was mostly a weekend thing, whenever some kids and I could score a six-pack. We'd get some older guys to buy it for us. I'd started working behind the counter making pizzas at Happy Joe's, so I now had more money.

Even in the beginning, drinking made me mean. I'd get mouthy, sarcastic, and even berate the kids I drank with. I was always challenging someone to show that no one had control over me and no one could do anything to me. No one was going to hurt me.

I hated getting up in the morning. It took me a while to wake up, and when Mom or Wally tried to hurry me up, I made them pay. Mom called me "Mr. Personality." She'd say, "Can this be the same boy who used to go to bed early and get up cheerful?" That irritated me even more.

I tormented Wally and drove him crazy. He had a wooden toolbox that he kept organized and neat. He didn't want me using his tools, so I'd ask him if I could in front of Mom, real sweet and innocent, and then pretend to be hurt that he didn't trust me. She'd take my side and he'd give in, and when I was done with the tools I'd throw them back in the box in a mess, or leave them laying around on the garage floor. Sometimes I hid them.

I caused conflict between Wally and Mom every chance I got. I loved getting him in trouble. Mom was always torn, but she was protective of me so I usually got her on my side. I had to be cautious, though. She was no dummy. She knew I was an agitator and spotted it if I got too obvious. I'd whine and explain how Wally was being a jerk, and at the slightest flicker of suspicion on her face I'd shift the story until belief reappeared. I was an expert at this dance of deception. Wally would protest what he knew were lies, but that was fine with me. If I could upset him enough he'd raise his voice. That would tick my mother off, and I would win. I had to be outrageous and subtle at the same time. It was power, and I loved it. I was a master manipulator.

Sometimes Wally and I couldn't even be in the same room together. His favorite hiding place was in the cellar, but I knew how to get to him even there.

It irritated him that my mother did so much for me. While he was down in the cellar, I'd sweet-talk my mother, be real friendly, and then ask her to make me something to eat. Then I'd yell down the cellar stairs, "Hey, Wally, Mom just made me some cookies. I might not eat them all. If there's one left, you want it?"

CHAPTER SEVENTEEN

A SCHOOLTEACHER FRIEND of mine once said jokingly that boys went nuts in seventh grade. Testosterone poisoning, he said. For sure, I crossed a line in seventh grade. I got more outrageous and even meaner.

Henry and I raised continuous, unmitigated hell, and the class loved it. They were bored, too. In history class, Henry sat in the row behind me. One time when I got up to get something, he sharpened a pencil and stuck it through a hole in my chair. I came back and sat down on it and drove the pencil a good inch into my buttock. I let out a screech and jumped up. "You stabbed me in the butt!"

He was laughing so hard he could hardly talk. "Gotcha! Gotcha! Shove that up there!"

The teacher threw both of us out of class, and the school nurse had to pull the pencil out. I still have a piece of that lead in my rear. But I got even the next day. During lunch, I got a straw in the cafeteria and made a spitball out of the paper wrapping. I chewed it until it was all wet and nasty but still in a solid lump. Back in history class, I turned around and saw Henry reading. I yelled at him and he looked up, his mouth open, his eyebrows up and his eyes wide. I was deadly with a straw and spitball, and I couldn't miss at that range. I nailed him right in the eye.

He let out a shriek and jumped up, putting his hands over his eyes. "You shot my eye out!" He started staggering around, banging into desks, squealing like a pig, and crying and shaking his head. I was laughing so hard I was choking, and the whole class was in an uproar.

Henry's eye was red for a week. I got two week's detention.

I learned about the Romans in Winter's history class. They fascinated me because they were always waging wars, and I thought fighting and combat were cool. They had shiny armor, cool uniforms with leather padding, intricate shields, spears, bows and arrows, and they fought on horseback. I thought the chariots and the fights at the coliseum were incredibly cool. Fighting had always interested me, and the Romans were a bunch of fighting fanatics who took over everybody. They were powerful warriors. What's not to love about that? What wasn't interesting? History class was storytelling time, basically, and what kid doesn't love a story? What geek wants to sit and do math problems instead of listening to a cool story about a society of warriors who took over the whole world? It was a no-brainer.

I loved history throughout the rest of my years in school. I loved to hear stories of the past, other civilizations and their cultures, and their wars. No matter how bad my marks were, I always got an A in history.

I liked Mr. Winters, too. He continued to treat me with respect even though I was aggravating to him. He gave me options. He'd tilt his head, give me a look and say, "Billy, come on, let's be part of this." He'd let me get away with just so much and then he'd say, "OK, now that's enough. I want you to do this. If you get the work done I'll let you go out in the hallway and hang out." Of course, it took me almost all of class to do the work, but getting out of class even a minute ahead of everyone else was cool. Winters gave me boundaries, and I accepted them. I knew he liked me.

When I acted out, Mr. Winters usually gave me extra history projects to do instead of stupid detention punishments. He didn't like what I did, but he didn't judge me. I did the extra history

CHAPTER SEVENTEEN

projects without raising hell. I enjoyed them. I felt pretty smart, too; I knew more about history than the other kids in my class.

The common denominator between Mr. Winters and Mr. Fisher was that they both gave me respect. They knew how to treat me.

That fall, the glandular light bulb went on, and it hit me that the school was swarming with girls. Female stimulus was everywhere: clothing, hair, animated faces, giggling, rounded chests and hips. The position of class clown took on new importance. Girls looked at me and laughed. I was cool! I got louder and more brazen.

One girl always grinned at me when I acted up. One day I bumped into her in the hall, and we both stopped and looked at each other face to face. She smiled, but my mind went blank. I couldn't talk.

I grabbed her purse and pulled it out of her hand. "You girls sleep with these things? What's in them that's so important you gotta carry them around all the time?"

Her face fell.

I panicked; I wanted her to keep smiling. But I couldn't help myself. I opened her purse and started poking around inside. "Looks like junk to me."

"Jerk!" she said. She grabbed her purse and stomped off.

That became my pattern. Every time I opened my mouth to say something friendly to a girl, an insult came out. "Man, those braces must suck. Your teeth must be pretty messed up, huh?" Finally I gave up. Any girl I was interested in or who tried to be friendly—in the end, any girl who paused nearby—I was mean to. I stole their purses and books and hid them. I mocked their voices and their movements. I insulted their hair and clothes. Eventually, they all avoided me.

It was the familiar pattern: I was destroying what I wanted. I wanted the friendship of girls, so I drove them off. I let no girl get close to me. All around me I saw boys and girls laughing, flirting and pairing up. Everyone else seemed normal and happy. I watched, furious and resentful and despairing. The belief that I was defective was too strong, the urge to be destructive too overwhelming.

My first thoughts of suicide occurred in the seventh grade. They were just thoughts; at that point I was far from actually doing it or even harming myself. Two situations seemed to trigger it. When I felt defective, it made sense that I should be eliminated. Throw out the damaged goods. When my fear got overwhelming, I wanted to not feel anything, like booze numbed me but more effective, more permanent.

The idea would pop into my head without any real emotional impact, like a mechanic considering a solution to a vehicle problem. Maybe I needed a new alternator. Maybe I should kill myself. The idea wasn't obsessive yet.

One student, Bo Krebs, was a jock. He picked on me, slapped me on the back every day when I was at my locker, shoved me and laughed at me. The other jocks that followed him around laughed at me, too. He was big and muscular, and I knew he could beat me up so I took it and tried to hide my shaking hands. Sometimes I fantasized about kickboxing his face, but that brief surge of power had a price—the return of my shame at having failed to take karate.

Sports fascinated me, just as they had since I was a kid. Competition and physical activity. But I was afraid I wouldn't be good enough.

I went out for football. During my second practice I did something wrong, just some stupid mistake, and the coach said, "Billy, quit messing around. Run four laps around the field."

It was routine coach stuff, but I took it to next level. "You think you can make me run around the field four times?" I yelled. I swore at him, stomped off and never went back.

I went out for wrestling, too, but quit because I couldn't take orders. Eventually I gave up going out for sports, although I really wanted to play. Whenever an authority figure tried to give me directions, even casually, I got nasty.

But mainly I quit because I knew I'd fail.

CHAPTER EIGHTEEN

IN SEVENTH GRADE I met Todd Cale. He was my height but stocky and muscular, rough looking, with shoulder-length dark hair and hands beat up from fighting. I liked his tough appearance and his surly attitude, and he liked how I defied the teachers. One day he asked if I wanted to go to his house that weekend. He and his older brother were known tough guys, and this was a clear invite to join the rough crowd.

Todd's brother, Wally, went to high school. He was a good looking kid, about six feet tall and real muscular, with a dark-complexioned Native American look, high cheekbones and long dark hair. He was a nice guy, but violent if you made him mad. He had a reputation for being a vicious fighter. He belonged to a gang called The Rednecks. There were about 12 of them, and nobody messed with them.

Wally and Todd were tough. They each had a few twisted fingers that they had broken while fighting. They fought physically all the time, even with each other. I mean, they pounded each other, even drew blood sometimes. The first day I went to their house they had a knife fight in the kitchen.

I showed up in the morning. Wally was making breakfast, and he said, "Todd, you want some eggs?" Todd probably should have known something was up; I was to learn that they weren't usually that considerate of each other. But Todd said, "Yeah!"

So Wally started cooking Todd's eggs. From where I sat at the table, I saw him dump about half the contents of the peppershaker into the eggs. Then he flipped the eggs over so the pepper didn't show and put them on Todd's plate.

"Eggs are ready," he said and set the plate on the table. He stepped back and stood by the stove, snickering. I was holding in a laugh too; it was exactly the sort of thing I'd do.

Todd took one big bite and started choking. He didn't even hesitate; he whipped his knife across the kitchen at Wally, and it stuck in the wall beside him.

Wally threw a big sharp cooking fork at him, and they started pounding each other. I crawled under the table; there were knives and forks and plates flying everywhere. Their mom came running downstairs and yelled, "Knock it off!" They stopped fighting instantly.

That was my first experience at the Cale's. There was always something exciting happening there. I just loved that place.

Wally and Todd's house was a hangout for six or eight of us. Most of them were older than me, in high school. The house was a two-and-a-half story building that looked kind of like a barn. They lived right on the main street in downtown Bettendorf. Everybody always came in the back door, which led up a couple of steps into the kitchen. Todd and Wally's dad was always sitting beside the window at the kitchen table. He was a real end-stage alcoholic who drank two fifths of whiskey a day. He'd sit in the window and cook those off. He had names for us all. When we came in, he'd look at us all and yell, "You get out of here!" He wasn't kidding; he meant it. Todd and Wally would come in from the other end of the house and yell, "Dad, shut up!"

Todd's mom was great. She always cooked for us all. Everybody called her Mrs. Cale. Todd and Wally fought each other all the time, but no matter how violent the fight got, when their mom said, "Knock it off!" that ended it.

CHAPTER EIGHTEEN

I felt safe with the group even though they were hardcore tough guys. They had experienced a hard life growing up. I never had any of my usual fear with them, and I never felt like I was bad or different around them like I did with other kids. I felt safe. We were all misfits, and I received total acceptance from them. I was a defiant troublemaker with no fear of authority, so even though I was a small guy, I was accepted immediately. I was one of them.

We all teased and insulted each other constantly. We were cruel and outright nasty. I was hands-down the best tease in the group. I was an artist in verbal torment and mockery. I was mouthy, sarcastic and relentless. No matter how anyone insulted me, I had an instantaneous comeback, and they always looked like a fool. I could never have held my own physically, but they were afraid of my mouth.

That was my role, and I was grateful for it. It gave me power, control and approval. I had nothing but admiration for these guys, because absolutely no one was going to hurt them. They were warriors, and they let me hang with them.

I was the center of attention when I was on a roll tormenting someone, the life of the party. I'd start in on someone, and pretty soon the rest of the guys would be cracking up. They valued physical strength and skill and appearance, so I picked on physical weaknesses. Let my victim pretend I wasn't bothering them; I knew better. I kept pounding away until they blew up. Then everyone joined in, and we all laughed. My ultimate goal was to get Wally laughing. He was the toughest of the group, and I idolized him.

Todd had a big sort of lump on his forehead, so I called him "Caveman." He hated it. Wally was really good looking, so I named him "Pretty Boy." That always got laughs, but I didn't push it. If you torqued out Wally, you knew it. He had a look that could terrify you. His eyes got really black, and his face became empty and expressionless. The other guys warned me, "When Wally gets that look, he's ready to blow, and if he does he'll kill you."

Sometimes tempers flared and we fought and pounded on each other. I never knew when to stop teasing. I almost always went too far, and I often got beat up for it. I paid that price willingly.

Wally loved it when I teased people, so when they finally snapped and started beating on me, he'd step in and make them stop. I knew he'd protect me, so I took on anyone. I'd tackle anybody, no matter how big or tough.

I mean, we were all friends. We'd beat on each other, give each other some bruises or a black eye, but it was in fun. Nothing serious. Broken bones—that was when those guys meant it.

Hanging around with Todd, Wally and the guys, fighting with them, and getting slapped and shoved around on an almost daily basis hardened me. I learned to take pain without complaining. Black eye, split lip, blood, it didn't bother me. We fought all the time. It was more of a playful thing, but it did hurt—I mean, we really did beat on each other. Fighting with them just made you tough. When you were running with the big dogs, you didn't whine. It was a sign of weakness. These guys weren't TV or movie actors. They were the real thing. They were warriors.

This was the beginning of my serious, steady drinking. I drank with Wally and Todd at first, but as my drinking progressed, I hung out more and more with Wally. Todd didn't drink too much, but Wally did. He drank a lot.

We usually got our beer through Wally. He worked at a gas station, and he bought it there. We never had any problem getting alcohol. Either somebody would buy it for us or, later, we would use fake IDs. I was a beer drinker at first. Later I got into vodka.

At school, Bo Krebs was an almost daily humiliating ordeal. I didn't mention it to Todd or the rest of the group, because I was afraid they'd see it as weakness. I could guess their response. I could hold my own with them, so why was I afraid of Bo Krebs?

I fantasized about beating his face shapeless.

Todd and I did a lot of dangerous stuff. In the winter we went bumper skiing. After a big storm hit, we'd wait for cars that were going slower because of the snow. We'd hide in the bushes by a stop sign and wait for a car to stop. When the car started to drive off, we'd run and grab the bumper and, using our feet as skis, we'd

CHAPTER EIGHTEEN

slide behind the car as it took off. Sometimes the drivers would get going 30 to 40 miles an hour. We never knew when we were going to let go. We lost a lot of gloves, because they got stuck in the bumper. You really had to watch it, because if people knew you were on their bumper they'd slam on the brakes and you'd slide under the car. That happened plenty of times. The driver would jump out, but we'd be up and running. Nobody caught us.

One time, Todd and I made a raft out of Styrofoam blocks, the kind that hold up docks. We tied them together with ropes and made this little raft, maybe four-feet-by-four-feet square. There was barely room for the two of us to stand, but the raft was plenty buoyant. There had just been a major flood, and Duck Creek was overflowing. We put the raft in way up by Palmer Hills Golf Course and rode it all the way down into the mouth of the Mississippi. The raft bobbed and lurched and spun, and we staggered, flailed our arms, clung to each other, let go and clung again. We stayed upright all the way down Duck Creek. It was a blast.

But the river was raging, and because we didn't have paddles or anything, we couldn't get off the raft. We got carried out into the Mississippi itself. The current was really strong, and we were carried along, helpless, shifting and weaving to stay upright. There was a dike along the river with huge fans in it. You didn't want to get near those. We were scared we'd get sucked in and drown, but we got washed right by them.

Todd lived by the twin bridges that crossed from Illinois to Iowa. We rode that little raft all the way down to the bridges and by luck floated up against shore there. We just got off the raft and walked to his house.

CHAPTER NINETEEN

DURING THE SUMMER between seventh and eighth grade, I started sneaking out at night. We lived in a one-story house, and I just opened the screen and slid out. The bottom edge of the window was only five feet off the ground. I had a way of pulling the screen back down to lock it, and I made little holes in the screen to unlock it.

Hanging out at the Cale's was heaven. There were absolutely no rules. We'd watch TV and drink a few beers, and then Todd and I would go screw around by the railroad tracks. The tracks ran along the Mississippi River, through downtown, past factories, and through industrial areas. The tracks became our hangout. When we heard the whistle of a train coming, we'd run down to the track and hide behind some structure so the train guys couldn't see us. They were watching for people jumping the trains—bums, but not so much kids.

The train slowed way down to about five miles per hour when coming through the city, but we still had to run alongside at a pretty good pace to grab onto the ladder that ran up the side of a boxcar. Then we'd climb up in there. Or we'd wait for an open boxcar and run and jump inside the door. The floor was probably four feet off the ground. We'd dive in and grab hold of the floor.

CHAPTER NINETEEN

We waited for flatbed cars with brand new automobiles on them. We'd get into the vehicles and pretend we were driving. We'd turn the lights on and climb around. Sometimes we'd jump into an open boxcar and find a couple of bums, rummies, sitting in there. We'd talk to them, and sometimes they'd talk back. Sometimes they'd just sit there and stare at us.

The train would travel through town at the same slow speed. We'd ride it down to the other end of Bettendorf and get off, and then wait for another one coming back and jump it. It was probably a couple of miles each way. We did it all the time.

Every once in a while the trains would stop in the city, and while they were sitting in the yard we'd go along the sides of the boxcars and check out the contents. One was full of new furniture, too big for us to haul out. We got into a freezer car that had Wendy's hamburgers and French fries and lugged boxes of fries back to the Cale's.

Once we broke into a caboose and found a wooden crate full of explosive charges, called track warning detonators. They were about the size and shape of a pack of cigarettes, with lead straps to attach them to the top of a rail. A single charge was placed where a caboose would run over it when the engineer was backing the train up. The weight of the train blew the charge and warned the engineer not to back up any further.

Todd decided he'd have a fireworks show. He strapped some charges against each other in a line on one track, and then another line the same length on the other track directly across from it. A train backed up and hit the charges, and they blew with a WHAM!

The more I hung out with the Cales and their gang, the less I saw of Tony. But he and I still did some things together. One night when I got drunk with him, we were walking toward a landscape tie wall at a McDonald's. I thought there was level ground on the other side of the tie, so I stepped over it. Actually, there was a five-foot drop on the other side, and I went down and fell on my right knee. It swelled up bad, but I covered it up by telling my mom that I had sprained it while we were goofing around. It was never treated, and to this day the kneecap bone still bulges out along the edge. But it was worth it. I loved booze and what it did for me. I didn't care what price I had to pay.

Todd and Wally went to keg parties, and one time they asked me to come along. It was down by the river at Lock & Dam #14. There was a small island connected to shore by a dike, and we walked across the dike and went to the upstream end of the island where there was a sandy beach. It was about a half-mile hike, and we carried a keg the whole way. It was a common partying spot, and when we arrived we found about 20 boys and girls there.

There was plenty of fighting and teasing of one another, but I was always secure with Wally and Todd around. There were some fun times at those kegs.

I thought of Bo Krebs, and my hands shook with fear and anticipation. I wanted to kill him.

Dan Johnson had been in some of my seventh grade classes, and we became friends that summer. He was another sort of misfit. His mother and father were divorced and he lived with his father, Floyd, one block over from Todd and Wally's house.

Dan was a nice guy and became part of our group. Sometimes we'd meet first at Dan's and then go over to Todd and Wally's. Sometimes we'd go to Cale's first and then to Dan's, because Dan usually drove if we were going out.

Floyd Johnson was in his fifties, rugged, with a full head of hair. He was kind of an adoptive dad to us. We'd all sit down together before we'd go out for the night, and Floyd would be sitting at the table with his usual cup of coffee and his non-filtered Camel cigarettes. He always had a cup of coffee and a cigarette. He'd give Dan $20, and sometimes he'd give me $20 because he knew I didn't have any money. He knew we were going to go out drinking and would get into trouble, so he'd give us a little speech.

"Now, you guys don't get into too much trouble tonight, and don't get any girls pregnant. I don't want any calls from the police tonight." He was basically saying, "Go ahead and be boys, I already know you're going to, but don't get into too much trouble." We took it to heart and said, "OK."

CHAPTER NINETEEN

Floyd was really straightforward with us. He'd rough us up kind of affectionately—he'd grab us by the shoulders, shake us and say in a mock mean tone, "You behave yourself!" He was a rough, tough old guy. He'd give us the truck to drive and say, "Dan, you're driving, so no drinking. Everybody else can, but you keep a lid on it." Dan wasn't really a big drinker like the rest of us anyway; he could take it or leave it. He was the designated driver.

Floyd knew what we'd go out and do, but it was because he was real with us that we actually tried to keep it somewhat under control. We did it out of respect for him.

Dan was goofy and clumsy, a tall and lanky kid with a long face and chin. We called him "Horse" and teased him. "Come on, horse face," we would say. He was into punk rock and we weren't, so we razzed him mercilessly about that. He gave it back to us as well, but he wasn't really a fighter, and when he got physical he got beat up. He was a great artist and could draw anything, and an absolutely fabulous pool player. Today, he plays professionally in pool tournaments.

CHAPTER TWENTY

BO KREBS STARTED in on me again on the first day of eighth grade. He came up behind me in the hall and whacked me on the back of the head. A couple of his jock buddies laughed.

Two days later I was at my locker when Bo slapped me from behind again. Something snapped in me, and my fear turned to a cold, controlled rage. I turned around and said, "That's the last time you'll ever do that."

"Really?" he said, grinning. "Let's talk about it after school."

I was fearful but excited all day. After school, Krebs and I met in someone's back yard. About ten other kids were watching. I was still kind of small and skinny, about five-foot six-inches and 130 pounds, and Krebs had gotten even bigger and more rugged over the summer.

He stood in front of me and said, "So, what are you going to do?" All my fear evaporated. I'd been toughened by a year of roughhousing with the Cales and their gang; Krebs couldn't come close to dishing out what I'd tolerated in fun. The Cales would have mopped the ground up with him—and I was one of the Cales.

I didn't even bother to answer him. I just attacked him and started pounding him in the face. I was deeply angry, yet strangely

CHAPTER TWENTY

calm and lucid. I remember thinking, *I'm not taking any more from you! No more!* And I kept thinking, over and over, *I'll show you what pain is.*

His face was bleeding in seconds, and he went down quickly and lay there whimpering. I stood over him, exultant. For a long time this guy had tormented me, and all of a sudden, just like that, it was over. I'd ended it. I felt enormous triumph, and hope. Dominant. Free of fear. I said nothing as Krebs got to his feet and left in humiliation.

The word spread fast, and I gained enormous respect. Todd told Wally and the rest of the guys, and I basked in their grins and slaps.

I was a warrior.

My encounter with Krebs marked the beginning of my serious fighting. From then on I looked for fights. There would be many more, and during each one I would silently chant, *I'll show you what pain is. I'll show you what pain is.* It was my war mantra.

That fall an older black man, LaVerne Dixon, used to take me and Todd and other guys raccoon hunting. Everybody called him Dix. He was a schoolteacher and lived by the high school.

We loved going coon hunting because it took place in the middle of the night. A couple of us would ride in the front seat of Dix's old beat up '71 Chevy pickup, making fun of him because he drove at least 20 miles an hour under the speed limit. It would take us forever to get to the hunting places. We'd keep saying, "Dix, would you hurry up?" He'd smile and shake his head. "Boys, there's just no hurry."

He loved sour cream and onion potato chips and orange pop. He'd have his potato chips on the dashboard and his orange pop in his lap, and he was constantly crunching chips and slurping pop while we crawled along. Crunch, crunch, slurp, slurp. It drove us crazy. I'd say, "Do you do that because you're black?" He'd just laugh. He had chips and pop for us, too.

He had six raccoon dogs, and we chased after them through the woods in the dark while they chased a coon, baying. When the coon was treed, Dix would let us shoot it. He taught us how to skin the animal right in the woods. He was incredibly fast; he could do it in less than 45 seconds. He'd just make a couple of cuts and use his weight—he was a big guy—and peel the skin right off. I mean, he was really good.

At the end of the night, we'd be dead tired and fall asleep in the truck on the way home. We loved it. It was a great adventure, running through the woods in the dark after the hounds with this big black man. Dix was good to us, an older guy who gave us teenagers something to do.

The other high point of eighth grade was my discovery of trapping, which became a lifelong passion for me. Tony, Todd and I had been reading *Fur-Fish-Game* magazine, and the trapping articles fascinated us. My first real big paycheck from Happy Joe's was for $202, and I spent the whole thing on trapping supplies. Dix showed us how to make a few simple sets, and when trapping season opened that fall, Tony and I set traps in the woods and fields by Palmer Hills Golf Course.

My first catch was an opossum. The long, silky thick fur was beautiful; white underneath, then dark, then silver tipped. Next was a raccoon, with its dense luxurious grizzled coat. I loved stroking the fur.

It was a beautiful time of year. The changing vegetation was rich with reds, browns, yellows, oranges and the deep greens of conifers. The weather was dramatic and changing; rain squalls, clear, crisp blue skies, dramatic moving clouds, the first light drifting snowflakes. I felt clear, healthy and strong. I didn't want to go indoors.

We caught more raccoons and opossums, and I discovered that I had a gift for understanding animal behavior and a fascination with it. I learned how to identify droppings, tracks and trails, scratches on trees, a hair caught in the brush. I developed an intuitive sense of where to find the animals and what they'd do. I was a natural hunter.

CHAPTER TWENTY

I felt no fear and no anger while trapping. It was taken out of me, gone. When we caught something, I felt successful and competent. I loved handling the furs, and they were worth good money, especially the raccoons. We made back my $202 within a couple of weeks, which made me feel successful, too.

In school I spent hours going over our trapline in my mind, thinking about our catches and planning improvements. I stopped raising hell in class; I didn't want detention because I wanted to get home as fast as possible after school to skin our morning's catch and prepare equipment and bait for the next day.

It was good to be with Tony again, too.

Winter snows came, and the trapping season ended. I was bummed for a few weeks, but then I started planning next year's trapline. I knew it would be longer and better. I dreamed of trapping for a living.

We did crazy stuff. In winter Duck Creek froze over, and when the spring thaw came the creek would rise over the banks and the ice would break up in chunks and float downstream on the flood current. Some of the floes were easily six feet across. Tony and a couple other older kids and I would jump on the big ones and ride them downstream. The floes were fairly stable, and sometimes we were able to ride one all the way to the Mississippi. The floes shifted and tipped and spun in the current enough to make it somewhat dangerous, and therefore an adventure. We figured it was like surfing.

It was much more dangerous to jump from floe to floe. I was fast and light and had great coordination, so I was good at it. It was a blast.

One time we floated way downstream, half a mile from the Mississippi. When I jumped to another floe, I hit the edge instead of the middle and slid into the water. I thought I was a goner; the current was strong and I was numb with shock from the frigid water. I wouldn't have made it without Tony and the others. We were completely soaked, and it was a cold, miserable three-mile walk home. My clothes froze almost solid.

We drank almost every weekend. At this time I was still somewhat in control of my drinking. I was afraid to go home drunk, which made me stop when it was almost time to leave. Dan acted as a control on me. He was much more responsible, and I listened because he was my ride home.

Always, though, drinking gave me relief from fear. Always.

CHAPTER TWENTY-ONE

THE SUMMER BEFORE high school, I snuck out at night on a regular basis. Todd, Wally and the guys would creep the car down the street with the lights off at about 1 A.M., and I'd crawl out my window and join them. If a bunch of us were going, we'd ride in Mrs. Cale's big Vista Cruiser station wagon. It was a long four-door car with a big trunk-like storage space in the back that was open to the back seat. We could jam six guys in easy. We called it the Vista Bruiser.

My drinking really picked up. We had our own parties, crashed other parties, but weren't drinking in bars at this point.

They'd take me home just before dawn. Todd and Wally were usually driving. As soon as I was crawling in my bedroom window, they'd start blowing the horn and yelling, "Bill's home! Bill's home!" Then they'd peel out. I could hear Mom coming up the hall, and I'd close the curtains and fly into bed with my clothes and shoes on. I could hear her open the door and look in, and I wouldn't move. I'd freeze. I never got caught.

They did it to me every time I got out of the car. I'd say, "Now, don't do that, I'm going to get into trouble, stop it." And they'd say, "Oh, no, no, no, we promise, we won't do it no more." As soon as I was going through the window, they'd lay on the horn and yell and peel out. I'd threaten, beg and try to reason with them. We'd have these serious, in-depth, meaningful conversations. I'd say, "Now, look, I'm really going to get into trouble. Promise me you won't do it." And they'd say, "Yeah, OK, we won't do that anymore. We know you'll get into trouble, so we promise we won't do that tonight." It was this sincere, almost tearful moment between us. But it always ended the same way. HONK! HONK! HONK! "Bill's home! Bill's home!" Then squealing tires and beer bottles being thrown into the front yard.

Todd and Wally did it to everybody. At the end of the night we'd make the rounds and drop everybody off. I always hated to be the first one dropped off because everybody was all riled up, and they'd be screaming and lights would be coming on up and down the street.

I was 15 now, and I had more freedom. My parents were losing control over me. Some nights I'd tell them I was staying overnight at a friend's house. I could usually find a place to crash, but if I couldn't I'd go to a nearby apartment complex. The main entrance was always open, and I'd go down one flight of stairs to the basement and sleep under the stairs. No one ever went down there at night. I used it so regularly that I kept a pillow and blanket down there. Nobody ever touched it. The next morning I'd go home around noon and clean up.

When we were out drinking, anything could trigger a fight with us. We'd be at a party and everyone would be making fun of everyone else, and too many people would start laughing at someone. The guy would get worked up and start swinging. I was always agitating; even if the whole party went ballistic and a big fight started, we always had a chance because Wally could take on ten people himself. I got pounded on, but I did some pounding. All fear left me when I attacked someone.

We had keg parties, usually outside along the river or at somebody's house. People always cringed when Wally, Todd and I showed up. I loved the looks on their faces when we walked in, because they knew something was going to happen. I was with these guys, and I felt powerful.

CHAPTER TWENTY-ONE

Pleasant Valley was a rival town, and we went to parties there. At one Pleasant Valley party some kids there said, "No, no more, no starting anything tonight, please." Of course, we promised we wouldn't do anything. This one guy was known to be the toughest in Pleasant Valley High School, and at some point he walked up to Wally and said, "Yeah, I've heard of you." They got in a fight, and Wally beat him up bad.

One night when Wally and I were out drinking, we went into a Mexican restaurant to use the bathroom. We were minding our own business. There were two guys in the rest room, and when I was using the urinal one came up from behind me and slapped me on the back of the head. I turned around and shoved him. The other guy came for me, and Wally grabbed him and threw him against the wall.

The fight moved out into the entryway of the restaurant. I was barely holding my own with one guy, taking more punishment than I was giving. The other guy charged Wally and knocked him through a round glass entryway table. There was broken glass everywhere. Wally dropped the guy and then grabbed the guy who was beating on me and thrashed him.

Wally pounded both those guys. In my mind, Wally could have been the world's ultimate fighting champion. To me he had absolutely no fear of anything. I admired him tremendously.

Cale's house continued to be the hangout where everything happened. Mrs. Cale was our adopted mother. She fed us, took care of us and cleaned us up the next morning. She was a tough old woman herself; I mean, she'd knock you senseless if you gave her grief. We did what she said and didn't mess with her. We had great respect for Mrs. Cale.

I gradually began to lose touch with Tony. He'd hang out at the Cale's for a few days, and then he'd fade off again. He wasn't into the drinking and fighting like I was.

I had believed in God ever since I was a child, even though I didn't like going to church. I'd been told that God had made the whole world and that He loved everyone, and I believed it. The overwhelming beauty of the natural world alone showed me that He existed and was good.

I never gave God much thought as a child. But that summer I started to wonder about Him. Who was He, anyway? If He loved me, why did He let me be so miserable? Was He punishing me for being bad? I didn't want to be bad. Did God make me bad? If so, He did not love me; in fact, that made Him bad.

I was terrified that He would punish me for even thinking such a thing about Him, but the part of me that suspected it might be true made me angry with Him. My twin companions, fear and anger, starting dancing a new step. I had entered the convoluted, tortured thinking of adolescence.

I started high school that fall. We lived across the road from Bettendorf High, but I was late to school every day. Mom would try to get me going in the morning, but I'd mess around and deliberately go slow. She'd make me breakfast and call the school to tell them I'd be late.

Over the summer I had done anything I wanted to do, pretty much without restraint, so it was almost impossible for me to go back into an environment where people told me what to do every minute. I was in serious trouble instantly.

I chewed snuff in class, ate in class, talked in class, cussed in class, and showed the teachers absolutely no respect. I got kicked out of classes on a regular basis. I got thrown out of every class I was in at least once. I was in the principal's office constantly. I just laughed at them. I knew they couldn't really do anything except expel me, and that was fine with me. I didn't want to be there anyway.

My stepfather, Wally, was outraged. He ranted about how I was disobedient, disrespectful, didn't follow through on assigned tasks, and cared nothing for the family. I just laughed at him.

I had to wear a tie when I worked at Happy Joe's. One day I forgot to bring one, and the manager sent me home to get it. I never went back.

Wally was furious.

CHAPTER TWENTY-ONE

My interest in girls increased, and I always had my eye on one in particular. But I'd tease her about her name or clothing, steal her purse or books, or do other juvenile stuff to drive her off. I always knew I would never have a relationship with a girl because I was nothing, a nobody. When I liked a girl, I'd dream that I could be with her, like my friends did with their girlfriends. But I knew I couldn't.

I was afraid of girls. I associated dating with sex, and for some reason, even though I'd never had sex, I thought it was a horrible act. I had discovered masturbation, but while it was unbelievably enjoyable, afterward I always felt tremendous guilt and shame. It made me feel terrible about myself. I believed that somehow I was being bad—that it was wrong and good people didn't do it. But I continued to do it, and I continued to feel worse and worse about myself.

I had a crush on this one girl. I forget her name. She was beautiful, just beautiful. She had a cool car, a Cobra, and we'd go for rides or just hang around and talk. We never did anything physical, never even made out. The relationship, if you can call it that, only lasted a couple of weeks. We never really dated. But I had a really bad crush on her for a long time. I think she was interested in me. I'll never know now.

I didn't date in high school until almost the end. My entire social life consisted of hanging out with my buddies and drinking, and later, drugging.

That fall, Tony and I trapped together again. Raccoons were our main targets; they were now worth $40 or more. We checked the traps in the morning before school, on foot. We had a longer line than the previous year, and we walked miles and carried the heavy animals back to my house. Raccoons can weigh up to 30 pounds, and some days we caught several. We skinned them in the garage after school.

Once again my fear evaporated while I was trapping; it was like it had never existed. The fall weather and colorful foliage I loved so much invigorated me and healed me. My thoughts were clear and positive when I was trapping. I couldn't wait to get out of bed in the morning. We caught a number of raccoons, I think more than 20. I felt tremendous accomplishment; I was good at something. Really good. I dreamed of making a living trapping. And it was great to be with Tony again.

It would be my last trapping season for a long time, and my last interlude with the boy who had been my best friend for so long. Alcohol and drugs would take them both from me.

My behavior in school got so bad that my parents and the school referred me to the Vera French Mental Health Center. I went from January 4th to the 18th. I don't remember much about the experience except that I had to talk with these two therapists. I wasn't interested in anything they had to say; I listened because I had to, and I said what I thought they wanted to hear so I could get out of there. I tried to convince them that Wally was the problem.

Vera French did no apparent good; I continued to make life hell for everyone, at home and in school.

That summer when I wanted to get away from home or go drinking, I told Mom I was staying over a friend's house. The next day I'd stroll into the house around noon to clean up, eat and sleep.

I was always looking for a fight. I didn't care how big a guy was; I'd torment him until he attacked. Wally saved me many times. At one party, a guy charged at me with a baseball bat. I put my arm up to protect myself, but he still nearly broke my head, and I fell on the ground. He was coming at me again when Wally came out of nowhere, grabbed him and humbled him. He beat him up pretty good.

Wally was superman. If I was in trouble, I'd call him and he'd come to my rescue out of nowhere.

I only crossed him once. We were at a party in a basement, and I started teasing him. Everybody was laughing. I'll never forget what happened next. Wally was pouring a beer from the keg. I made some crack, and he glanced up at me with that look on his face. "That's enough," he said quietly.

I teased him one more time.

CHAPTER TWENTY-ONE

I never saw it coming. He dropped the keg hose, whirled around and drove his fist into my face. BOOM! He probably knocked me backward six feet. I lay there on my back and thought, *I'm done.* I was sure he was going to kill me.

He came over and picked me up. "You gotta know when to stop," he said calmly. I stood there, shaking and dazed. "Come on," he said. "You're all right. Just knock it off." I never mocked him again.

Wally and his bunch were experienced, hardened fighters. Some of the toughest guys in the world came out of Bettendorf. Pat Miletich was a contemporary of Wally's and went to school with him. Pat became UFC Lightweight/Welterweight Champion, and then a fighting coach. In 1997 he founded Miletich Fighting Systems (MFS), a mixed martial arts training organization. MFS is still headquartered in Bettendorf, but has other locations across the United States and Canada. MFS trained several former mixed martial arts world champions, and its elite-level fighters mostly compete in Ultimate Fighting Championship promotions. MFS also works with law enforcement agencies to provide mixed martial arts training to police officers and security personnel.

We had keg parties almost daily at Lock & Dam No. 14 on the Mississippi. At one party, I saw Miletich carrying a keg on his back through the woods. I followed him and kept calling him an old bag of bones, like the donkey on *Grizzly Adams*. Finally he got bothered and set the keg down and pounded me a bit. I didn't fight back; I just tried to protect myself. It wasn't too serious—Miletich was just tired of hearing my mouth. I just wanted to be able to brag that I'd taken him on and lived through it.

Wally and Miletich ran with the same crowd. They were known as the two toughest fighters in the area. Everyone wanted to see them fight each other, but there was no animosity between them. They respected each other. In later years Miletich tried to get Wally to train with him but Wally didn't want to. I don't think Wally really liked fighting; he just fought when he had to do it.

I sparred and then trained with Miletich years later during my brief fighting career.

CHAPTER TWENTY-TWO

DURING MY SOPHOMORE year in high school, my drinking got out of control.

I tried everything to get out of going to school. I discovered that drinking would somewhat mentally prepare me for a boring day in this life, and I began to steal liquor from my parent's supply that they used for socializing. I'd pour small amounts of different kinds—vodka, whiskey, scotch—in a plastic butter container, stir them up, and drink the whole thing behind the garage before school in the morning.

On the weekends I was able to get into a bar called The Goal Post in downtown Bettendorf. The bar was known for serving underage kids. We'd play pool and darts and drink all weekend.

That fall, I got into a serious fight with another student. A bunch of us guys were hanging out at a school dance. We used to come up behind each other and poke the other guy in the side, trying to irritate him. Standard procedure, like saying hello.

This one guy didn't care much for me, and I felt the same. In an attempt to sort of include him, actually in a friendly gesture, I came up behind him and gave him a good solid jab in his left side with my left fingers out straight and rigid.

CHAPTER TWENTY-TWO

He screamed and clutched his side. "I got broken ribs!" he yelled. "I just got out of the hospital!"

I felt awful. "I'm really sorry," I said. "If I'd known, I never would have done that."

The guy wouldn't let go of it. "If I didn't have these broken ribs I'd kick your head in!"

"I'm really sorry," I said. "I didn't know."

He kept swearing at me and threatening me, and a crowd soon gathered. I kept trying to quiet him down. "Calm down, I didn't mean to hurt you."

But he got more aggressive, and louder. "Christman, you think you're so tough, but you're just a punk. I'd mess you up if my ribs weren't broken!" He was practically spitting in my face.

I tried to get away by walking around and between the tables, but he followed me. He probably thought I was backing down, because he started saying, "See? He's a coward!" He kept taunting me, trying to humiliate me. As far as I could see it was working; by then the crowd was snickering and laughing at his remarks. Laughing at me.

Until that point I'd been in a pretty good mood. I hadn't really started drinking yet; at most I'd had maybe a couple of beers in the parking lot. I usually didn't get hammered until after the dances.

I really didn't want to fight the guy. I must have apologized a hundred times, but he kept following me and abusing me. By now people were openly laughing at me. I actually saw the instant my patience ended. It did not seem to be a conscious decision; it just happened. I watched my irritated frustration change instantly to rage. I remember thinking, *Uh-oh.* I knew I'd crossed that line and was incapable of going back. I knew what was coming.

I stopped and faced him. I wanted to kill him.

He stood in front of me and leaned forward until his face was only inches from mine. He swore at me one last time. Suddenly, I had the clear thought, *It's my turn. I'm gonna cause some pain now.* I raised my left hand, palm open and facing him. He shut up. A look of awareness came over his face; I think he knew.

"You think you're in pain now?" I asked quietly. "I'm gonna show you what pain is."

Then I punched him right in the face as hard as I could, and then proceeded to the ribs!

Anyone who has had a broken rib knows even a sneeze can be excruciating. A direct blow is unspeakable agony. He screamed and doubled over. With my left hand I grabbed his shirt collar and held his head against my side, and with my right fist I proceeded to pound him over and over on his ribs. This was no blind fury; I was cold and calculating. I wanted to cause as much pain as possible. *I'll show you what pain is*, I chanted silently. *I'll show you what pain is.*

He was staggering, and I staggered with him to hold him up and keep pounding. We ended up outside. I got him on the ground on his back, and then I sat on his stomach and pounded his left side. I raised my right arm above my left shoulder, arched it down and thudded the heel of my right fist into his ribs. He screamed and begged me to stop, but I kept it up until all he could do was squeal with each blow. Finally he was silent, almost senseless.

People were pulling at me and trying to stop me. I got up, shaky but exhilarated. I felt powerful, invincible. I drank until I blacked out. The guy went to the hospital that night, and he never spoke to me again.

I don't remember getting into any trouble for the incident. My friends said he got what he deserved. The whole thing reinforced my reputation as a tough guy in my mind.

I didn't go a week without a fight of some sort. One winter night, Todd and I were out drinking, and at dawn we went back to Todd's, wasted. Wally was already home, passed out on the couch. Todd and I came in the back door, laughing and being loud, and Wally started yelling, "Shut up! Shut up!"

We yelled back, "Shut up! Shut up!" We didn't push it. We knew that if he got up he'd kill us, so we went outside onto the main street.

CHAPTER TWENTY-TWO

Along came a big Chevy Blazer. We made ice balls, and when the Blazer came within range, BOOM! BOOM! We dented that sucker!

The brake lights went on, and Todd and I ran laughing back inside and sat in the kitchen. The Blazer came in the back alley and pulled up into the driveway, and four big guys got out. One of them came to the back door and knocked, and Todd opened the door.

The guy said, "You just throw ice balls at our car?"

Todd said, "Yeah, so!"

The guy turned around and went back to his Blazer. As it turned out, there were eight guys in the Blazer, and they started piling out like ants. Todd said, "Come on!" and charged them. I followed him.

Three guys ran at me, while the rest jumped Todd. I fought as best as I could and got in some hits, but I was getting pummeled and blood was running down my cheek.

I yelled, "Todd, help me!"

He yelled back, "I'm busy!"

I looked over and had to laugh. Todd had ripped the drainpipe off the side of the garage. A guy ran at him, and Todd whipped the drainpipe back and wrapped it around the guy's head. I heard this TING! and the guy dropped. Knocked him out cold.

Guys kept trying to close in on Todd, and he kept swinging. I continually heard this TING! TING! TING! By then I was on the ground with the three guys pounding on me. I was getting banged up bad. I was just protecting my face.

Finally, Todd was done with his guys and came over and started wailing the guys on top of me with the drainpipe. He finally chased them into the Blazer, and they all left.

We went into the house. We were scared we were going to get into trouble with the law, so Todd said, "We gotta call the police on them first, or we'll be in deep trouble."

When the cops showed up, we told them that eight guys in a Blazer had attacked us. We were all cut up and bleeding, so there was no question there had been a fight. The cops were pretty skeptical; they all knew Todd and Wally. One cop asked us, "What did you guys do?"

"Nothing," Todd said. "We were minding our own business, walking down the alley, and they jumped us."

"Sure," the cop said. "Right. OK."

They didn't even write a report.

CHAPTER TWENTY-THREE

I DON'T REMEMBER much of my last two years of high school. It's a blur. There are some vivid fragments, but mostly it's big gaps of missing time. Blanks.

I started getting arrested. Disorderly conduct, public intoxication, resisting arrest, interference, that kind of stuff. "Interference" is interfering with police duties; such as harassing them and talking back. I'd start something in a bar, and they'd call the cops. Bar fights were routine.

My anger always got worse when I was drinking. I'd be drinking alone in a bar and see a guy and a girl together, a couple, laughing and flirting. I'd become convinced that they had a healthy, normal relationship, had great sex, felt deep love, and had found happiness together. Everything I could never have. I'd become jealous of their relationship, even though I didn't know them. I'd become terrified that I could never have a normal man/woman relationship, and hot on the heels of that fear would come rage. I'd become infuriated that I was being forced to watch what I could never have.

I'd walk over to the couple, laugh at the guy, slap him on the back of the head, shove him and do whatever would start a fight. It usually resulted in me getting kicked out of the bar or arrested. And getting my head beat in.

I didn't win many fights. I wasn't a big guy, and I was usually too drunk to fight well. But I hurt people. I had experience and no fear of physical pain, and my rage gave me power beyond my size.

My junior year I completely missed the fall trapping season. I drank through it.

Older guys bought us booze on the weekends. During the week, I did most of my drinking during school lunch break. The dad of a girl I knew had a well-stocked refrigerator and a garage full of beer and vodka, and we drank at her house almost daily.

Every morning, I woke up scared. I was scared to go to school and of what the day ahead held. I increasingly compared myself to my brother, Jeff. He was a hard worker and a straight-A student, and he always seemed to do the right thing.

More and more, I wanted to die. I hoped something would happen, like getting hit walking across the road. I wasn't planning anything specific, but I thought about being dead a lot. I was still too scared to do it myself.

My anger at God increased. Why did He allow me to suffer so much? Why wouldn't He help me? But I refused to ask Him for help. I was afraid He wouldn't. That would have been the final rejection.

One of my few clear memories is a good one: Buying my first vehicle, in my junior year, from my grade school gym teacher. He had an old 1971 Chevy pickup parked in front of his house. It never moved; it just sat there. I asked him if he'd sell it, and he said, "Give me $300 and it's yours."

It was all beat up, but I was immensely proud of it. It was blue and white and had a wood bed. I loved that truck. I used to polish it and admire it. I wanted to redo the whole thing. I was constantly working on it. The starter was always going, and I couldn't afford to put it in the shop, so I'd replace it myself. I must have replaced a dozen starters; I got pretty good at it. Dix helped me occasionally.

I really wanted to fix up the truck's appearance, and later, at the end of my senior year, I finally got the money together to get it in a

CHAPTER TWENTY-THREE

body shop for some basic work. When I got it back it was all covered with primer because I couldn't afford a paint job, but I thought it looked great. A week later I totaled it when I was drunk.

One night we were at a party at some girl's house. Her mom and dad were gone. There were about 70 kids there, and all of a sudden half the Bettendorf police force showed up. I'd gotten arrested the night before for public intoxication, resisting arrest and interference, and I knew I couldn't get into trouble again this soon. Kids were scattering everywhere. I couldn't go out the front or back doors, so I ran upstairs into the girl's parents' bedroom and turned on the light. I could hear the cops already coming into the house downstairs. Where was I gonna hide?

I looked into the closet and saw all these dresses and suits hanging there, and all these shoes lined up on the floor. Aha! I turned the light off and squeezed in behind the clothes, putting my back against the wall. The closet door was half open, and I could just make out the shoes at my feet. I was wearing cowboy boots, and I positioned them directly in line with all the other shoes. Just another pair, blended perfectly in with all the rest. *I'm so sharp,* I thought. I was laughing to myself.

A cop came in the room. I could see his flashlight going around the room. It came to the closet door, and he walked over and opened the door the rest of the way. I held my breath and didn't move; he was only a couple feet from me, but I was completely hidden. It was all I could do to keep from laughing. This would be a great story!

The flashlight beam shone across the clothes, and then along the whole line of shoes, from one end to the other. It passed right over my boots.

Then it came back and stopped on my boots.

"Nice try," he said. "Come out."

I stepped out, and he shined the light in my face. "How did you see me?" I asked. "I was perfect! Before you arrest me, you have to explain how you got me."

He snickered. "It would have been perfect, except your jeans came out from under the clothes and went down onto your boots. Those boots had legs!"

"But that was so good," I said. "You gotta admit, that was good. Will you let me go?"

I had him laughing now. "No."

"I can't get arrested again tonight. I swear I'll go home. I'm going home right now."

In the end, he let me go. Of course, I didn't go home. The night was still young.

Jeff and I never really fought. We argued at times, like brothers will, but it only got serious once. He was home from college, and he barged into my room and started yelling at me. I don't remember why; he'd probably discovered that I'd stolen something of his. I did that often enough, to sell stuff for booze.

Whatever happened, he was infuriated. I stood up, and he shoved me. I was instantly angry—nobody touched me! "Back off!" I yelled.

I'd never seen Jeff lose his cool, but he did this time. He kept shouting and shoving me, and I kept backing up. I almost fell several times. I knew I couldn't lose it. I couldn't hit my brother. And I didn't.

Abruptly, Jeff turned and stomped out of the room. I was shaking. It was the only time I can remember being able to control my rage.

I have almost no recollection of my junior and senior year classes, and I have no idea how I graduated. By my senior year I was drunk throughout the day in school. I drank in the morning and at lunch break and usually did not return to school in the afternoon.

I drank and drove constantly. I got picked up eight times, but the cops always let me go. They knew me, plus I could always talk my way out of getting arrested. One night a cop stopped me when I was coming home from the Buckhorn at 2 A.M. on a motorcycle.

CHAPTER TWENTY-THREE

I was blistered. He let me go with a warning. The very next night I was coming home from the Buckhorn on the same motorcycle at exactly the same time, and the same cop stopped me again. He let me go again. With the same warning.

Then I wrecked my truck.

On Senior Skip Day, just before graduation, I'd been drinking all day and night. At 3 A.M., I was driving my pickup and had a blackout. I went off the road into the ditch. The ditch kept the truck going straight, and I drove to an embankment with a set of railroad tracks along the top. I hit the embankment at 60 MPH, breaking the drive shaft and skyrocketing the truck up over the side and onto the railroad tracks. I was airborne. There was a creek on the other side, and I would have landed in it except that the drive shaft was hanging down. It caught the edge of the railroad tracks and ripped the end of the truck off, stopping the truck.

I regained consciousness and found myself piled up on the floor under the glove compartment. I got out of the truck and was standing there when lights shone on me. Two cops had been having coffee in a restaurant across the road and had seen the truck leave the road. They ran over to the edge of the embankment and shined their flashlights on the wreck.

"What are you guys looking at?" I demanded.

They came down to help me out. I gave them a false story, insulted them and cursed them. They stayed calm and tried to calm me down, which really exasperated me all the more, so I swung at them. No contest, I got roughed up a bit. I blew a .31 on the Breathalyzer, and this time I went to jail. It was my first recorded OUI.

I was sentenced to a 21-day outpatient treatment at the Center for Alcohol and Drug Abuse (CAD). I have no idea why they passed me; I was a complete jerk. I drove there drunk and was sarcastic and hard to deal with throughout the whole course. I don't remember any of it.

I replaced my truck with another one, a 1969 Chevy for $700. My uncle Roger paid for it, and I worked it off. I didn't like the Chevy as much as my first one.

By the time I was a senior in high school, I thought constantly of suicide. I was much closer to actually doing it now. My first thought was to do it like my dad did—in the garage, with carbon monoxide. I thought this would be the easiest and most painless way. I was still concerned with how bad it was going to hurt, and, absurdly, with how I would look when I was dead, so gas in the garage seemed to be the best choice. The thing that always stopped me was my concerns about my mother. I knew it would destroy her to find me dead, and she would have to live the rest of her life knowing that her baby boy had killed himself. This thought would always cancel any serious thought I had of actually doing anything.

Early one morning I came in the Cale's back door, wasted. I had no memory of what I'd done all night or where I'd been. Mrs. Cale looked at me and said, "Bill, you're dying. You're gonna die an alcoholic death within a year."

That scared me. If anybody could recognize the signs, it was her. She knew alcoholics. When Todd and Wally were little kids, their dad owned a bar in LeClaire, Iowa. They grew up behind the bar. I felt doomed, because I knew I wasn't going to stop. I knew I couldn't.

I started dating Lisa Bregman at the end of my senior year. She was my first actual girlfriend. She was my age, went to Bettendorf High School, and had even dated some of my friends. She was a brunette, about 5-foot 6-inches tall, pretty, with an athletic build. She ran five miles a day, but she was a smoker.

Lisa was a nurse's aide and took care of elderly people. She was a pleasant, friendly girl, but she loved to party and got real crazy when she was drunk. I saw her frequently at parties. I was attracted to her partly because she was pretty, but also because she was crazy like I was when I drank. One night when I was drunk enough, I screwed my courage up and asked her to go out with me. I was amazed when she said yes.

We soon were doing everything together, including drinking and all that went with it. I was at the peak of my heaviest drinking, and Lisa always drank with me. We were drinking buddies.

CHAPTER TWENTY-THREE

I had my first real sexual experiences with Lisa. I loved it and hated it at the same time. I was sure that sex was bad. I already knew that I was bad, so having sex now made me worse. Sex also convinced me I was inadequate. I was certain that I was no good at it.

Lisa lived at home with her folks. Her mom was mommy dearest; her dad was principal of a local elementary school. They were both very proper, respectable people. I only slept over when I passed out there. Her dad once found us sprawled out naked, passed out in the basement. I wasn't his favorite person.

Lisa and I fought a lot when we got drunk. We fought about childish, stupid stuff. We were always breaking up and getting back together again.

Lisa's dad used to let us use his car, a four-door Ford LTD. One night the Mississippi had flooded, and we were driving to a party on a road that closely followed the river. We came to a flooded section, and Lisa told me to stop and go another way. I thought I knew better, so I drove on. The water soon got too high to see the road, and I drove into the ditch. The car hood went under, the back end lifted up out of the water, and the water poured in when I opened the door. Lisa was screaming at me, but I just got out and started wading to the party. She followed me, still screaming. When we got there she called her dad, and he called a wrecker.

Lisa had a girlfriend I couldn't stand. The girl was promiscuous and slept with everybody. One night I passed out on a bed, and when I woke up the girl was in bed with me. I had a particular horror of someone doing something to me against my will while I was asleep or passed out, and I went into an instant rage. I drove the girl out of the room and then fought with Lisa about letting it happen.

I hated it when other guys paid attention to her. I was always afraid she was going to leave me. I knew I could never measure up. I wondered why she was even with me.

Lisa introduced me to cocaine. She was into it heavily. I didn't want her using it, and we fought about it. An active alcoholic giving someone grief about abusing cocaine—how rational is that? But, then again, none of the things we fought about were ever rational. Later that summer I got into cocaine myself.

At this point, when I drank I almost always got mean. Lisa used to say she knew when to get away from me because my right upper eyelid would start to droop. That meant all hell was ready to break loose.

One night we were leaving the Buckhorn at 2 A.M. I was driving her dad's LTD, and we were fighting about something. She started yelling, "Stop the car! Get out of the car!" I kept driving, and she kept screaming at me to get out. I stopped the car and kicked her out, and then drove off and left her. When we drank together it usually resulted in fights like this. That would always result in my drinking even more heavily—and my increasing realization that someday I was going to kill myself.

I graduated in June 1985. No school, no job, no responsibilities, no need to do anything but drink. All day. Every day.

CHAPTER TWENTY-FOUR

I STARTED DRINKING when I woke up, drank until I passed out, woke up again, gagged down a beer to stop shaking, and then drank until I passed out again. The hangovers were horrendous. Home was a pit stop—free food, a shower and laundry room; a place to steal a drink and maybe sleep a few hours. My parents were blurred figures in a fractured stream of confused images.

One night, Wally got in my face, and I couldn't seem to get away. I remember thinking, *This time I take you down*. We'd never come to blows before, but that night I decided it was time to teach him a lesson. I taunted him mercilessly to get him to make the first move so I'd have a good reason to unleash. My mother was alternately begging me to stop and raging at me. "You're just like your father!" she said.

All of a sudden the room was full of cops, four or five of them. Everything stopped and went silent. Nobody moved.

Mom was sobbing and barely able to talk. "You have to leave," she said. "You can't stay here anymore. I can't watch you destroy yourself. I can't let you destroy our home. You have to leave."

She kept saying that I had to leave. I didn't get it. I looked around at the wall of faces and saw a unified agreement set in stone against me. I finally got it. She was throwing me out. Tonight. Right now.

I was paralyzed with fear. I couldn't think. The cops walked me out the door.

I spent the rest of the night at a neighbor's house, drank the next day, stayed at another house the next night, and drank the next day. I drank as hard and fast as I could to numb myself. My fear increased a hundredfold; I knew I wasn't going to make it on my own. I knew I couldn't work.

Pat Miletich's girlfriend let me stay at her apartment for a week or so. I stayed out of their way; I was ashamed. Pat was in control of his life, and I wasn't.

I'd call my mother at the beauty shop and beg her for money. She always refused. I'd get nasty and swear at her, and when she wouldn't give in, I'd hang up on her.

Two of my drinking buddies let me stay in their apartment for a couple of months. It was right next door to the Bettendorf police department. One day my mother came to the apartment. It was the first time we'd seen each other since she threw me out.

The apartment was small—just two little bedrooms, a kitchenette, a living room and a cramped bathroom. I had used to be extremely neat and clean, but those days were long gone. The place was a pigpen and filthy. Dirty dishes were piled in the sink and on the counter and table, the garbage was overflowing, there were clothes strewn everywhere on furniture and on the floor, the floors were filthy, and the bathtub was so grimy you could almost stand on the black ring. The whole place stunk of booze, cigarettes and puke.

I told Mom I slept on the couch. She asked me where my stuff was, and I took her in a bedroom and pointed at a small, neat stack of folded clothing in a plastic milk crate in one corner. The police hat was on top of the clothes.

"That's my space," I said. She started crying.

She'd brought me groceries, but she wouldn't give me any money. I was nasty about that. She never visited me again.

CHAPTER TWENTY-FOUR

I no longer kept in touch with my family, except to call Mom at the beauty shop and harass her for money. I never asked her how she was; I just demanded money and cursed her when she wouldn't give in.

But she kept track of me. She wanted to know if I was still alive. She'd go to her mother, and Grandma would say, "He'll come back; he'll be OK." Grandma had total, utter faith that God would save me. She said the rosary constantly for me.

The police hat became very important to me. Almost daily I'd pick it up, look at it, put it on, take it off, and look at it some more. It was my only connection with my father; all I had of him. In some weird way I thought that by carrying it around he'd rescue me somehow. I wanted him and God to rescue me. I hated God for not saving me, but I was willing to forgive Him if He did.

There was a bar a couple blocks from the apartment, and I drank there. I went to a lot of parties because the booze was endless and usually free. Sometimes I wouldn't make it back to the apartment for days. If my roommates were out they'd lock the place, and I'd have to sit on the steps for hours waiting for them to come back. They wouldn't give me a key.

Sometimes the sun on my face would wake me up, and I'd find myself laying flat on my back on the rocky ground in the alley behind the apartment. I'd have no clue how or when I got there, which terrified me.

When I woke up after drinking, I'd walk past the back of the police department to get to a gas station and buy beer to calm the shakes. Sometimes cops would be coming out to get into their squad cars, and I'd get that look of disgust and pity, the "what a waste" look. I knew they were right, and I knew I couldn't do anything about it. I hated myself. I tried working, but I kept getting fired for coming in drunk or not coming in at all.

That summer I got into snorting coke with Lisa. I loved it instantly; it made me feel powerful, invincible, brilliant, tireless and sexy. Lisa introduced me to the biggest dealer in town. I told him, "I really like this stuff. I can get rid of some for you." He didn't really want me to deal for him; I had a boyish look, and he thought

I was too young, just a kid. But he kind of liked me, so he tried me out. He gave me six grams ($600 worth) to sell, and he told me I could have $100 (or a gram) for myself. He also told me the deal: "You mess with me, and I'll kill you."

I'd sell the coke no problem, and, of course, I always took the gram over the $100. The gram was always gone within an hour or two at the bar. Then I'd go get another $600 worth and do it again. And again, and again, and again.

Dealing coke scared me, but it was a rush at the same time. This was a much bigger deal than getting kegs in high school. I was hanging around with the real tough guys; people who had Uzis and brought real drugs up from Texas. I started having ambitions of being a big drug dealer, although I knew there was no way I could, because I could never control my day. The dealer I worked with started his day at ten o'clock at night. He would always show up at the bar at ten, which was where you knew to find him and turn in your cash to get more dope. The bar was his office. He always seemed controlled. He could sit there and drink all night long without showing it.

I was hanging around dangerous people now—a whole different crowd—and I had this sneaking suspicion that I was going to die soon. A few times the dealer invited me to go with him to all-night coke parties, and I'd get so messed up I'd be in a blackout for most of it. I tried to control my mouth around those guys, but I was afraid that during a blackout I'd do my usual thing and start running my mouth and insulting someone. I was scared I would antagonize them and they'd kill me.

I went to the dealer's apartment once. He rarely let anyone go there. All he had was a beanbag chair, a little black-and-white TV, and a scanner. I couldn't figure that out. He was a big drug dealer and made a lot of money. So where did it go?

Suicide was always on my mind. One night, I was at a keg party in an upstairs apartment in an industrial area by the old International Harvester plant. Out back was a narrow strip of grass and then railroad tracks. The apartment was crowded and noisy,

CHAPTER TWENTY-FOUR

with easily 20 people jammed in there. At one point, we all quieted down to listen to a train rumble by. Just then, a calm, clear thought came to me: I would kill myself on the train.

I went outside and watched the train roll by a few feet away. It was going slow through town, and I was an old hand at jumping trains. I hopped on and stood on the coupling between two boxcars, the place where they hitch together, just a couple feet above the tracks.

The train left town and picked up speed. It was a hot night, and I was wearing shorts and a short-sleeved Hawaiian shirt, no shoes. The breeze felt good. I figured the train would eventually go fast enough that I'd lose my balance, be bounced off, and get crushed. I was gripping the car in front of me, and as the train went faster I had no trouble hanging on. So I let go, stuck my arms out to the side for balance, and rode the coupling like I was surfing.

The train went faster and faster, and I swayed and waved my arms and shifted my feet to stay on. Somewhere deep inside, something wanted to live. It wasn't fear of death; I wanted that.

I stayed upright for what seemed hours. The glaring lights of town stopped whipping by, and there were long minutes of black with dim lights flickering by in the distance. Occasionally, I'd see a burst of lights as we passed through a small settlement. We were well into the countryside.

Probably going 50 or 60, I thought with clinical detachment. Then I had a bizarre thought. *Man, I'm getting far from home! Probably go to Michigan if I don't get off.* I was considering suicide, and here I was worried about how far I was getting from home.

I closed my eyes and jumped. Not under the wheels, but to the side, as far from the train as I could.

I hit the ground with tremendous impact and rolled and rolled through weeds and dirt. When I stopped it took a minute to get my breath. I felt like I'd been beaten with clubs. I was sore and shaking. I stood up, very wobbly, and moved my arms and wiggled my fingers and ran my hands over my body. Nothing broken. I was bleeding everywhere from dozens of small cuts and scratches. I brushed gravel out of my skin.

There was a main road about 20 feet away that ran parallel to the tracks, and I walked to it. My feet were cramped and cold from miles of clutching at the irregular surface of my vibrating steel perch, and the warm pavement felt good. I started walking back to Bettendorf. Where else would I go?

I came to a trailer park and recognized it; I was about ten miles from the apartment. I figured I could walk that. When I had passed the trailer park, a Scott County patrol car stopped behind me. The sheriff got out. "Need a ride?" he asked in a friendly tone.

"Naw, I'm good," I said.

"Where you from?"

I pointed back at the trailer park. "I'm from there."

He looked at me for a minute. I could see him think, *Sure.*

"We heard a guy from Bettendorf hopped a train to kill himself," he said. "Know anything about it?"

"Really?" I said, trying to look surprised. I must have opened my mouth at the party. I jumped rear-first up onto his hood, sat there, and asked him for a cigarette. He gave me one and lit it for me, and then arrested me. He was real nice about it.

I spent the night in a cell; I don't remember much of it. The next day the judge gave me the disgusted "what a piece of trash" look; I'd been in front of him before for the usual drunken behavior, and I looked like hell. He fined me $50 and said, "I'm tired of seeing you. Next time, no fine. I'll lock you up for a while." I had no money, so I made payment arrangements—lies, basically—with the clerk and walked out of the courthouse.

I was hung over bad, nauseous and shaking. I needed a drink, but I was broke. I didn't want to get picked up again, so I went back to the railroad tracks and started walking along them toward Bettendorf. The sharp crushed stones hurt my bare feet, so I tried hopping from one wooden railroad tie to the next. The ties were spaced farther than a normal stride, and my balance wasn't too good, so I kept missing them and landing on the stones, which hurt worse because I was jumping. The jumping made me nauseous, too, and a couple of times I fell. I tried walking on the rail, but I couldn't keep my balance.

CHAPTER TWENTY-FOUR

It was a warm, clear morning with no breeze. I swayed, hopped and limped along as the sun rose. It got stiflingly hot, and my head, arms and legs started turning pink. Sweat stung my eyes and scratches. I was desperately thirsty.

When I reached one small town, the ties and gravel stopped and the rails ran through tar. The tar was hot but smooth, so I left the tracks and got back on the road. Outside town I walked out on the tar, limping onto the gravel shoulder when cars passed. People looked at me, but nobody stopped to offer a ride.

I shuffled along. The tar got hotter, and my feet started to blister. I blacked out a couple of times, but I must have kept walking because each time I came to I was closer to Bettendorf. By nightfall I was sitting in an apartment in Bettendorf with a couple of friends, my skin beet red, the soles of my feet raw and propped up on a coffee table. I was drinking. I don't remember the rest of the night.

I got thrown out of the apartment for not paying rent. I stayed at three or four different places for about a month each, freeloading until people got sick of me and kicked me out. I was basically homeless. Lisa and I were still dating, getting drunk and stoned together, fighting and making up.

I stayed briefly in the basement of my childhood friend Dean Snyder. He lived with his parents in a split-level home, and they let me sleep downstairs in the utility room on the concrete floor. I had a pillow and blanket, but no mattress.

I came home drunk one night at 2 or 3 A.M., upset about something, and went into a blind rage. I was sick and tired of myself and exhausted by the fear that constantly consumed me. I decided that tonight I was going to end it all.

I knew Dean kept a shotgun in his bedroom up on the main floor, so I went in and turned on the lights. I was ranting and raving, yelling that I'd had it and I was going to kill. Dean woke up fast and lay there watching as I ransacked the entire room. When I found the shotgun in his closet, I started screaming, "Where are the shells?" I started tearing the room apart, yanking clothes out of the closet and throwing them across the room. I pulled drawers out of dressers, dumped them on the floor, kicked at the contents and screamed, "Where are the shells?" I vaguely remember yelling, "Screw 'em! Kill 'em!" At that point Dean ran out of the house and down the street in his underwear.

I found the shotgun shells in a dresser drawer. I was going to blow my brains out, because I knew it would be quick. I was in a state of complete rage and self-pity.

Dean called the Bettendorf police, and their SWAT team surrounded the house. Decker Ploen was chief of police at the time. He lived next door to my mom and was a good friend of our family—and plenty familiar with my problems. The SWAT team called him and told him they had surrounded a house with Billy Christman in it. They said I was raging and had a gun and that they were going to shoot me if I came out with it. They were concerned I'd go out into the neighborhood and kill someone.

Decker told them not to shoot. He got dressed and came to the house and waited with his men. I finally passed out inside, and the police eased in cautiously and took the shotgun. They left me there to sleep it off.

The next day, Decker sat with me on the front steps and asked if I was willing to go to treatment to get help with my alcohol and drug addiction. I told him I was. There was no arrest and no paperwork. It was as if it had never happened. And I didn't get help.

After that incident, I had a panicky urge to clean up my act. A previous employer, Mr. Wilky, had told me that if I was ever in Marysville, Michigan, I could work at the Wilky Brothers Conveyer Factory. I told Lisa I'd take the job and find a place to live, and she could follow me. I took a Greyhound to Marysville, found the company, and walked in unannounced. Mr. Wilky was startled to see me, and skeptical, but finally he said, "We'll try you out. But come to work drunk once or miss one day because of drinking and you're fired."

This created even more fear, because I knew I wasn't going to be able to do it for long. I had to drink; it was the only thing that kept the fear at bay.

CHAPTER TWENTY-FOUR

I rented a single room in a hotel for $75 a week. It nearly took up my whole check. I didn't have much left for food. For the first time, I tried to control my drinking. It worked for two days.

My next door neighbor in the hotel was a Coast Guard officer whose wife was divorcing him because of his drinking. The third night I was there, he gave me an extra hamburger he'd bought and a beer. I drank the beer, and he offered me more.

He knew I wasn't eating, so he brought a hamburger home for me every day. It became a daily ritual. I'd get home from work, he'd knock on the wall, and after I cleaned up I'd go to his room for my burger and beer. If it weren't for him, I'd never have eaten. He bought all my beer, too. He wanted someone to drink with.

At first I managed to stop drinking in time to get to bed and make it to work sober the next day. Some evenings I'd go down to the lake and sit on the dock and drink. I could see Canada. I missed Lisa a great deal and felt so lonely I could barely stand it, even drunk. Somehow I was able to go without missing work for three weeks. Abruptly I began drinking to the point of passing out every night, and one morning I was too sick to work.

I didn't bother to call my job. When my hangover died down later that day, I bought a Greyhound ticket to Bettendorf. All my possessions fit into one cardboard box. I was careful packing the police hat. I taped the box up good and addressed it to my mother.

It was too late to mail it that day. "This stuff is real important to me," I told my Coast Guard drinking buddy. "Will you mail it tomorrow?"

"No problem," he said. "Absolutely. I'll do it first thing."

I got on the bus that night and showed up at home the next day. The box never arrived. I think my friend meant to mail it. Maybe he got drunk and lost the box, or maybe he forgot about it. I had no idea how to reach him. I didn't even know his full name.

Something died in me when I lost the police hat.

A friend of mine let me stay with him for a couple of months in Bettendorf. I was back with Lisa again, doing the same old stuff, drinking and fighting daily. Sometimes it got physical. Once when I was sitting on an ottoman, she punched me in the face. I fell off the ottoman, jumped up, punched her in the eye and knocked her down. Her dad put up with a lot from me, but that time he hunted me down and really chewed me out. I thought he was going to kill me.

I drank every waking hour. The only money I made was from selling coke, and that all went to buying coke and booze. My friend got sick of me and threw me out. No one in town would let me live with them. As a last resort I asked my step-grandmother, Wally's mother. She reluctantly said I could stay with her, but that she would not tolerate any drinking. There was no way I could not drink, so I thanked her and declined the offer.

A friend of mine had just moved to Dallas, Texas, for a job, and he had told me that if I ever needed a place I could stay with him. I flew to Dallas. He took me to the small ranch-style house he lived in with a friend and the friend's girlfriend. Within a week they were disgusted with my drinking and constant blackouts and the fights I picked with people who came over for parties.

At one party I saw a guy across the room look at me with what I thought was disgust and then turn to some people and say, loudly, "Bill's a cornstalk." *A cornstalk?* What did that mean? I had probably just hallucinated it, but I decided that it was some sort of rural Texas insult. I walked across the room and hit the guy smack in the face, with no warning.

We were promptly thrown out of the party and started fighting out on the front lawn. I had long hair, and the guy kept pulling it. I asked him to please stop—a ludicrous request considering I'd started the fight. He just laughed and kept pulling my hair. "I'm telling you," I warned him. "Don't do that."

He laughed and kept yanking away.

I went ballistic. I threw the guy against a truck, stunning him, and then started kicking him. We ended up on the ground together, and I bit his finger half off, almost severing it at a joint. I beat him and kicked him until he stopped fighting back.

CHAPTER TWENTY-FOUR

One night, I had the classic fight with God. I lost it with Him. I'd had it. Who did He think He was, doing this to me? He was a sadistic monster.

I'd long ago lost any fear of going to hell; I figured I was already in hell and that nothing could be worse than how I now felt. I stood in the backyard of the house, drunk, shaking my fists at the black sky, screaming and swearing at Him, asking Him why He ever allowed me to be born. I told Him I hated Him and was disgusted by Him. I begged Him to come down so I could beat Him up. It was a real temper tantrum; I stomped my feet, swung my arms, screamed and spit until I was hoarse, exhausted, shaking and weak. It must have been a pathetic, ridiculous spectacle.

God ignored me. That killed me even more.

I came out of a blackout a few nights later in some sort of industrial area filled with huge metallic tanks and buildings, with vehicles on pavement that stretched all around. I could see an office building with a staircase going up the side to the top. I counted five stories. A thought came clear from outside of me, like a voice: *Climb up to the roof and jump off.* Like a robot, I walked to the base of the ladder and grabbed a rung. Then I had a visual image of my body rupturing against the ground and blowing open, guts and bones and raw meat. What if the fall didn't kill me? I lost my nerve and walked away.

After this, I got a job driving a forklift in a warehouse in Dallas, but I got fired for showing up drunk. My friend threw me out because I couldn't pay the rent. Two girls let me stay at their place, but within two weeks they told me to leave. Every day they begged, "Please leave, you have to leave." I saw the look: disgust and pity. Get out of our sight, we don't want to look at you anymore.

But there was no place left to go.

I stayed in bed in my room for three days, staring at the ceiling, paralyzed with fear. I didn't eat or drink. My life was over.

The only friend I had left was a guy named Todd. He called my mother. She said I could stay with her and Wally if I entered treatment. I agreed; I was out of options.

A day later I flew home and checked into inpatient treatment at Riverside Retreat in Rock Island, Illinois. It was November 24, 1986. I'd been on my own less than five months.

CHAPTER TWENTY-FIVE

I WAS TORQUED about being in the treatment center, because every minute of my life was controlled. But I was relieved to have a place to stay. I was resting, detoxing, getting fed, and I was going be staying at my mother's later. I wanted my life to be different, but I still didn't know how I was not going to drink.

My memory of treatment is pretty foggy. I couldn't think straight or comprehend simple things. I stayed in Riverside for a couple of weeks until I got kicked out for breaking the rules. I mouthed off in group therapy, made sarcastic remarks all day, got caught shaking the cigarette machine to get quarters, constantly got room detention, and was a general pain.

We had to attend therapy groups, and I hated the lady who ran one of them. One day, I felt she was attacking a guy in the group. He was actually crying. He didn't seem to be able to defend himself, so I spoke up for him. I always had a protective instinct, so I took the attention off him and put it on me.

"What are you attacking him for?" I said. "He's supposed to be here to get well, and you're messing with him. Why don't you mess with me?"

She asked me if I wanted to continue treatment.

"You can do whatever you want with me," I said. "Kick me out; I don't care."

She spouted off back at me, and that triggered Evil Bill. "You're just a worthless counselor who thinks you know what you're talking about, but you don't have a clue. You're worthless." I really laid into her, until she was crying.

Afterward, a male counselor took me aside and said, "Bill, you attacked that woman today. You can't do that."

"Well, I did. What are you going to do about it?"

"Your mother will be called for a meeting this evening, and then you'll be discharged."

I wasn't too worried about it. I knew outpatient treatment was an option, and I knew my mother would let me stay at home if I stayed in treatment.

After the meeting with the male counselor, I decided that since I was going to be discharged, I might as well do whatever I wanted. I left the grounds and walked to a burger joint. Leaving the grounds was a big no-no. When I got back, a female counselor came into my room and told me I'd been discharged and had to leave immediately.

"What?" I said. "I just went to get something to eat."

That didn't cut any slack with her. Within minutes my mother showed up, stone faced, to take me home.

I went to outpatient treatment, and somehow I graduated. I don't remember much about it except that I had to attend AA meetings. I thought that was a joke. But it changed my life.

I'd managed to stay sober during treatment, but I knew I'd drink as soon as I was on my own. I could feel the self-hatred and despair of my last days of drinking hot behind me, waiting, greedy for me. I shook with the fear of it. Finally, from the depths of my soul, I turned to God and begged Him to help me. It was the first real prayer I had ever said in my life.

My first AA meeting was in the basement of a church in Bettendorf. All I remember was that a guy with round glasses came up to me afterward and said, "I'll be glad to be your sponsor." I had no idea what a sponsor was, but I knew he wasn't going to be mine.

CHAPTER TWENTY-FIVE

"No," I said. "You're not going to be my sponsor. Just get away from me."

"But you're new," he said. "You need a sponsor."

"You don't know what I need. *I* don't even know what I need."

I only stayed sober for two weeks. I was twiddling my thumbs at my mother's house, bored, and the fear returned big time. I called some old buddies, and we went out drinking and doing coke all night. The next day I was hung over, sick, horrified and terrified. What had I done? I prayed again, full of remorse and guilt, and begged God for another chance.

After that I went to AA meetings almost every day. Someone would talk about how he hated himself and felt like he was nothing when he was drinking, and someone else would talk about how fear had dominated his life, and I'd think, *Yeah, that's how I feel*. God had led me into a community of people who thought and felt exactly as I did.

The atmosphere at meetings made me calm. All around me were people who said things that proved they'd been just as crazy as me, but who now seemed to be leading fairly normal lives. I had no idea how they did it, but I wanted what they had. They would talk about horrible times they had been through and horrible things they had done, and laugh at themselves. Seeing them laugh and talk gave me hope. I could feel sanity and health returning.

Those first days in AA represented the first time I could remember actually feeling good since I was a kid. But fear was still a persistent factor. I never talked at meetings. I'd watch people walking around the room, talking and getting coffee, and I'd wonder how they could do it. If I did that I knew I would stand out and people would notice me. I was afraid of that.

I was going crazy hanging around the house, and I needed money, so I got a job at Hardees flipping burgers. It was boring and depressing, and I only made about $60 a week. But I didn't have to interact with anyone, so I stuck it out.

I didn't start hanging out with anybody in AA until I started going to a meeting attended by a lot of guys my age. They'd invite me out to coffee at the Village Inn afterward, and we'd sit there and have pie and drink coffee until 2 in the morning. They'd ask me about myself and I'd tell them a bit, and then we'd talk motorbikes or whatever. I started to relax. They accepted me, laughed when I tried to be funny, and acted like they liked me. I started feeling as if I were part of the group. I still didn't trust anybody, but I started doing things with a few different guys.

I was soon at meetings all the time; it was my social life. These people were just like me. By now I had a good idea of what a sponsor was: a person with experience in sobriety who took you under his wing and instructed you, one-on-one, in how the AA program worked. He helped you stay sober and showed you how to deal with practical life problems using spiritual tools.

I'd wanted a father all my life. I wanted a sponsor.

Some of us started The Last Chance Group. An older guy named Danny was a regular at the meetings. He was a biker—rough and tough—who grew up in a bad neighborhood. He had done a lot of fighting when he drank, and you could tell from how he looked and carried himself—muscular and beat up a bit, calm and confident—that he was a guy you didn't want to mess with. I always admired people like that. He talked about his anger, how destructive his rages had been, and how he had been mad at God for messing up his life until God showed him how to live. I asked him to be my sponsor. He was the first positive male mentor I sought out. God would send more.

Danny was very helpful in the beginning of my sobriety. He immediately got me started on the 12 Steps, which was the spiritual part of the program. I took a Fourth and Fifth Step with him, examined some of my character defects, and started taking responsibility for them. I began to see, dimly, that I had created at least some of my problems. It was a new concept; until then I'd been a complete victim.

My fear subsided. I still woke up with it, but by noon I was OK. I had moments of confidence. I had spiritual tools; I had friends; I was somebody. At times I actually sensed the presence of God. During meetings I would suddenly become aware that people were being more honest and stronger, and I felt a healing presence.

CHAPTER TWENTY-FIVE

I began to pray when I was alone. I had no idea how to do so at first, but people at the meetings talked about prayer and meditation a lot, and my understanding grew. I did the recommended daily morning prayer—asking God to keep me sober for another day—but I found myself praying during the day, too. I had these quick internal conversations with God, always asking for something. *Help me with this.* I assumed He was listening.

Danny soon had me shaking hands and pouring coffee, and he urged me to speak more often. I started cautiously asking for help, my heart pounding as I raised my hand. Once I said, "I'm always afraid some bad thing is gonna happen. I don't even know what it is."

A guy raised his hand. "A sense of impending doom is common early in sobriety. It will pass. Keep coming back." Another hand went up. "Fear is the opposite of faith. You couldn't get sober alone, but you did it when you asked your Higher Power for help. Pray for help with your fear, and have faith that the same Power that got you sober will help you."

I'd heard some of these things before, but I'd considered them sanctimonious babble from people who didn't understand how bad my life was. But they made sense now. God gave me the grace to hear.

Danny was my first sponsor and over time I had a couple more sponsors. Then I met Carlos. He was in his mid-forties, with sandy red-brown hair and a moustache. He was about 6 feet tall, 200 pounds, and in good shape. He worked outside, had a tree service, tore down small buildings and did other odd jobs.

Just being around Carlos made me feel good. When I was scared or confused, he had a calming effect on me. He was my sponsor for many years and played a major role in my life. Carlos was probably the closest thing to a dad I've ever experienced.

Carlos kept in daily contact with me. He took interest in me and helped me get through my daily fears. He was a hard-working man, and he insisted that anybody close to him work just as hard.

I left my job at Hardees to sell motorcycles at Brenney's Cycle Works. I didn't make much money, but I loved handling the bikes, and the younger customers looked up to me. I was comfortable talking to them. I was knowledgeable; I was somebody.

I bought a Kawasaki KZ 1000. I'd always wanted one. I rode it a lot. I was starting to enjoy myself.

Raging and fighting no longer dominated my life. The blowup at the woman in the treatment center had been my last. I still had some anger, but I could easily keep it in the background. A few times I had differences of opinion with guys in AA, and after the meetings I would start with the sarcastic insults. However, instead of allowing the insults to escalate, I backed off.

I was barely surviving on the pay from Brenney's, so in March 1987 I took a job with TruGreen Chemlawn, a nationwide lawn fertilizing company. I drove a flatbed truck with a tank of chemical fertilizer on it and sprayed lawns. The pay was better, but the work was repetitious, boring and physically demanding. I worked 70 to 75 hours a week and was exhausted all the time. I hated it. The only good thing was that I learned to clean and prep the truck after work and plan my route for the next day. That organizational training would serve me well when I started my own business.

I was sick of doing menial dead-end jobs and barely making enough to survive. I figured that if I were going to have a real chance in life—a chance at a real job—college was the only avenue. So, in September I quit TruGreen and started classes full time at Scott Community College in Bettendorf.

CHAPTER TWENTY-SIX

I WAS A criminal justice major. It was a two-year, 64-credit degree. I was specific about what I wanted: to chase down and capture fugitives from the law. I felt I'd be good at it, based on my early years of trapping. My ultimate goal was to be a U.S. Marshall.

I loved the classes and aced them, especially criminology. After all, I was a bit twisted and a criminal myself; I seemed to understand exactly how they thought. One of my teachers was a murder investigator for the state Department of Criminal Investigation (DCI), and he told me I was a natural. For one of my assignments, I critiqued the Son of Sam serial killer investigation. I pointed out where they made mistakes that had cost them time and how they could have solved the case faster. My DCI teacher said the critique was excellent and that if I'd been involved in the case, it would have made a difference.

That November, I celebrated my first anniversary in AA. My head was clearing. I talked more at meetings and made more friends. Sometimes I felt no fear for days, although I still had bouts of anxiety.

During my second year at school, I took the Bettendorf police exam and placed in the top ten of the 400-plus people who took it. I blew the interview, undoubtedly because my attitude and immaturity showed through. Plus they were looking for college graduates.

Jim Sweeney, a lieutenant in the Bettendorf police department, had recently left the department to work for Per Mar Security, a private investigation firm. He approached the Scott Community College criminal justice department looking for potential employees. My DCI teacher told Sweeney, "Christman's amazing, he'd make a great detective. Grab him."

Sweeney offered me a detective position with decent pay, paid expenses and benefits. I was only four credits short of graduating, but it was an opportunity I couldn't pass up. I figured I'd finish my degree later.

I loved the job immediately. One of my first assignments was a worker's comp case. The worker was getting big checks because he claimed he was almost totally disabled—injured for life. He said he couldn't raise his right arm or shoulder at all and that he could only sit behind the counter of his small gun shop, where, he said, he made practically nothing. The company paying his claim knew he was lying, and they hired us to prove it.

I studied him like I'd studied the animals I wanted to trap. I found out the guy was a vendor at gun shows, and I went to one he was set up at. I walked up to his table carrying a camera and tripod and told him I was a student doing interviews on gun control. I said an expert had recommended him to me. He liked that.

"Mind if I film the interview?" I asked.

He almost visibly swelled up. "No, no, go ahead," he said, waving a hand dismissively as if it happened all the time.

I had a list of questions written on a clipboard to make the interview look official—his opinion on the Second Amendment, and that kind of stuff. I'd read a question and he'd answer it, and every now and then I'd look up and ask a casual question as if for my own edification—what was the best self-defense pistol, and that sort of thing. He strutted his stuff to impress me, and I acted impressed.

Then I slipped in, "You make any money at these shows?"

"Yeah," he grinned. "I've never made less than $1,000 at a show, and the best part is it's all under the table."

CHAPTER TWENTY-SIX

He said that on film! Man, I was clever! I loved this job!

I found out that he sometimes spent the weekend in his SUV at a certain campsite. I had no way of knowing when he was going to be there, so for about five weekends I spent Friday afternoons and all day Saturday there in a rented camper, just waiting for him to show up. My company paid for the camper and my time. Finally, one Saturday morning he pulled in and rented a spot. I immediately abandoned my site and rented the one right beside him. I set up the camera and tripod inside my vehicle, aiming through a window at his camper, just like in the spy movies.

I watched him set up a folding lawn chair, park his butt in it, and then sit there for three hours drinking beer and listening to the radio. I thought I'd go nuts. I had to get him moving.

I drove to town and bought half a dozen small balsa wood model planes. Back at the campground, I put them together and started throwing them around. I made them fly and ran behind to catch them like a ten year old. People in other campsites stared; they undoubtedly thought I was whacked.

Finally, I threw one up over the guy's camper. I was lucky that day, and it landed on the roof! I went into my camper and turned on the camera, and then I went back outside and walked up to the guy.

"Excuse me, sir," I said, "I'm sorry to bother you. My model plane landed on your camper roof. Mind if I climb up to get it?" There was a narrow vertical ladder leading up the side of the camper.

He didn't recognize me from the gun show. I figured he wouldn't want a stranger climbing on his property, and he did exactly what I hoped he would. "No problem," he said. "I'll get it for you."

This was just like trapping, only with a different kind of bait! He climbed the ladder easily and smoothly, reaching one arm after the other up over his head to grab each rung and pull himself up. All on film.

"I don't know how to thank you," I said, shaking his hand. "You have no idea how helpful you've been." He looked at me like I was nuts.

I promptly packed up and drove off, pounding the dashboard and cackling. This was more fun than a man ought to be allowed!

At the gun show the man had mentioned that he burned firewood, and after some investigation I learned that he had it delivered tree-length. It was getting cut and split somehow. I drove by his house, but his backyard wasn't visible from the road. The land behind rose up in a small hill, and the top was covered with brush. A map showed railroad tracks on the hill. I parked my car two miles away on a back road, grabbed the camera and tripod, hiked through weeds and briers to the tracks, and followed the tracks until I was fairly sure I was above his house. I pushed through the brush, and, sure enough, I was overlooking his backyard about fifty yards below.

I had just set up the camera when I saw him come out into the yard and start cutting up firewood with a chainsaw. For an hour he cut and split wood, handling the chainsaw with ease as he swung the splitting mall up over his head and down hard enough to send the pieces flying. I could hear the impact up on the hill. Nothing wrong with this guy's arms! Then he stacked the split wood and mowed the lawn. I filmed the whole thing.

I went back to the van and drove toward the office. I figured I had all the evidence we needed. Then, a quarter of a mile ahead, I saw his truck pull out of his subdivision. I decided to follow.

About a mile later, his brake lights went on and he started to pull over. A road-killed deer appeared ahead on the right shoulder. *You gotta be kidding me,* I thought. *He's gonna grab that deer.*

He stopped beside the deer and got out and looked at it. I stopped not 20 feet behind him and started filming through the windshield. It was a good sized doe, maybe 150 pounds. The man grabbed the legs, dragged the deer to his dropped tailgate, and then hoisted it up onto the truck bed by sheer muscle.

Finally, he turned and saw me. I was laughing. He wiped his hands on his pants and walked over to me, looking puzzled. I rolled the window down and grinned.

He stopped beside my door and bent slightly to look in the window, frowning. "What are you doing?" he asked.

CHAPTER TWENTY-SIX

"Filming you," I said. "Don't you remember me? I'm the guy who interviewed you at the gun show, and I threw a model plane onto your camper roof and you climbed up and got it. I got everything on film. I filmed you putting up wood in your backyard, too, and loading that deer. You've been screwing the company on your worker's comp claim, and now you're screwed!"

His mouth dropped open, and I drove off.

The company that hired us was ecstatic, and my boss was ecstatic. I was the man.

Detective work challenged me and used my abilities to the fullest, and I got better and better at it. I received constant compliments from my boss, and the pay was good. Between AA meetings and my job, the fear died to an occasional faint background growl.

Then, in early 1989, an unexpected new door opened.

Decker Ploen, the Bettendorf chief of police, called me and said a citizen's two Dobermans had been badly torn up after a tangle with a large raccoon that was feeding every night in the guy's trash cans. Decker knew I was a trapper, and he wanted to know if I could catch the raccoon. I said that I could.

I turned the man's trash cans on their sides, blocked the sides to keep them from rolling, and set cage traps in them. On the first night, I caught two large male raccoons. I became an instant hero to the homeowner and a regular contact for the city's police and animal control departments. They told me they received lots of nuisance wildlife calls and were desperate to refer the calls to someone. I told them I was their man.

My first real paying wildlife job was for a Davenport man and his wife who had raccoons in their attic. I caught several in cage traps on the ground outside the house, but I couldn't understand how they were getting into the attic. It took me four days to figure out that they were going underneath the front porch, crawling up inside the porch's hollow columns, and then going up through the porch roof to the main wall of the house. There they had chewed a hole in the wall, and they went through that hole up between the wall studs and into the attic. When I finally discovered their route,

I was convinced I was an expert. I not only caught the rest of the raccoons, but I also screened off the bottom of the porch to prevent any more from entering. I was paid $575, and promptly bought more equipment.

The nuisance wildlife calls increased until I had at least one job a day, and usually more. Groundhogs ate people's flowers and vegetables, skunks dug holes in lawns looking for grubs or sprayed the family dog, squirrels chewed holes in roof trim, and raccoons ripped off roof vents to get into attics. I bought more cage traps and got better at catching animals. Word of my skill spread, and the calls multiplied.

I fit the wildlife work around my job with Per Mar as best I could, setting traps after work in the evening and checking them before I went to work the next morning. As the calls increased, I started to think maybe I could trap for a living.

Once that idea took hold, I was obsessed with it. I became extremely excited about providing this type of service to the community—possibly even turning it into a career. Ever since Tony and I had trapped together as kids, I'd wished I could do it for a living, but I had always assumed it wasn't realistic. Now it looked like it might be possible.

I was plagued daily by the possibility that I could do wildlife work full time, although I didn't know how to run a business and was sure I'd fail. Carlos encouraged me to keep taking animal jobs. He told me I should follow my dreams and do what I really wanted to do. He said he'd help in any way he could. He told me the worst thing that could happen was that it would not work out, but that didn't mean my life was over. At least I'd have tried.

CHAPTER TWENTY-SEVEN

THERE WERE WOMEN my age at the AA meetings, but at first I was too shy to approach any of them. One woman named Jody was absolutely beautiful, with long brown hair and a striking build. That summer I asked her out, and she accepted.

We connected instantly and began to see each other daily. She was bright and outgoing, and we enjoyed each other's company. We were soon sleeping together, and I loved it. I felt none of the shame afterward that I'd had with Lisa. I'd always wanted a woman to think I was special, and Jody obviously did.

Ever since I was a kid playing with Duke, I had wanted to get a German Shepherd. I bought a female and named her Ellie. She was friendly and dedicated, and her companionship brought both of us a lot of pleasure. We had moments of real contentment together.

Jody told me her ex-boyfriend had taken Tae Kwan Do from a guy named Joe Mesa in downtown Moline. I watched one of Mesa's classes. It was my old dream, kickboxing. I told Mesa I'd think about taking classes.

Later, I confided to Carlos that I was scared to take the class because I didn't know anything. "You're not supposed to know anything," he said. "That's why people take classes."

"I'll look stupid, 'cause I don't know anything," I said.

He snorted. "You want to learn how to kickbox?"
"Yeah, I really do."
"Then you're going to have to go to class."

I enrolled and discovered I had a natural aptitude for it. I went to class three or four times a week and practiced daily for hours. I loved it. I quickly became very good at it. Even as a white belt beginner, I was beating the blue and red belts.

I was dating a beautiful woman, I loved both my jobs, and I was becoming good enough at kickboxing to consider fighting professionally. My demons were at bay.

Actually, they were just waiting.

In November, Jody told me she was pregnant. I didn't want to marry her, and I was scared to take on the responsibility of a child, but I felt I had to do so. I believed my family would not tolerate my getting a woman pregnant without marrying her, and both Jody and I felt this was the only responsible thing to do. I clearly remember thinking that marriage would be a mistake, but I felt I had no choice.

Jody and I moved into a little apartment in Moline, and two months later, in early 1989, we got married.

The honeymoon was over fast. I spent most of my time away from home. If I wasn't running the wildlife business or doing private investigator work, I was at Tae Kwon Do classes. I'd come home and eat supper, ride my motorcycle to the class, work out for an hour and a half, spar for another 45 minutes, come home, practice Tae Kwon Do for an hour, do paperwork for the business, get four or five hours of sleep, and then get up and do it again. About the only time Jody and I spent together was when we went to AA meetings. She was riled about me being gone all the time. I avoided her as much as possible.

Jody and I didn't really know each other that well, and another major problem quickly reared its head. I've always been almost compulsively neat and organized; I can't stand clutter. However, Jody didn't seem to mind it at all. I felt she didn't know how to clean properly, which infuriated me. And she slept a lot because

CHAPTER TWENTY-SEVEN

she was becoming increasingly depressed about her pregnancy. It aggravated, and I let her know it. We soon began to argue.

Our daughter, Brooke, was born on June 10, 1990. Jody and I tried to create our own little family unit as best as we could, and we started going to AA meetings together again on a regular basis. But we fought constantly about control of the household and how it would be run. I was gone until dark every day and out most nights. Working in the public all day was like going out into a jungle, and when I came home I wanted peace and quiet and a neat, organized home. Invariably the place was, to me, a mess, and we fought. We gradually stopped going to AA meetings together.

My wildlife work was becoming everything to me, and I didn't allow anything to get in the way, including my new family. Or Ellie. My job took all my time. I always had something job-related to do, even after I got home. The truck had to be unloaded and cleaned and reloaded for the next day, and I had paperwork. There weren't any computers back then, so everything was handwritten.

Jody developed a separate life. Her mother lived only a couple of miles away, and she spent a lot of time there. We argued constantly, mostly about how the house was kept and my lack of attention to the family. When I talked to Carlos about how Jody and I fought, he'd always calm me. He'd talk to me, make me understand, and get me to make amends to Jody if I needed to do so without condemning me or making me feel bad.

My wildlife work started to interfere with my job at Per Mar Security. I realized that I had to either start turning down animal jobs, which I was terrified would destroy my dream of a trapping career, or quit Per Mar. That scared me too. I liked the work and the good money and the security.

"Follow your dream," Carlos told me. "If it doesn't work out, you can always get another job. Actually, Per Mar will probably hire you back. So what if you fail? At least you tried." He was always encouraging me to try things and do my best and not worry about failure.

In September 1990, I left Per Mar Security to start a full-time wildlife business. My family thought I was crazy to give up my job and insurance to—as they saw it—catch raccoons. I worked out of a small Mazda pickup truck with a camper shell, ladder racks and ladders longer than the truck. I was immensely proud of the magnetic signs with my company name, "Christman's Animal Relocation," on both front doors.

Jody wanted me home more often, but I had no interest in being a husband or a father. I did what I had to do out of responsibility, not desire. My wildlife business totally consumed me. I paid no attention to my daughter for her first several years of life. I missed most of her first talk, her first steps, and everything else. The only thing I cared about was that she was fed and well groomed. I was continually trimming her fingernails and toenails. That was my main concern with my daughter during her first few years of life.

I worked locally, and almost every day I came home in the afternoon, unannounced, to try to catch Jody not doing housework or in bed napping to prove she was sleeping the day away and not attending to our home. The place was always clean, but it was cluttered, and I complained constantly about it.

I had less time for AA meetings, and when I was there I spent most of the time thinking about work. I obsessed about it. My fear soon returned, but with a different face. I became convinced the business would fail. The more calls I got, the louder a voice in me said, *This could all end tomorrow. You'll go bankrupt. You'll be homeless. You'll be a failure.* It was ludicrous. I was getting better at the work, my reputation was spreading, and I was starting to make good money. But the fear had a life of its own.

I was absolutely driven. There was no way I was going to let Jody or Brooke interfere with the business. At supper I snapped at Jody when she tried to drag me into discussions I had no interest in, and then after supper I went into the garage to build exclusion devices. I had realized early on that removing nuisance wildlife was only part of the solution; it was just as important to prevent the problem from happening again. That meant stopping wildlife from getting into people's houses. Animals like squirrels and raccoons usually got into attics through vents on roofs, gable ends and soffits and through attic fans, so I designed animal-proof wire mesh covers for

CHAPTER TWENTY-SEVEN

those places. I ordered rolls of wire, cut and hand-bent the pieces, spot welded them together, and painted them. When I was done in the garage, I went back inside and did paperwork.

Jody and the baby went to bed early, usually before I was finished. At about 9 P.M. I'd quit for the day and sit alone in front of the TV and think about the next day's work. I'd stay up watching all those kick 'em-up movies: Chuck Norris, Jean-Claude Van Damme, Steven Seagal. I still wanted to be a kickboxing champion. Nine o'clock was my relaxation time, the 5 o'clock most people experience.

While I was doing a job I was completely absorbed and happy. I enjoyed figuring out where an animal traveled, what bait and trap to use, and how to make the set. I felt confident when I left a job knowing I had a good chance of a catch. Checking the traps the next day was always exciting, and when I made a catch I was filled with exhilaration. I'd think, *Man, I'm good. I'm the best.*

But whenever I slowed down, such as when driving between jobs or at night, the confidence would fade and a cold, clear thought would rise: *This won't last. You'll fail. You're defective. Something horrible will happen.*

Success led inevitably to fear of failure. The only solution I had was to do more work. The more I worked the more I succeeded, and the more I succeeded the more I feared failure, so the more I worked.

My madness had returned.

I was down to going to about one AA meeting a week, a Wednesday night men's group. My connection with God faded. I was far more concerned about failing in business than in my marriage. I became harsher and more controlling. I didn't allow Jody to argue or disagree with my desires for a spotless house and perfect child.

Jody started hanging out with a different group at AA, and she got a sponsor who I felt interfered with our marriage. Jody was desperately unhappy and undoubtedly told her sponsor about our problems, just like I complained about her to Carlos. Jody's sponsor was probably telling her how to deal with it, such as by demanding that I spend more time at home. I saw it as meddling with our marriage. The rift between Jody and me grew wider.

During it all I kept taking Tae Kwon Do classes and practicing. I got better and better. There are nine belt levels, and I got my black belt, the highest, within three years. I sparred in class a lot, and I became the best in the school. I was Joe Mesa's best black belt.

I had my first competitive fight in the early nineties at The Mark, a big 9,000-seat multipurpose arena in Moline. I was accepted in an event called the Tough Man Contest. There were 40 fighters in all. My corner man was Mr. T—*the* Mr. T. When I walked into the ring I was scared to death, although I knew I was good. I was especially good with what's called a reverse side kick. I was very accurate, very fast, and I could knock people across the room.

When the bell rang, this short, stocky bodybuilder came running across the ring. I was only about 155 pounds, and this guy was rugged. This muscle-bound bodybuilder knew he was just going to eat me up. He came running right at me and couldn't wait to tear me up. I waited until he got in range and then spun around and did a sidekick. I broke three of his ribs and knocked him out. They took him out on a stretcher.

I thought, *Wow, I'm a god!*

The next night I got beat by a boxer, a three-time Golden Glove winner. He knocked me down for more than ten seconds. I didn't care. I was running with the big dogs. I was a success.

My back started to hurt. I knew something was wrong, so I trained and fought as much as I could.

My wildlife business was exploding. I worked from the minute I woke up until I dropped into bed. Jody and I barely spoke anymore, except to fight. Ellie sensed our anger and hid the second our voices rose.

I left business cards everywhere, and I got referrals from police departments, animal control people and local Humane Society shelters. Most of my early jobs were for individual homeowners with raccoon, skunk, groundhog and squirrel problems. As word

CHAPTER TWENTY-SEVEN

spread I started to get calls from schools, municipalities and corporations.

Increasingly, I talked with Carlos about divorce. He told me repeatedly that I didn't need to make that decision today and that I should sleep on it. He told me that all relationships end sooner or later. "Enjoy the relationships you have," he'd say. "People come and go. It will always happen. It's a fact of life, and the sooner you get used to it the better off you'll be. Enjoy the relationships you have now to the fullest, every day, because the next day they may not be there. The relationship you and I have, as much as you don't want to think about it, will be gone some day. I don't know when, but it will happen."

I used to get upset when he said that, because I didn't want it to ever happen. But it did. Shortly after that, he moved to Louisiana.

I was now making good money, and in 1993 Jody and I bought a house in Moline. It was the American Dream: self-made man buys home and installs happy wife and kid.

One of my first large commercial customers was International Harvester. They had a big plant located on about 200 acres near the Mississippi, and they had a chronic problem with raccoons, skunks and opossums that came in from the surrounding areas. The plant doors were open 24/7, and animals were always ambling inside. The directors at the plant were always calling me, and by 1993 I was removing about 70 raccoons, 70 skunks and 50 opossums each year for them. I finally said to them, "I'm here all the time anyway, so why don't you just hire me to do an ongoing preventative maintenance program? Then you won't have to keep calling me, and I can work it into my schedule better instead of getting crisis calls all the time."

They agreed, and I signed my first commercial contract. I basically surrounded the plant with cage traps and reduced their complaints to next to nothing.

In 1994, two beavers started eating the bark off expensive ornamental trees in Moline's Ben Butterworth Parkway, a public walkway along the Mississippi. The animals did thousands of dollars of damage in a few nights. Newspaper headlines read, "The Beavers That Ate Moline." Officials from the city called me, and I caught the beaver the first night. It was average size but made huge headlines at 83 pounds.

The story was on the front page of the local papers, with a big color picture of me with the beaver. To my astonishment the story went national, and TV footage of me appeared on the nightly news across the country. All of a sudden I was a celebrity, and it seemed as if everyone in the Quad City area knew me. I couldn't go into stores or gas stations without some stranger saying, "You're the guy who trapped the beaver, right?"

If I needed proof I was a success, this was it. I was ecstatic.

I was also in instant, constant demand. The phone rang off the hook with wildlife calls. I pushed Jody and Brooke further into the background. There was no way I was going to ignore my adoring, needy public. I had never in my life been the center of this much attention, and I loved it. I was not going to let anything interfere with it.

Alcoa Aluminum called. The plant was one of the largest in the world at a mile long and a quarter-mile wide. It sat on about 300 acres of prime wildlife habitat, and animals were a constant problem. The water the plant used had to be run through a series of filter ponds along small discharge streams (called outfalls) before it could be dumped into the Mississippi. The EPA scrutinized the outfalls closely and did not tolerate anything interfering with the correct flow, or with the dikes. Groundhogs dug dens into the pond dikes and caused them to fail, and beavers came upstream from the river to dam the outfall streams. Skunks and raccoons wandered into the building, creating health and safety issues. Alcoa wanted my help. I told them I was their man and that they could call me any time.

My back pain got worse. I ignored it. Nothing was going to get in my way.

CHAPTER TWENTY-SEVEN

My marriage deteriorated steadily. Jody wasn't a real touchy-feely person, so there wasn't any major conflict with my not liking to be cuddly or physically affectionate. But one night while I was sleeping, she laid her hands on me like she had seen a TV evangelist do and prayed that God would remove the devils that resided in me. She prayed a little too loud, and when I woke and found her hands on me, trying to do some sort of exorcism, I freaked. Someone was touching me without my knowing it, and the idea of someone casting demons out of me scared me to death. I immediately became furious. I took it as an extreme violation, and we got into a vicious fight.

Jody never told me exactly what she thought the evil in me was. But that act triggered my now continuous thoughts that there was something seriously wrong with me. In the summer of 1994, I stopped sleeping with Jody and began spending my nights downstairs on the couch.

CHAPTER TWENTY-EIGHT

AROUND THIS TIME, an older guy started coming to the Wednesday night men's group, the only AA meeting I still attended. He was about 60, balding, about five-foot eight-inches, and a bit chunky but solidly built. He was quiet at first; all he said was that his name was Barks and that he was newly sober. I saw him sometimes at other meetings, too.

After a while he began to raise his hand to speak. His comments were short, concise and had strong spiritual overtones. I liked his honesty and humility. He intrigued me. I wondered what his background was, what he did for a living, and what he was like outside AA. A bunch of us usually hung around socializing after meetings, and I began to approach him. He told me his real name was Richard Barclift; "Barks" was an old college nickname. As time passed he fit in with the group, and he and I became casual acquaintances.

Then I discovered Barks was a Catholic priest. I was impressed that a priest had the humility to admit he had a problem with alcohol and to turn to lay people for help. I was impressed, too, that the Catholic Church itself had the humility to let one of their own designated spiritual guides attend a non-denominational group for help.

CHAPTER TWENTY-EIGHT

From then on I watched Barks closely. I scoped him out. I've always held priests in slightly higher regard than other people. Priests are spiritual professionals, picked and trained for the job of going between God and man. They have rules to live by, and they have to give up certain things. Like sex. As a kickboxer, I understood the importance of discipline and training, and I felt priests lived by a similar code.

At first I didn't think Barks liked me. When I spoke at meetings, I tended to joke and kid around. He always listened intently when anyone spoke, and I thought his serious look was disapproval of my attitude.

I watched him closely; how he acted, what he said. He wore normal street clothes, never preached or talked religion or dogma, admitted his foibles, and was quick to laugh. He was honest and matter-of-fact. One would have never suspected that he was a priest, although there was a consistent spiritual element in his comments.

I was feeling out whether I wanted to approach him. I had questions about God and spirituality. Without really being aware of it, I had begun a slow, cautious approach to a man of God. It would be six years before I really reached out to him.

In September 1994, I had made an appointment with my attorney to start divorce proceedings. The day I walked into his office, I was served with papers from my wife's attorney.

I knew my connection to God was slipping, and I struggled to hang on to it. In the spring of 1995, I bought the *One Year Bible*. It had daily readings from the Bible divided into segments. The idea was that if you read an excerpt every day, at the end of one year you would have read through both the Old and New Testaments. The readings calmed me. Even when I didn't understand the passage, I felt serenity and acceptance. My favorite reading was the parable of the Prodigal Son.

Pat Miletich had been trained in martial arts by Nick Tarpien, and Pat became good enough to run the Nick Tarpien School of Karate franchise in Davenport. I started attending in the summer of 1995, and I went for about a year, mainly to spar with bigger and better fighters to improve my ability. I only weighed about 160 pounds, but I routinely sparred with six-foot, 200-pound guys, and I practiced at home every night. I was in the best shape of my life. I was sculpted.

I had succeeded in my dreams of being a professional fighter and trapper. But I had failed in my marriage. In November 1995, the divorce became final. Even though I had wanted it and knew it was coming, the actual event affected me deeply. I felt terrible and guilty. I knew I'd been a poor husband and father. I believed I was incapable of love. The only thing that kept me going was martial arts and work. So I buried myself in both.

That fall, Barks had hip surgery. Half a dozen of us from the Wednesday men's group held a surprise AA meeting in his hospital room, and he loved it. We all got closer that night, and something clicked between Barks and me. We were drawn to each other. It was the beginning of our friendship.

Barks and I began to hang out together occasionally after meetings, and we slowly got to know each other. I was curious about his life—how he became a priest and what he did with his time off. When I told him I was raised Catholic but was no longer practicing, he just nodded. His attitude toward me and treatment of me didn't change. The Catholic Church forbids divorce, but he didn't reject me because I'd had one. He was an absolutely non-judgmental man, accepting, kind, compassionate.

Barks never acted aloof or superior. The very fact that he was in AA showed that he was willing to look to others to heal. He once said at a meeting, "We're all imperfect. We help each other. This is a like-to-like ministry." I could recognize humility when I saw it, and I knew instinctively that it was a deeply spiritual characteristic. I was attracted to Barks because of it.

Barks understood only too well the tragedy of addiction and the devastation it caused. I saw sadness, concern and empathy on his face as he listened to stories of personal anguish and loss. Yet he was essentially a cheerful, optimistic man. He had faith. That

CHAPTER TWENTY-EIGHT

puzzled me. How could he be so accepting when life could be hell on earth? His faith intrigued me.

I'd never known a priest personally before. Slowly, I began to trust him. But I was still cautious.

Our relationship was basically social at first. We didn't get into long, detailed discussions about sobriety and spirituality or my personal issues. A few times he asked how I was doing with the pain of my divorce. He was opening a door, but I wasn't ready to bite, and he didn't push the subject.

I think Barks learned a lot from being accepted into a group of laymen as an equal. He was one of the guys. He definitely got an education on what life was like for the layperson; he heard detailed stories about struggles with relationships, children, finances, work, everyday life and about our rewards and joys. I think it made him a better priest. Any priest or minister would benefit from attending some open AA meetings and just listening without judging.

In the spring of 1996, I was best man at the wedding of my friends Chris and Lisa, and Barks was the priest. For the first time I saw him actually perform as a priest, administering the sacraments of Matrimony and the Eucharist. Until then I had known him primarily as a friend; that day the full impact of his priesthood sank in. He was Father Barclift. Father B.

He knew I was interested in vehicles. At the wedding reception, he told me he'd just bought a fairly new black Jeep Cherokee Limited, and he invited me to his apartment to see it. I went, and we ended up talking for hours. We'd discovered a mutual obsession with vehicles of all sorts. Four wheels, two wheels, three wheels, land, water, air—as long as it was a vehicle, it didn't matter.

I began to visit him occasionally. We'd have supper and talk cars. I was building my Monte Carlo, and at one point he'd had an Audi S4. He was in way over his head with it—it was too expensive to maintain on a priest's salary—so he got rid of it. I told him that was a good thing, because it was too dangerous for an old guy to drive a car like that. He liked speed.

We'd talk about high performance muscle cars: the Shelby Mustang Cobra, Dodge Challenger, Charger, Camaro, Firebird,

Corvette. I'm a sucker for the latest electronic gear, and he'd torment me about how much money I spent on gadgets. He'd accuse me of having a fax machine in my vehicle, or a blender built into the back seat, or night vision cameras on the bumpers. We talked constantly about the new cars coming out. I was always trading my work trucks in for the latest models, and he ragged on me for that. He read in the kitchen, and the table was covered with what he called his prayer books: *The Catholic Post* and the *National Catholic Reporter*, but also *Auto Week*, *Road and Track*, *Motor Trend* and *Sports and Exotic Car*.

"You know," he said one time, "our cars are like our horses. What you drive is your horse."

He had just bought a Volkswagen. "If that's the case, your Volkswagen is a donkey," I said. "You're a humble priest; you should be driving a donkey. I want an Arabian."

"Pride," he sniffed. "Jesus rode an ass."

"That's the only thing I don't really like about Jesus," I said. "He should have ridden something classy. I understand this whole humility thing, but have a little pride in how you get around, for God's sake. He could have been riding an Arabian."

"Yeah, but He had a roomful of trophies that is rarely referred to in Scripture. He won all kinds of races with that shabby little animal He rode. The thing with Jesus is that you can presume He had a roomful of trophies because He never mentions it; He's too humble to talk about it."

"Trophies?" I snorted. "He could have mentioned them at least once. That would have really impressed people."

Father B put on a snooty look. "He wouldn't be my personal Lord and Savior if He talked about His trophies all day, like we talk about cars."

"I don't have a problem with what He wore," I said. "The robes, that's accepted savior stuff, that's cool. It's just what He was driving. As a matter of fact, when I get up there I'm gonna talk to Him about it. He gets a kick out of me, and He's gonna let me up there to at least talk to Him. I don't know whether I'll get to stay

CHAPTER TWENTY-EIGHT

or not—that's another story. But I'm gonna have a talk with Him about the ass."

Father B looked thoughtful. "What would Jesus be driving today?"

"A Pacer," I said. "A Gremlin, a …"

"No, no, no. It would be a plain little Jetta with a turbo on it, super charger and pumps. He would need to cover a lot of ground, and economically, too. Although he hobnobbed around all those oil wells in the desert, He was poor. He could do miracles—he would be driving a TDI and could back up to any rubber tree …"

"Wait a minute. He was a carpenter, so He'd drive a truck. Probably a Ford Expedition King Ranch."

Father B shook his head, giving up on me.

The pain of my divorce was easing. My work was going well, although I was still driven by a fear of failure. I was going to AA meetings more regularly now that I was single. I was still reading the *One Year Bible*. The chronic fear began to fade into the background. I had moments of contentment.

It didn't last.

CHAPTER TWENTY-NINE

MY WORK AT Alcoa was becoming almost a full-time job in itself. During the first few months, believe it or not, I removed 336 groundhogs from the dikes. That's not counting other animals: raccoons and skunks inside the plant or hanging around the loading docks, beavers damming the outfall streams, overpopulated deer causing vehicle accidents on the public road in front of the property.

In 1996, I signed a maintenance contract with Alcoa. I now had more work than I could handle myself, so I hired my first technician, a guy named Gene. He was on probation, and I was supposed to meet with him and his probation officer to prove he had a job. "Wait until you see my probation officer, Michelle," Gene said. "She's drop-dead gorgeous."

We met at Gene's house. Michelle was beautiful. She was trim with an athletic build, had long blond hair and blue eyes, and was wearing a short skirt and colorful flowery blouse. I couldn't get her off my mind, and a few days later I called her at her work and asked her what crimes I'd have to commit to get her to be my probation officer. She laughed, and within a week we had our first date.

She was self-conscious at first, but she relaxed enough over dinner to tell me that she had two tattoos. I'd just gotten one on my right shoulder, so we compared. By the end of the date we were

CHAPTER TWENTY-NINE

old friends, and on the second date we were in bed. I spent almost every night at her apartment. We were infatuated with each other and had sex constantly.

I bought another German Shepherd, a male I named Bach. He and Ellie became instant friends, and Michelle loved them both. The four of us spent hours playing together. But my serenity went out the window. I was anxious and unfocused again. I knew Michelle and I weren't right for each other; we both had emotional issues that conflicted dangerously. Even though she was beautiful, she was very insecure about her looks. My nature is to joke and poke fun at myself and others, but that was completely off limits with Michelle. She could not take even the slightest kidding, particularly about her appearance. If I teased her about anything she got really offended, and I'd end up placating her for the night. I had to watch what I said, and that made me mad. And when people made me mad, I punished them. Within a month, we were arguing.

But I could see that the real Michelle was kind, considerate and loving, and I believed that if I worked with her she'd get through these issues. She didn't feel good about herself, so I'd help her. She was a damsel in distress, so I'd save her. I'd make her happy. People had helped me, so I felt I had a duty to help her.

We continued to make love on a daily basis. I was sure I wasn't any good at sex, and because it was a major part of our relationship, I felt I had to become an expert lover. I'd become successful at kickboxing and wildlife control through study and practice, and I thought sex was just another skill that could be learned. I read books, watched videos, studied and practiced until I became, in my mind, an accomplished lover.

Michelle liked to be touched. After sex she liked to cuddle, and with her I was OK with it. I willingly provided it because it made me feel special, needed and important. It got to the point where she gave me that look—that I was somebody who was special to her.

She was a military police officer in the Army and had done a tour in Desert Storm, where she had been a sergeant. She talked often about becoming a police officer, and I encouraged her because I knew it would make her happy.

Michelle wasn't comfortable in social situations. She was at her best when she was alone with me. She accepted the fact that I had a business to run and needed to put a lot of time into it, but when I was done for the day she wanted me to spend the rest of my time with her. We argued about it, but I usually gave in. More and more, we spent time alone at her place or mine. I began to fall away from AA. Sometimes I didn't go to a meeting for a month or more.

The fights got worse. I never knew when something I said would trigger her insecurity, and the second she started to react I jumped all over her. I was an experienced verbal fighter, and she wouldn't tolerate being attacked, so we'd end up screaming insults at each other. It wasn't just her being oversensitive—sometimes I'd be infuriated at her for something and I'd tell her she was messed up in the head, and off we'd go. Although I never hit her, my rage was back in full force. After each rage I hated myself for it. I was in despair; I was failing in yet another relationship.

Once again, the only pleasure I had was my work, and I dove even deeper into it. My business was still growing, and I added new species. I was now eradicating bats from people's houses, trapping moles on lawns, removing urban pet-eating coyotes, and culling urban deer. I was solidly established. Everyone in the area knew I was the best in the business, and the calls kept increasing.

Wildlife work is a constant challenge, and every job is different. I thrived on it. I had long hours of real happiness. But the thoughts always returned: *I can't have a normal relationship with a woman; the business could fail tomorrow; I'm defective and inherently flawed.*

I knew the relationship with Michelle was bad for both of us. I saw clearly what it was doing to us. So I asked her to marry me.

To this day, I don't have a clue why I did it. It wasn't a rational decision. I knew it would lead to disaster. Yes, I felt responsible for her and was convinced she'd be destroyed if I broke up with her. And yes, there was pride that I could save her, bring out her good qualities, change her and be her special one. But it was more than that. Once again, I willingly chose chaos. It's the old perversity of

CHAPTER TWENTY-NINE

the human soul: the ability to destroy what we want, what we love, what's good for us.

The Catholic Church defines mortal, soul-killing sin as a gravely destructive act committed with full knowledge of its seriousness and with deliberate, complete willingness. I sinned when I married Michelle—against both of us. Deliberately. I didn't do it to be destructive—I'll give myself that—but I knew full well it *would* be destructive. Sin ruptures the link to God's grace.

In January 1997, I bought a bungalow in Moline, and we moved in. We got married in March. Things got worse fast.

Our fights became more frequent and nastier. The slightest trivial disagreement triggered screaming rages in both of us. I was terrified that she was unhappy with me and that I might never make her happy, and in the old familiar alchemy my fear turned to rage. I hated her for not being happy. We'd shriek out each other's flaws; she'd call me a controlling, critical jerk, and I'd call her a psycho and threaten divorce. The dogs hid. We'd scream for a while, and then I'd jump in my truck and be gone for hours, waiting for her to call. She always did, crying and apologizing. I'd console her and assure her I wouldn't leave. I'd come home, we'd be forgiving and affectionate, have dinner and make up.

The year after we married, I bought house in Milan, Illinois. It was in the country on seven acres of pasture surrounded by woods. The property had two barns, a creek running through the front yard, and another one behind the house through the pasture. I wanted horses. I bought the place because I hoped we'd be happy there. We weren't. The fights continued.

Our fights always led to me threatening divorce. I was convinced that it was wrong to do, but I was desperate for the constant conflict to end, and I knew in my heart that the only solution was separation. I blamed myself. Why had I gotten in this mess? Why couldn't I make her happy? I hadn't been able to relate to girls back in school, my relationships with Lisa and Jody had been disasters, and here I was smack in the middle of the same chaos. I was terrified that I was incapable of a normal, healthy relationship with a woman.

We steadily became more isolated. I never wanted to have people over to the house or go to social functions, because I knew I'd say or do something that would offend her. I knew a shouting match would result, and I'd end up being embarrassed in front of everyone.

In October 1999, I was taking a 32-foot ladder off my truck when a lightning bolt of pain went down my leg. I dropped to my knees. I was in agony and could barely walk. My company had worker's comp, and I was covered because although I owned the company, I was also considered an employee. So I began rounds of seeing doctors.

I knew I should take it easy and let my employee do the work, but I was terrified to turn down any jobs. In agony, I handled ladders, climbed on roofs and loaded and unloaded the truck. I refused to stop practicing Tae Kwon Do and kickboxing, although the pain and stiffness slowed my movements.

In early 2000, Michelle became a police officer at the Moline police department. Many nights she worked second shift and didn't come home until midnight. I always pretended to be asleep when she came in. I left for work early in the morning while she was asleep, and by the time I got home she was back at work herself. I was glad for the time alone. I loved working around outside on the property.

Michelle became surer of herself as a police officer and started socializing with other people in the department. She started avoiding me. Many times while on my way home I'd see her out in her squad car, and she'd drive by with barely a nod, or just completely ignore me. When we were together, she acted detached. I felt she thought less of me because I was injured and weak. Defective.

I bought Michelle a German Shepherd, another male named Axel. Ellie, Bach and Axel got along great. When Michelle and I fought, the three dogs bolted for their room together. At least they kept each other company.

My back pain got worse. My work could be physically rough, with constant bumps and scrapes, and that, along with the impact

CHAPTER TWENTY-NINE

of years of Tae Kwon Do and kickboxing, had conditioned me to ignore everything but extreme physical discomfort. So I continued working. The doctors kept referring me to different back specialists. I evidently had some degenerative condition with a couple of my lower vertebrae, and the opinion was forming that I might need an operation to fuse my back. That scared me. What if I couldn't work afterward? I gobbled aspirin and kept working.

Michelle and I had moments of real happiness together. We still had sex often, went out to dinner and the movies, and played with the dogs. We were homebodies, just her and me together. I now rarely went to AA meetings. My world got smaller. And my fear increased.

By early 2001 I knew that I needed professional mental help, and in March I started seeing a psychiatrist. It was my first experience with psychotherapy and medication. The doc was about fifty years old, thin, with swarthy features. He immediately decided I was depressed and put me on Zoloft.

I had a weekly talk session with him. I liked him—he was a nice guy—but I was uncomfortable about the woman who sat in on every session taking notes. I told him that it made me uncomfortable, but he said he needed her as a transcriber. She never said a thing besides hello and goodbye; she just took notes. It was tough for me to relax with her there. After all, we're all human—how could she not react to what I said, form impressions or judge me? I was open and honest with the doc. I trusted him because he was a trained professional and was supposed to be non-judgmental. And he had a code of confidentiality. But I never trusted the woman.

We talked about my fear and anxiety, about Michelle and Jody, about women in general, and about my inability to love and trust. He analyzed my feelings, and it sort of made sense. I don't remember a diagnosis.

The Zoloft didn't help, and it reduced my sex drive. That was unacceptable; I had to perform often. The doc tried something else. I don't remember it helping.

I had back surgery scheduled for June 2001. I was concerned I wouldn't be able to take care of the bigger home in the country, so I bought a house in Moline, and in May 2001 Michelle and I moved in.

After the operation, the surgeon said that my spine had degenerated to the point that it was in pieces. They couldn't understand how I'd been able to walk. They fused the vertebrae with a bone graft from my hip and put in a cage. It was six months before I was able to work again. However, my business didn't collapse like I'd feared; by then I'd hired another employee, and the two men did the work while I did the paperwork. That should have relieved my fear, at least minimally. But it didn't.

The doctors had hoped the operation would relieve the pain. If anything, it got worse. And so the pain medication dance began. They started me off on a narcotics patch of some kind, and then steroids. Next came Vicodin, and then Ultram.

The pain meds had a drastic effect on my mind. I started experiencing extreme emotional highs and lows. It took me a while to realize that I was going through withdrawal several times a day. During withdrawal, I went into severe depression and anxiety and got really irritable. My psychiatrist monitored my responses, made recommendations, and eventually discovered that I had to overlap meds. He determined that Vicodin and Tramadon would be the best combo and have the least wacko effect.

While I was recovering, Michelle was working out daily, was in fabulous shape, and felt better about herself than ever. She needed me less and less. I also made her nervous when I talked about my fears of not being able to do my job anymore and possibly losing the business. In late 2001, my psychiatrist started seeing Michelle as a patient, to help the marriage.

I started spending some time socially with a woman who was friendly to me. I found that I could relax with her and be myself. I became attracted to her, and that concerned me. One day, I told the doc about it.

"We haven't done a thing," I said. "We just see each other socially; we're not dating or anything. We haven't even held hands or talked about having a relationship. But I'm attracted to her, and I'm concerned about the effect it might have on my marriage."

CHAPTER TWENTY-NINE

A few days later, Michelle came home furious from a session with the psychiatrist. "He says you're seeing another woman," she said. "You're having an affair. He says I might want to consider a divorce because of what he called your 'extra-curricular activities.'"

I denied it, and we had a big fight. I confronted the psychiatrist. He didn't admit or deny it. All he said was, "I can't help you. I can't see you anymore."

It was a shock. I had trusted him. I had gone to him hoping he could help both my mental state and my physical pain. I felt rejected, alone and in despair of a solution.

CHAPTER THIRTY

IN EARLY JANUARY 2002, the Catholic priest sex abuse scandal in Boston exploded on the national media. More than 130 people had accused Father John Geoghan of abuse during a 30-year period, and the Boston archdiocese had hidden it from the public, paying off victims and moving Geoghan from place to place, where he continued to find new victims. It seemed like there was a revelation about the Boston cover-ups almost daily through January and February. New reports revealed that cases against at least 70 other Boston-area priests had been settled and hidden by the Church over the past ten years alone.

The news disturbed me deeply. I was shocked and disgusted with the Church, which was a rational response. Emotionally I got agitated, and my fear increased. I always had FOX News on when I worked in my office, and I'd be at my desk and hear reports of yet another abuse case. I'd be captured by the flickering faces, the reporters' artificially dramatic voices, and all the sordid details. My heart would pound, my breath would get short, and my hands would shake. It would be long minutes before I could work again. Sometimes I had to shut off the TV.

To add to the madness, Michelle and I had a huge fight over some trivial item we were going to buy to fix up the kitchen. I demanded

CHAPTER THIRTY

a divorce, and this time I meant it. Michelle knew it, and she went completely ballistic. She threw everything in her path against the walls and floors until the whole house was a mess of smashed glass, dishes, pictures, knick-knacks, books and tapes. The dogs hid quaking in the basement.

I left for a few days.

The clergy sex abuse exposes kept coming. They seemed endless. Each one increased my agitation.

Michelle went into a rage and screamed at me before leaving. She had absolutely no fear of me, and although she made no move to do so, I became irrationally convinced she was going to somehow hurt me. I knew in my condition I wouldn't have been able to defend myself.

I was in a relentless state of fear. The divorce was impending, I worried obsessively that I'd lose my business and go bankrupt, and although I knew she was incapable of it, an illogical terror grew that Michelle would try to kill me. To add to the panic, I could see myself losing control of my thoughts and feelings. They raced in complete confusion. Then another clergy abuse scandal would hit the news, and my terror would ramp up another notch.

One day in early March, I started drinking again. The booze numbed me, but there was no real high—just flat deadness. I didn't get blind drunk like before; I stayed fully conscious, but I felt nothing. Just heavy gray emptiness.

I drank intermittently and always alone; I didn't want to talk to anyone. After each time I got drunk, my self-disgust increased. Thirteen years of continuous sobriety was gone out the window.

My divorce from Michelle was finalized that month. Scenes of fights I'd had with Lisa, Jodi and Michelle repeated obsessively in my mind. I couldn't shut them off. The familiar childhood goblin, gloating at my failures, came from hiding and gleefully wrapped its arms and legs around me in a relentless, possessive grip. It told me I was bad and that something horrible was going to happen.

I knew I was in danger. From some feeble buried resource, I got the courage to call a friend in AA and told her I was drinking again.

She was frightened by how I sounded and begged me to return to AA. I didn't. I kept drinking.

One night in late March, I pulled my truck into the garage, hit the automatic door closer, and sat in the cab, paralyzed. I couldn't even get out of the truck. I became filled with the conviction that I was a mistake, a defect in the world, a blight in God's plan. I could do nothing right, nothing good. I destroyed everything I touched.

I'd always fought that thought and pushed it away with desperate clutches at proof I was a success. *I'm an excellent trapper. I take good care of my vehicles. I'm professional about my paperwork.* Now I saw that all those attempts were business-related, shallow and pathetic. The full reality hit me: I was a failure.

I was exhausted. All my life I'd been tormented, and it would never change. There was no hope. At that moment I gave up. I cannot describe the despair. Living one more day like this, let alone the rest of my life, was beyond bearing.

The thought came clear and direct, as if from outside of me: *Kill yourself. Leave the truck running. It will be over. Kill yourself.* Then another thought came, this one mine: *All my life I've wanted to die. I've always tried to figure out a way to die. Now I have one. Just don't turn off the truck.*

I became calm; it was over. I had decided. I felt enormous relief.

I sat there a good twenty-five minutes in the truck, waiting to pass out. Suddenly, a clinical, emotionless observation came to me: *This is how my father died. At exactly the same age. I'm 35 too.*

At precisely that moment of abandonment of hope, God put the image of my mother in my mind. I saw her face and literally felt her presence. I saw her break down sobbing at the news of my death.

I saw my daughter, Brooke, now almost 12. All my life I'd felt that my father had abandoned me; now she would feel the same. She would remember me as a suicide. That horrified me.

God took me outside of my own anguish and showed me the devastation my suicide would wreak on those I loved. He gave

CHAPTER THIRTY

me a moment of clarity, and a choice. Something shifted in me. I turned away from my own pain toward the needs of others. I decided not to die.

I still wanted to. So I came up with a solution: *I'll sit here and think about it, not make up my mind yet, but I'll keep the motor running. That way I'll pass out before I make up my mind, and I won't be responsible.*

Then I thought, *How sick is that?* and I laughed out loud. Get rid of the guilt but still get to die? Everyone would still be hurt. I reached out and turned off the truck.

I called another AA friend and told him I'd come close to suicide. He said I needed professional help, and he arranged an emergency visit with another psychiatrist, Dr. O.

Dr. O was an obese man in his fifties, with a heavy face, black hair and glasses. I don't remember much of that first visit. He seemed professional and knowledgeable, and I put myself in his hands with relief. He wanted to see me daily at first because I was in crisis, and I agreed.

Dr. O became my lifeline. He was friendly, supportive and kind. He'd call me at home to see how I was doing. The urge to kill myself faded; when I was overwhelmed emotionally, I knew I'd be seeing Dr. O soon, which enabled me to put any decisions on hold until I could talk to him. And talk I did. Stuff poured out of me in a loosely connected torrent: my fears, failed relationships, drinking, business, back pain. At the beginning of each session Dr. O would ask me what was going on that day, and it was like pushing a button.

Dr. O taped every session. He did that with all his patients. He had stacks of labeled tapes everywhere—on shelves, on his desk, on tables. He wanted me to tape our sessions as well. I taped a few, but I kept forgetting to bring a tape recorder. It was a hassle, and I had enough on my mind. Dr. O said I could have copies of his if I needed them, so I decided not to tape the sessions myself. I would bitterly regret that decision.

My insurance didn't cover the sessions, so I paid the doctor out of pocket, usually with cash. Like many people who grew up poor, I felt insecure without cash in my pocket, and I sometimes carried as much as several hundred bucks with me in twenties and fifties. I liked the ability to buy a shirt or a tool or whatever on a whim, not because I needed it but because I wanted it. Impulse spending had become important.

A few weeks went by. I felt better after each session, but within a few hours I was a mess again. Dr. O reassured me it would take time.

I was sitting in my office when it happened. It wasn't a specific memory, at least at first, but more of a recollection of something long past. There was no blinding flash of light, no sudden shock of awareness—the scene simply appeared in my mind as if it had always been there, as familiar as any other vague image from my childhood.

It was a large, dimly lit room that looked like a study or library. I knew somehow, intellectually, that it was in the rectory of Our Lady of Lourdes Church, where Jeff and I would hang out with Father Wiebler. He had been our parish priest when we were in Bettendorf, and he'd spent time with Jeff and me as a sort of father figure. I could picture the full-sized pool table in the rectory and a couch and a couple of chairs. Two steps led down into it.

Things got clearer. I was standing against the pool table, facing across it. It was covered with red felt. I think I was getting ready to take a shot. Father Wiebler stood behind me, the front of his legs pressing against the back of mine, holding me against the table. He bent down over me as if he was trying to help me hold the cue stick, or make the shot. Then his hand was in my crotch, wiggling my genitals. I instantly froze, unable to move. The image abruptly ended.

Had the incident at the pool table really happened, or was I imagining it? I'd had a vague bad feeling about Father Wiebler since childhood, but nothing specific. About 15 years before I'd run into some people who had attended Lourdes when we did, and Wiebler

CHAPTER THIRTY

came up in the conversation. They said there was a rumor that Wiebler had left the area in a hurry because of allegations of sexual misconduct with children. The comment kindled my vague feeling of unease about the man, but I had pushed it out of my mind.

Then another scene appeared. Father Wiebler and I were at Buffalo Beach, on the Mississippi. We were beside each other, and he was helping me into my swimming trunks. Then his hand was in my trunks, and he almost gently grabbed my penis and began stroking it. Again I became physically frozen, and again the memory ended suddenly.

I'd never forgotten the night that Jeff and I had eaten dinner at Father Wiebler's, and how I had been so scared I couldn't eat. That scene returned, along with its position in time; it had happened right after the beach incident. I wracked my brain to remember if anything else had happened, but nothing came back. I've always hated blackouts, and I was frustrated at how the two memories ended so abruptly.

For the next two weeks I had constant flashbacks of those two scenes. Were they real, or was I nuts? It drove me crazy. The images haunted me. They came without warning sometimes during the day, but they landed with full force after work. I stayed up late watching TV, trying to block them, but they kept coming. And always the question: were they real? I was pretty messed up; I couldn't tell what was real.

I decided I had to talk to Father Wiebler and ask him if he remembered anything. I called Father B. I suddenly needed a priest.

CHAPTER THIRTY-ONE

THE NEXT DAY I met Father B at IHOP and spilled the whole story: the drinking, the suicide attempt, the supposed memories of Wiebler, and even some details of my failed marriages. I did it because he was a priest. It was different than talking to Dr. O. This was more of a confession—an official act of reaching out to the Church.

I still believed in the Church. On some deep level I understood that I needed help with my relationship with God beyond what psychiatrists and AA could offer. I believed that a priest was God's representative, and I knew Father B would take it seriously.

I couldn't stop talking. At times I was shaking and crying. Father B listened quietly, occasionally shaking his head and taking deep breaths. His face grew sadder and sadder. I could see that he believed me about the memories. It's impossible to describe how much that meant to me—that someone didn't look at me like I was nuts, or pull back, or walk away. He believed me.

When I was finally quiet he looked at me, his eyes filled with tears, and said, "Oh, Bill. I'm so sorry."

Something let go in me. He believed me.

I asked him if he knew Father Wiebler.

CHAPTER THIRTY-ONE

He nodded. "I've heard of his approach to people, and of what seemed to me to be his absolutely insane antics. He once put on a parade through Bettendorf on Good Friday, done in some kind of modern genre, depicting the Way of the Cross of Jesus in a way that would be hip to a bunch of teenagers he was teaching at Assumption High School. Another time he took a starting pistol into his religion class and set up an incident that would involve shooting someone to teach some sort of lesson. In the middle of religion class, a kid in the back stood up and said, 'Wiebler, you're full of it.' Some other kid across the room said, 'Aw, sit down.'

"The first kid didn't sit down, so the kid in the other corner of the classroom stood up, pulled out a starter pistol—the kind that shoots blanks—pointed it at the standing kid, and pulled the trigger. The class absolutely went bananas! The wheels came off. And Wiebler, of course, as the priest was in there trying to break everything up and settle everything down. He finally had to see who was knocking on the door, and it was the principal and the teacher from across the hall.

"There are plenty of stories about Bill Wiebler," Father B said.

I told him I was thinking of calling Wiebler to see if I could resolve whether or not the incidents had actually happened.

"Go ahead," he said. He paused. "We should get together again. How about next Saturday at 11 A.M., right here?"

That was the beginning of our real relationship. It was mid-April.

I told Dr. O about the memories and my doubts about whether they were real or just another symptom of how messed up I was. He reassured me that I wasn't crazy. He said repressed memories were not uncommon with child sex abuse victims. The experiences were simply too painful for a child, and a denial mechanism of some sort blocked them out so he or she could continue to function as if everything was all right. But it wasn't all right. The emotional damage of the abuse could be deep and last a lifetime.

On May 1, I called the diocese and said I wanted to get in touch with a priest who used to be pastor of Lourdes. Irene Loftus, the parish chancellor, came on the line.

"I'm trying to get in touch with Father William Wiebler," I said.

"Is this an allegation?" she asked.

I thought that was a strange response. "No," I said. "I just want to talk to him about something personal."

She told me he lived in St. Petersburg, Florida, and gave me his address and phone number.

On May 3, I dialed Wiebler's number. I had no idea what to expect. At that point I was so confused that if he had said, "Are you nuts? I never did anything like that!" I would have dropped the whole thing. In fact, I was hoping that was exactly what he would say.

He didn't answer, so I left a message.

On May 5, Wiebler called me. He apologized for not calling earlier; he said he'd been on a cruise ship as the chaplain and had just got in.

"My name's Bill Christman," I said. "I don't know if you remember me, but me and my brother, Jeff, spent some time with you in the early '70s, when we were kids. Our father had just died, and we'd moved to Bettendorf. My mother, Mary, had just joined Our Lady of Lourdes. You were the pastor."

"Sorry, I don't remember you," he said.

I described what Jeff, my mother and I looked like, how we hung out at the rectory playing pool with him, and how he took us swimming.

"I don't remember you," he said again.

Something in his tone told me he did remember; he just wasn't admitting it. "Listen," I said, "The reason I called is ... I'm just gonna come out and say it."

"OK," he said. "Go ahead."

"Did you ever abuse, rape, fondle, molest or sexually assault me or my brother when we used to hang out with you?"

There was a long pause. Then he said, "I don't recall."

I was quiet. I couldn't believe what I'd just heard, because I knew what it meant. I didn't really want it to mean that. When I made the call I was really hoping Wiebler would say, "Oh, I don't

CHAPTER THIRTY-ONE

know what you're talking about. I'm so sorry you feel that way, but, gosh no, I didn't do that!" In my mind, I was just crazy to even think it had actually happened.

I found my voice. "So, did you ever sexually abuse or molest or harm anybody in any way, shape or form, during your entire tenure as a priest, anywhere?"

There was another long pause, and then he said, "I don't recall."

I knew I was right. I knew I wasn't crazy. It had happened. You don't answer a question like that with, "I don't recall."

I became paralyzed with fear. I couldn't speak.

"I'm sorry," he continued. "I just don't remember you. I wish I knew what you looked like."

I really don't remember what we said after that. I don't think we said much. I was in shock.

I called Father B immediately.

He was extremely upset. "He said *what*? Oh my God. Bill, I'm so sorry. The handwriting is on the wall; it happened. He did it. You need to call the Bishop."

That afternoon, I called the diocese and asked for Bishop Franklin. Irene Loftus came on the line, and I told her about my conversation with Wiebler. She said she'd talk with Franklin and get back to me. An hour later she called to say she'd arranged a meeting with Franklin the next day.

At the meeting I told them about my conversation with Wiebler in more detail.

"Bill Wiebler is an odd duck," Franklin said. That would turn out to be the understatement of the century. They both felt the conversation indicated there should be an investigation. I wanted to meet Wiebler face to face; my fear was making its old transformation to anger. I was beginning to see I wasn't crazy.

The meeting ended with Franklin and Loftus saying they'd bring Wiebler to the area so we could all discuss this matter together. "I'll have him here," Franklin promised.

I felt a strange excitement. This was going to go somewhere. I called Father B and asked him if he'd go with me to the meeting, and he said of course he'd be there.

The next day Loftus called to ask if I could attend a meeting at 1 P.M. on May 10, with Wiebler present. I said I'd be there and would be bringing a priest friend. She agreed, and I called Father B immediately. He insisted we meet the next morning at IHOP.

I was chewing pancakes when Father B asked, "What is it that you want from the Church?"

I knew exactly. "I want the assurance that he will be off the streets and will never harm another child again."

"Well, let's do it," he said. "Let's ask for that. Let's get it."

On May 10, we had the meeting with Wiebler that I described at the beginning of this book. During the meeting, it was obvious Wiebler had abused me and many other children. Bishop Franklin acknowledged it had happened and offered me compensation. I told him I wanted no money, but that what I did want was a guarantee that Wiebler would be contained and prevented from harming other children. I also wanted a formal apology from Franklin, as a representative of the Church, for being fully aware of Wiebler's abuse of children for years and continuing to allow it to happen. Franklin assured me I'd get the apology and promised he'd keep me posted of Wiebler's actions.

CHAPTER THIRTY-TWO

THE AFTERNOON AFTER the meeting with Wiebler, Irene Loftus called me and asked me to sign some forms to release my medical records. "It's for compensation," she said. I told her I wasn't interested in compensation. I wanted to know where Wiebler was, and I wanted a formal apology from Franklin.

The next day, Loftus sent an e-mail asking for all my medical records, including my documents for therapy. I was cautious about why she wanted them, but I was too upset by the whole episode to think clearly about it. I e-mailed her back and agreed to sign the forms.

A few days later, Carrie Coyle, a close friend who was also a lawyer, met me at a pizza shop for lunch. Carrie knew about my marital problems and drinking problems, but I'd said nothing to her about my memory of the abuse or my meeting with Wiebler. She could see something was bothering me and asked what was wrong. I told her what had happened over the past several weeks, including my memory, my initial telephone conversation with Wiebler, and the meeting.

"Father B went with me," I said. "Bishop Franklin was there, and Irene Loftus. Loftus wants me to sign a release form so they can get my medical records."

"Wait a minute," Carrie said. "Do you know who Irene Loftus is?"

"Yeah, she's the chancellor of the Davenport diocese."

"No, not just that. Do you know who she is?"

I shrugged. What was she getting at?

"Irene Loftus is an attorney with Lane & Waterman," Carrie said. "That's the law firm that represents the Davenport diocese. Didn't she tell you that in the meeting?"

It didn't sink in at first. "You mean she's a lawyer?"

"Yeah—for the diocese. Didn't she tell you that?"

"No, she just said she was the chancellor. She never said she was an attorney."

"That's illegal," Carrie said. "That's a breach of professional conduct. There's no way she should have been at that meeting without telling you she was an attorney with the diocese's law firm."

Why didn't Loftus want me to know she was an attorney? Then I remembered that she and Franklin had asked me not to tape record the meeting—that she would take good notes. And that at the end of the meeting, her legal pad was almost empty.

For the first time, I had the horrible suspicion that the Davenport diocese might not really care about what had happened to me and that they might only want to protect their image. Did they have an agenda all along during the meeting with Wiebler? The Boston cover-up stories filled my mind. I had trusted Franklin and Loftus. I fought to control feelings of betrayal.

I told Carrie I had not asked for money, just an apology and a guarantee that Wiebler was out of circulation. That seemed simple enough to do. Why did they need my medical records?

"Don't sign anything," she said. "Hopefully they'll give you what you asked for and that'll be the end of it. But they don't need your medical records for that. There's a chance they're building a case in the event this turns into a lawsuit."

At that point I felt I needed legal help, so I asked Carrie to represent me. She said she wasn't familiar with this type of case but that she'd handle it if I wanted her to. I trusted her and her expertise,

CHAPTER THIRTY-TWO

so I insisted, and she agreed. She told me that once I signed an agreement with her, I was not to have any more communication with the diocese, Loftus or Bishop Franklin whatsoever; she would handle it from there on out. I promised her I wouldn't, and I said I'd let her know about any e-mails or phone calls that I got from any of them.

Carrie also said that she wanted to include her colleague Cindy Taylor as her partner, and I agreed. We decided to wait a while and let the diocese fulfill their promises. If they did, the whole thing would be over. "But don't sign a release for your medical records," Carrie said again. "Don't sign anything."

I was concerned about what was going to happen to Wiebler. Franklin had assured me that they were sending him for psychological evaluation, and I desperately wanted to know if that had been done. I wanted someone to keep tabs on him to make sure he wouldn't molest more children.

The apology from Franklin, as a representative of the Church, was important to me. I held the Church partially responsible for the abuse because they had known Wiebler was a pedophile for years. I told Carrie I didn't need a written apology; I wasn't interested in anything they might think I'd use as an admission of guilt so I could take legal action against them. But I take apologies very seriously. If I'm in the wrong, I have to admit it to have any peace about what I've done. And if someone honestly admits they've wronged me and is sincerely sorry, it helps me let go of any resentment I hold. I can forgive them.

Father B and I kept in close touch. I wasn't back at AA meetings, I was seeing Dr. O, and, to really add to the insanity, I had started dating Michelle again. I was a mess. Father B was worried about my mental state, and he called almost daily to check on me. We got together often, usually at IHOP.

Mostly, he listened while I rambled on. It just poured out of me. Talking to Father B was different than talking to the doctor. Dr. O was emotionally detached, as befits a professional, and he had begun to diagnose me. I couldn't help but feel at least some judgment in that. Father B never judged me, and he never lectured. He sat quietly with me, present, empathizing.

One day he made a suggestion: If I truly wanted to heal, I had to forgive Wiebler. I thought he was nuts, and I passed it off as a typical religious remark—something he was supposed to say because he was a priest. Whenever I thought about Wiebler, I saw red. I wanted him dead, in hell. I wanted him to suffer like all his victims were still suffering.

Father B meant it, though, and I would hear him say it again. It would become his one refrain. Ultimately, I'd understand. And make a decision.

In early June, Bishop Daniel Jenky, who was in the Peoria diocese of which Father B was part, removed eight priests because of sex abuse allegations. It was the first local clergy sex abuse scandal, and it was big; it was instantly all over the media nationwide. There was a story about it in all the local papers every day, and Father B called me almost daily to see how I was taking each new revelation. That precipitated a lot of meetings. He'd say, "Hey, what are you doing? Let's get together some time, tomorrow, Thursday, Saturday morning, whenever." The breakfast meetings at IHOP were becoming a regular thing.

He was having a hard time, too, dealing with the revelations of abuse in his own diocese. His parishioners were shocked, horrified and angry. Their faith had been shaken, and Father B had to not only deal with his own torment but also nurture his flock. What could he tell them to restore their faith?

He didn't talk about his own pain much with me, but I could see it on his face. His concern was for others. He wanted his parishioners to heal, and he wanted me to have a sounding board and not have to carry my pain alone. He had no agenda and played no obvious priestly role; he was more an older friend. He wanted me to know that he was there for me. It slowly dawned on me that this quiet man was a true priest. I wasn't aware of it at the time, but looking back, I can see that simply being in his presence was healing me.

CHAPTER THIRTY-TWO

I went to Las Vegas to take a break. I laid around a hotel room for five days and didn't do a thing—not even drink. Michelle broke up with me as soon as I got back. On June 20 I drank a couple of beers and then called my old AA sponsor, Carlos, in Louisiana. I was ready to stop. He invited me to come down, and I stayed with him in his little apartment for a week. All we did was go to AA meetings and talk sobriety. I came home in much better shape. Those beers on June 20 were my last, although it would be another two years before I began attending AA meetings regularly.

Father B and I began meeting at IHOP every other Saturday at 11 A.M. It wasn't a formal agreement; we just started doing it. It would become a regular routine.

I met Patty in July. She was a waitress, blond and slightly built, very pretty, cheerful and vivacious. My crew and I had stopped at her restaurant for lunch, and she had waited on us. I wanted to date her immediately. I asked her out, but she smiled and said no thanks. She was undoubtedly used to getting hit on all the time. I didn't give up. I kept going by and asking her out each day for a week until she relented. Within a week we were dating steadily.

Patty was different than Michelle. She was easygoing, cheerful and not at all possessive or insecure. For a while we were happy together, and I was glad to have the approval of a woman again. I felt special again.

When I talked about Patty with Father B, he just listened, smiled and nodded at appropriate places. He wasn't being socially correct or polite; he was simply happy that I was happy. He didn't say, "Bill, are you sure diving into a new relationship makes sense right now?" That was what I was asking myself, and I was pretty sure I knew the answer. But I didn't want to know, and I didn't want Father B to say anything about it. If I'd asked him, he probably would have responded, but he never gave unsolicited advice. That was important to me. I knew I could talk about absolutely anything with him and that if I didn't ask him what he thought, he wouldn't say anything. He wouldn't judge me.

Occasionally, though, he'd tell me that I had to forgive Wiebler if I truly wanted to heal. Forgive the person who had sexually abused me as a child? I bit my tongue.

All through June and July, I waited for the diocese to call. After each week without word from them, I'd call and ask for Loftus or Franklin, and the receptionist would tell me they weren't available at the moment but that they'd call me back if I left my number. I would, and they wouldn't, and a week later I'd call again.

"I'm supposed to be notified where Wiebler is," I'd tell the receptionist each time. That was my biggest concern. Each time she'd ask me for my number, as if she didn't already have it, and assure me they'd call back immediately. They never did.

Why? My requests seemed so simple. I'd vent my increasing anger to Father B, and he'd nod and agree it was frustrating. He didn't criticize the diocese, but he didn't make excuses for them, either.

By August it was blatantly obvious that I was getting the runaround. I felt I had to strong-arm Loftus and Franklin, so I called Carrie and asked her and Cindy to officially represent me and to approach the diocese for information. Maybe hearing from lawyers would get results.

On August 8, 2002, I signed an Attorney Representation and Fee Agreement with Carrie. She then informed Lane & Waterman, the law firm that represented the Davenport diocese, that she and Cindy of Kirkwood Law Offices in Davenport were representing me. They told the diocese that all future correspondence should be directed to them and that they should not attempt to contact me. Carrie again made it clear that I was not asking them for money; all I wanted was word of what had been done about Wiebler, and an apology.

I didn't even ask for reimbursement of my lawyers' expenses. I was willing to pay them out of my own pocket. I just wanted the business settled. Most of all, I wanted to know where Wiebler was and what was being done about him. The possibility of him out

CHAPTER THIRTY-TWO

there destroying other children, with the full knowledge of the Church, and me helpless to stop him was more than I could stand to even think about. I swung between aggravation and frustration with the diocese and rage at Wiebler. I started to fantasize about shooting him, stomping him, kicking his face in.

When I signed with Carrie and Cindy, I didn't tell my daughter, Brooke, about the abuse because she was only 12 and I wanted to protect her. But I did tell her mother. Jody was stunned. For the rest of that summer and into the winter, I continually pestered Carrie about where Wiebler was. She contacted the diocese repeatedly, but had no luck. The diocese did, however, keep asking for my medical records.

Some of the diocese's reaction was understandable, because I was now being represented legally. The diocese had circled its wagons. But I couldn't understand why they had kept Wiebler's status secret. It would be two years before we learned what had happened to him, and the details of that story would be a shock.

During this entire time, I saw Dr. O about once a week. Our sessions had begun to change, and I was becoming increasingly uneasy about it. Sometimes he contradicted himself. In one session he'd encourage me to go to AA and tell me it was necessary, a proven way to get sober, and that if I was alcoholic I could never drink again. Then, a few sessions later, he'd say he had patients who were alcoholics but had managed to control their drinking and have just a couple a day, and that they had done it without AA.

Increasingly, he talked about himself and his achievements, sometimes for most of the meeting. He'd go on about articles he'd published, seminars he'd run, and how he was considered an expert in this field or that. He'd use clinical language—shrink talk—to explain diagnoses and origins of problems, and sometimes I couldn't understand what he was talking about. I was beginning to think he didn't like me anymore. His usual warm greeting and smile had changed to a short, clipped, "Hello, Bill." He acted as if he weren't glad to see me.

At first I wrote it off to my excessive sensitivity and made excuses for it. Maybe he was being hard on me to help me. Maybe

I was being paranoid. I kept telling myself that I should give him the benefit of the doubt.

Sometimes I'd be late to a session due to a work emergency. As a businessman, I understood well the importance of scheduling, and I always called ahead to tell him I was running behind. I always offered to pay him for the session if we cancelled, but he'd refuse and then, obviously irritated, snap at me for being late.

The sessions were not bringing the relief he had assured me they would. My emotions were as crazy as ever.

CHAPTER THIRTY-THREE

BY JANUARY 2003, I knew I'd never get an answer from the diocese. They really didn't care. They had seemed to care at the meeting with Wiebler, and I'd trusted them, opened myself up to them, and they had taken advantage of me. I was furious; somebody had betrayed me again. I didn't take that well. I decided to ask for money.

Carrie, Cindy and I calculated the cost of past counseling and potential future counseling, negative impact on my work and income, mental anguish and legal costs and came up with a figure of $750,000. I thought that might get their attention. Carrie said we had a good case but that it might take a while to settle it. That was an accurate statement.

At IHOP, I told Father B we were asking for $750,000. He asked how we'd arrived at the figure, and then he told me he thought it was fine that I be reimbursed for my losses and the lawyers get paid for their time. I started ranting again about all the legal proceedings. Father B listened, quietly chewing his breakfast. After a minute I stopped, a bit mortified that I'd lost it once again.

"Does it bother you when I get like this?" I asked.

"No, no, it's honest," he said. "But all this legal wrangling is snuffing out what I think was initially a healing process. It bothers me that it's turned into a legal and financial settlement issue."

When I told Dr. O, he asked if I was sure I wanted to sue the Church. He said he didn't think it was a good idea, because the Church had powerful lawyers who would crush me. I was astonished. I'd kept the doctor informed of my frustration with the diocese all along, and the previous fall he had encouraged me several times to sue them. In his own words, I needed to hit them where it hurt—in the wallet. I had told him I didn't want to do that. I'd still hoped, naively, that I'd get my apology and get Wiebler off the streets.

On January 23, 2003, Carrie wrote to Lane & Waterman attorney Charles Miller to ask for a settlement of $750,000. The legal dance had begun. I had no idea what an endless, convoluted ballet it would be.

On January 29, Miller wrote to Carrie asking for more information about the abuse, for insurance purposes. Specifically, he wanted to know what happened, where and when. Carrie wrote back a brief summary of the abuse circumstances. On February 12, Miller requested more specific information. Carrie referred him to Irene Loftus. She told Miller that Loftus had been at the meeting with Wiebler and had supposedly taken "good notes."

Miller didn't respond. In early March, Carrie wrote asking if Miller had spoken to the insurance company, and he responded that he couldn't ascertain the status of insurance coverage for the diocese, but that they would be glad to offer pastoral counseling. They knew full well I didn't want pastoral counseling. The stonewalling had begun in earnest.

Patty and I were getting along great. In February we got engaged, and she moved in with me with her ten-year-old daughter, Lindsey. We set a tentative wedding date for that December.

CHAPTER THIRTY-THREE

On March 21, Carrie wrote Miller, "We find it difficult to believe you have not been able to ascertain the status of insurance coverage for the Davenport diocese. Do you intend to make an offer on their behalf?" He didn't answer the letter, or return Carrie's repeated calls.

I called Carrie and Cindy weekly, hoping for an answer. After a month of absolutely no word from Miller, I asked, "Why are they doing this? And why won't they tell me what's up with Wiebler? This is driving me nuts! I want this settled. What else can we do?"

"If we have to," Carrie said, "we can file a lawsuit for the amount we are seeking. The official term is filing a 'Petition at Law,' and it's a definite threat to take the case to court. It's the next step. Hopefully they'll cooperate and we can settle before it gets to that point. If they don't we can file, but you better be sure you want to do that. Filing a Petition at Law shows the other side you mean business and that you're willing to take the case to court. But if it does go to court, it means they can publicly disclose any evidence they think will help them, which includes intimate details of what happened in the abuse. They're going to try to destroy your case, and if that means discrediting or humiliating you, they may do it. You better be sure you're ready for that before we file."

I was horrified by the thought of Miller putting me on the witness stand and forcing me to describe all the details of the abuse in front of the court and the press. "He wouldn't do that, would he?" I asked Carrie.

"Oh, he'll do it all right," Carrie said. "It's his job. If we file a lawsuit, the diocese can legally demand all kinds of personal information about your mental condition, therapy, marriages, work history, specifics of the abuse—that kind of thing. And they can use whatever they feel is necessary to defend themselves at the trial."

I couldn't understand why the Church would want to do that to me. They knew the abuse had happened.

Things with Dr. O had degenerated further. I knew now he didn't like me. I had no idea why, but it triggered feelings that I was somehow defective. I continued to treat him politely. I'd talk, and his responses would seem cold and clinical, detached, like I was a job he disliked but had to do. He kept telling me how messed up I was and how serious my mental problems were. No kidding. That's why I was seeing him.

He had diagnosed me as bipolar, with post-traumatic stress disorder (PTSD) because of my father, and said I needed medication. He was a big believer in medication and tried a number of them on me. None seemed to help; if anything, they seemed to make me crazier. We talked a lot about my responses to the meds. I was taking four or five different ones at one point, plus the pain meds for my back. I'd tell him whether my anxiety or depression or whatever had gotten worse or better, and when, and how long the attacks lasted, and he'd fiddle with the prescriptions, raise or lower dosages, or add or stop a medication. The one drug he kept me on consistently—the one I was on the longest—was Adderall. He said it was essential.

I began to wonder if there was something wrong with him. He continued to say one thing during one session and then say something completely different the next. I kept thinking, *This guy doesn't know what he's doing. Or he's messing with me.* Then I'd feel bad. Maybe I was crazy. I gradually stopped seeing him, until I was only going once every couple of months. I had to see him at least that often to keep the prescriptions going. The thought of not taking the Adderall physically frightened me.

My emotions seemed more out of control than when I'd begun seeing him. I had constant anxiety attacks, and my mood swung wildly—sometimes daily—from black depression to bouts of high octane workaholic energy, during which times I stayed up almost until dawn frantically, but productively, doing paperwork. The moods were punctuated with panic attacks that paralyzed me for long minutes and left me shaking. When I was finally exhausted, I'd yearn desperately to get off the endless whirlwind. Thoughts of suicide started popping up again, unbidden. They promised peace.

CHAPTER THIRTY-THREE

I was the first to approach the Davenport diocese with an abuse allegation, but I wasn't alone for long. In May, a man identified anonymously as John Doe I filed a sexual abuse lawsuit against Reverend James Janssen and the Davenport diocese. It was the first officially filed abuse lawsuit against the diocese, and against Janssen. The name "John Doe I" suggested to me that others were in the works. I called Carrie and Cindy immediately. My first impulse was to also file, but Carrie suggested we wait. She thought this lawsuit might make the diocese more anxious to prevent us from filing, to save face. Maybe they'd be more willing to settle out of court.

But Miller continued to not return calls.

By now I had a real resentment against the diocese, and complaining about them became a regular component of my IHOP meetings with Father B. He took it in stride, but now he started telling me that I needed to forgive both Wiebler and the diocese. It was the only thing he said that I hated hearing. During our entire time together, his only theme was forgiveness. He talked about how Jesus had done it—how He even said, as He hung dying in agony on the cross, "Father, forgive them for they know not what they do."

The very thought of Wiebler made me grind my teeth. Sometimes I did try to imagine forgiving him, and even having a casual conversation with him, but my mind always rebelled, and I would end up seeing myself beating his face to a pulp.

Father B continued to never tell me what to do; he believed in free will and choice. He saved me by not messing with me or pushing me to make decisions. He made it clear that he was available any time I needed him and that he would do whatever was in his power to help, but he didn't claim to have any magic cure or special phrases. But without trying, he had the ability to make me think. "Forgive Wiebler and the Church," he said, and he allowed me the years I needed to approach that possibility.

At home I tried to be a father to Lindsey. To me that included disciplining her. When I asked her to do things we'd all agreed she should do, like help with housework or clean her room, she'd ignore me or take forever to do it. It was typical rebellious adolescence, and nowhere near as bad as I'd been to my parents. But I took it as deliberate defiance, which infuriated me, and I'd demand that she behave. Patty would step in and ask me to be more lenient, and Lindsey would smile. I felt like she was playing us off against each other. I'd tell Patty the girl would never grow up if she got away with everything, and then we'd argue.

The sad part was that Patty and I got along well when we weren't fighting about Lindsey.

On July 18, Father B called me. "Have you seen today's *Des Moines Register* headline?" he asked. "'Diocese Faces Abuse Lawsuit: The Davenport Vicar General Identifies Himself As the Priest Accused of Abusing a Parishioner.'" Another anonymous defendant, also named John Doe, had filed a sexual abuse lawsuit against Monsignor Drake Shafer and the Davenport diocese.

Shafer was the man who had put his arm around my shoulder and squeezed it after the meeting with Wiebler a year ago. The invasive, false intimacy of the gesture returned vividly to me, and I was instantly furious—irrationally, with myself, not him. I had allowed him to touch me!

July passed with no formal response from Miller, and then the first week of August passed. Incredibly, he had stonewalled us for almost five months. I was still afraid of going to court, but I was so furious at that point that I told Carrie to file the lawsuit. So, on August 14, Carrie wrote Miller: "We have not heard any response from you since our letter dated March 21, 2003. Enclosed please find a Petition at Law.... We have been authorized to wait five days ... before filing, in hopes that this matter may be resolved in an amicable fashion."

Miller immediately wrote that they'd be in touch by September 15. That deadline passed, and on September 19, Carrie wrote threatening to file the lawsuit if there was no response by the 23rd. Exactly on September 23, we got a letter from Miller saying they needed more information for the insurance company—including the exact dates of the abuse! That was patently absurd. Was a

CHAPTER THIRTY-THREE

seven-year-old boy supposed to know the dates on which he had been abused? Do children carry notebooks in case they get abused and jot down the dates for future legal use before blocking out the entire experience from their memories?

Then two more lawsuits against the diocese were filed. On September 16, James Wells filed against Father Janssen and the diocese, and on September 25, John Doe II filed against Father Janssen and Father Francis Bass and the diocese.

There would be more.

On September 24, Miller wrote suggesting a conference call on October 14. Carrie wrote back agreeing to the call. No response, as usual.

Carrie threatened a lawsuit again. On October 14 she wrote Miller, "You were to contact us to schedule a phone conference to be held today ... we have no correspondence ... concerning this matter ... we will be filing a Petition at Law on October 15." This time the threat produced immediate results. The conference call was held the next day, the 15th, with Mikkie Schiltz and Robert McMonagle, two other attorneys for Lane & Waterman, my attorneys Carrie and Cindy, and Irene Loftus participating.

At first it seemed to be a productive meeting. Carrie and Cindy agreed that I'd sign an authorization to release my medical records, with a confidentiality agreement. We would also agree to provide a brief narrative of specific allegations. In return, we wanted any and all of Wiebler's diocese employment files, sexual abuse allegations, and information on his treatment. It was a reasonable request, and they seemed agreeable.

Carrie wrote a follow-up letter on October 20 listing the agreements. As usual, there was no response. On the 24th she wrote, "We have not heard from you since our letter of October 20 ... in the event we do not hear from you by October 31, we will be forced to file our Petition at Law on November 3."

A few days later, Miller wrote, " We are attempting to locate insurance coverage.... Our first task is to identify the insurance carrier, then locate a policy if possible, and then establish the effective dates of that policy. Unfortunately, the diocese does not have a copy of any insurance policies which were effective in the relevant time frame." He said they were trying other avenues, but that it was "very time consuming and difficult."

He continued by stating that when coverage was established, the insurance company would want to know when the abuse occurred and the subsequent treatment. "That is why," Miller wrote, "we have asked that Mr. Christman provide us with an authorization for medical records, which are certainly to be kept confidential."

Then came the real kicker: "Understandably, you have asked for similar information about Father Wiebler. Unfortunately, that information is not available without Father Wiebler's consent, which we don't have."

That absolutely blew me away. They could legally demand information from me because I wanted a settlement, but we couldn't demand information from Wiebler because he didn't want to give it? Wiebler obviously didn't want to cooperate, because he had nothing to gain and everything to lose; I had to cooperate, because I wanted a settlement. He was the perpetrator and I was the victim, yet we had no power over him. Instead, the diocese had power over us. How did this get so horribly twisted?

The diocese had stonewalled for more than a year now, and the conviction was growing in me that they had no intention of ever settling anything. Going to trial was beginning to look like a real possibility.

I had absolutely no trust that the diocese would keep my medical records confidential. They hadn't kept a promise yet. If the case went to trial, I was sure the information would be used against me. And then it would be public knowledge. That horrified me. I was a respected local businessman, and the last thing I wanted was the intimate details of my sexual abuse, emotional problems and personal life made public.

Still more lawsuits were filed against the diocese. On October 28, John Doe III filed against Father Janssen, Father Bass, a Father Theodore Geerts, and the diocese. On November 18, Donald Green

CHAPTER THIRTY-THREE

filed against Janssen and the diocese. On November 24, Stephan Davis filed against Father Bass and the diocese.

By October, Patty and I had postponed the wedding indefinitely. I had become increasingly irritable

It seemed like I was irritable all the time. Traffic, employee mistakes, people who didn't answer the phone fast enough, everything exasperated me.

Work, as usual, was my only release. Temporary insulation from hell. No two wildlife jobs were the same, and I loved the challenge of finding out how raccoons or bats or squirrels were getting into a building, or how to catch a trap-shy beaver or coyote. I liked working with wildlife, and I liked helping people with their wildlife problems. I was a good businessman, organized and efficient. My insomnia and hyperactive mind were great paperwork tools. So my business kept growing.

Bizarrely, though, the more money I made, the more convinced I became that bankruptcy was imminent. So I took on more jobs, worked longer hours, succeeded still more, and obsessed more about failure. It was insane, and I knew it, and I did it anyway. I couldn't stop the thoughts, the fear. When I slowed down for a minute I shook with a sense of impending doom.

Every other Saturday morning I'd be at IHOP, ranting to Father B about something or the diocese or whatever, or near tears with despair, or frantic with fear that I was insane and that one day my head would just explode. Father B listened calmly through it all. Eventually I'd deflate, and we'd end up joking or talking cars. Almost always, he'd manage to fit in, "Bill, you'll never heal until you can forgive."

Forgive Wiebler, right. Hardly a day went by without me wishing he was in hell.

Carrie continued to try to contact Miller, but he stayed silent throughout November and December. The diocese was continuing to be deliberately uncooperative and obstructive. It didn't make any sense. They'd had seven sex abuse cases filed against them in about six months; wouldn't they want to avoid yet another one?

By then, stalling was commonly acknowledged to be the standard Catholic Church policy when dealing with abuse cases. In a July 2, 2003 article in *The World Today*, reporter Tanya Nolan wrote that the head of the Jesuits at the time, Mark Raper, admitted that the order had been deliberately employing legal stalling tactics in sex abuse cases. "That," Nolan stated, "comes as no surprise to lawyers who've represented victims of sex abuse."

A year and a half had gone by since my meeting with Wiebler. Nothing had been resolved, and it didn't look like it would any time soon. I struggled with despair, but I still hoped we could resolve the issue in, as lawyers say, an "amicable" way.

I had no warning that the next year would be even worse.

CHAPTER THIRTY-FOUR

WITH THE ARRIVAL of 2004 a new actor entered the drama, a lawyer for Lane & Waterman who would turn out to be, in my opinion, an absolute master of stonewalling, obfuscation and intimidation. Miller had been Santa Claus by comparison.

On January 12, my attorneys received a letter from Attorney Rand W. Wonio, saying he was now representing the diocese in my case. He said they had nothing conclusive yet from the insurance companies. That had been their refrain for over a year; no news there. Then he suggested private mediation and gave the names of two mediators he knew. Maybe we were getting somewhere.

Before mediation could happen, however, Wonio wanted information on the nature and extent of my psychological injuries. He asked for a signed Patient Authorization for Release of Information and a list of the healthcare professionals I'd seen regarding my claim. He also wanted a description of my personal situation since the abuse, including a summary of my marital status, work history and how my life had been impacted. "We sincerely wish to resolve this situation without resort to litigation," Wonio concluded, "and assist him with any pastoral care he might desire."

Right, pastoral care.

I could sense the man's personality through the letter. He seemed more articulate than Miller had been, more demanding, somehow colder. Meanwhile, the cases against the diocese continued to pile up. On January 14, John Doe IV filed against Father Janssen and the diocese. On the same day, John Doe V filed against Father Janssen, Father Bass, and the diocese. On January 26, John Doe VI filed against Father Janssen. On February 4, John Doe VII filed against Father Bass and the diocese.

In early February, Carrie wrote to Wonio that we didn't want to go to court either, but that we were adamant we wouldn't provide the documents he had requested until he provided all diocese records on Wiebler. She said we'd consider mediation, but suggested another mediator. She finished the letter with, "If mediation has not been scheduled within seven days, we will file the petition [lawsuit]."

There was no response from Wonio, so on February 26, Carrie wrote, "Please be advised that we will be filing a petition ... on March 2, 2004."

Wonio answered the next day.

"I'm very disappointed to receive your letter about the filing of the petition," he wrote. "I don't see what good it will do to file a lawsuit when we have demonstrated our willingness to try and resolve this situation through mediation."

Willingness? That was ridiculous. He'd never followed up on Carrie's attempt to arrange mediation.

He continued, "Your letter demonstrates an apparent unwillingness to share information with the diocese about the nature and extent of your client's claimed injuries." More smoke and mirrors. We had been willing to give the information; we just wanted the same about Wiebler.

Further stonewalling followed, and then on March 15 Wonio sent a Tolling Agreement, which is a legal document that allowed everyone in the case to extend the time to file an action, subject to a statute of limitations. "Let me know if you and your client are

CHAPTER THIRTY-FOUR

willing to enter into such an agreement and attempt mediation," he said.

We had tried to pin him down on a mediation date for a month now; he was evidently just buying more time. We hadn't asked for a Tolling Agreement, and it wasn't necessary for mediation anyway. Signing it would have just given him more time to delay.

Maybe it was just me, but it seemed like the diocese was taking out their big guns. It seemed as if Miller had been a bit too gentle for them, so they had replaced him with this guy. Now they were taking the gloves off.

On March 30, Wonio wrote that he'd be willing to accept service of the lawsuit when we filed it, and the next day, on March 31, we officially filed: Jack Doe v. Father Wiebler and Diocese of Davenport, Inc.

The next afternoon, Carrie got a call from the *Des Moines Register* asking about the lawsuit. She was told that the Davenport diocese had issued a press release saying "Jack Doe" had refused mediation. The next day an article appeared in the *Quad City Times*, titled "Davenport Diocese Faces New Sex Abuse Lawsuit." It explained that the lawsuit, filed by "Jack Doe," claimed that Wiebler had molested Doe when he was a child. It included an erroneous comment by Wonio that said, "The diocese has made numerous offers to mediate Jack Doe's monetary demands, but his attorneys have not provided some necessary information regarding damages." The article concluded with, "Wiebler remains in a treatment facility in Missouri, the diocese said."

I literally slumped with relief. Wiebler was isolated from children.

I would later discover that within days of our meeting with Wiebler and Franklin on May 10, 2002, Franklin had ordered Wiebler to the St. John Vianney Renewal Center in St. Louis, Missouri. Why hadn't they told me? It wouldn't have hurt them, and it would have given me immeasurable relief. Much of my anguish since that meeting had come from my fear that the diocese was refusing to tell me anything about Wiebler because he was still loose, out there abusing children with impunity. The thought of that old predator still distorting children was intolerable.

I'd made two simple requests: Let me know Wiebler was off the streets, and apologize. If the diocese had granted these requests as they had promised, the whole matter would have ended back in 2002. But they chose to do neither. So here we were, embroiled in battle.

Carrie immediately wrote to Wonio concerning his remark that we had refused mediation. "This is absolutely untrue," she said. "If these blatant misrepresentations of facts continue to be released to the press, we do not intend to proceed with mediation. We told you that Mr. Christman did not want to enter into a Tolling Agreement, thus the necessity of filing before mediation."

Wonio's comeback was typical: "I made no misrepresentation to the press," he said. "We offered you mediation several times, and that offer included a simple Tolling Agreement. Your refusal was not only of the Tolling Agreement, but also of mediation. In our view, you refused mediation. I don't think there's any other way to look at it."

I was upset that the news about the lawsuit was now public, although I knew it had to happen. I felt it was inevitable that my anonymity would be broken. I had hoped, naively, that the whole business could be kept private, but I knew how invasive and persistent the press could be.

I was humiliated that the sexual details of my abuse might become common public knowledge, but I was particularly upset about what it would do to my family. Brooke was now 13 and probably knew just enough about sex to be embarrassed, confused and disturbed. I could imagine what the other kids at school would say about me, and her. She'd be the object of gossip and speculation. I ground my teeth. Why was the Catholic Church allowing another child to be punished?

The claim that we'd refused to supply information or go to mediation was, to me, sleazy twisting of facts to make us look bad. As far as I was concerned, the diocese, through Wonio, was deliberately trying to smear me publicly. I was appalled.

CHAPTER THIRTY-FOUR

There really wasn't anything I could do except be furious. My hands were tied. I was getting raked over the coals, and I was becoming more frustrated with my own attorneys because I felt they weren't protecting me. I wanted them to get mean and nasty, and I told them that. In their defense, this was their first abuse case, and they were putting a lot of effort into educating themselves.

Wonio acted as if nothing had happened. On April 12 he wrote to Carrie and said, "I'm not sure what you want to do with this, but we are going to have to reveal the name of your client to the court, Craig Levien [who was representing other victims], Mike McCarthy [representing Father Bass], and Ned Wehr [representing Father Jannsen]. I assume you want to take some steps to protect the identity of your client."

Protect my identity, right. I could see myself on the witness stand, the public leaning forward, drooling over every humiliating detail like the audiences in those sick TV talk shows where people confess their sordid acts to the host.

CHAPTER THIRTY-FIVE

Now that a lawsuit had been officially filed, there was a real possibility that the case would go to court if it couldn't be settled in mediation. That meant lawyers on both sides had to begin preparing their cases, which included accumulating information to defend their position. The legal dance was about to get even more complex—and, of course, slower.

There are many rules governing how this information can be collected. The legal term for the process is called "discovery." Discovery is a formal investigation, conducted according to court rules, that takes place before the trial. Its purpose is to let one party question other parties, or their witnesses, and to let one party request, or force, others to produce documents or other physical evidence. Besides gathering information to use at the trial, discovery allows the parties to assess the strength or weakness of an opponent's case, with the idea of opening settlement talks.

One kind of discovery is called "interrogatories," which are written questions that must be answered in writing, truthfully, under penalty of perjury. These can be quite complex, as I was to find out.

Another type of discovery is a deposition, during which one party to a lawsuit, usually a lawyer, verbally asks questions of the

CHAPTER THIRTY-FIVE

other party or their witnesses. The party is under oath to tell the truth. A court reporter is present to make a written transcript, and the session is also videotaped.

A lot of people have been the subject of a deposition and have generally found it to be unpleasant. The job of the lawyer doing the questioning is often to discredit the person and his or her testimony. While some lawyers do this with true respect for the witness, others are experts at insinuation, intimidation, putting words in people's mouths and twisting their meaning. I was to discover that Wonio was a master at running a deposition.

Other types of pretrial discovery are written requests to produce documents and "requests for admissions," in which one party asks the other to admit or deny key facts in the case.

We'd made little progress in our requests for information about Wiebler. All we knew about his whereabouts came from the newspaper article that said he was in a treatment center in Missouri. The diocese still hadn't given us any satisfaction on that question.

Jack Brooks and Brian Fairfield of Brooks & Trinrud were representing Wiebler. On May 20 Carrie had written to Brooks, saying she had contacted him the previous week concerning accepting service of the lawsuit for Wiebler, and Wiebler's whereabouts. "To date we've had no response," she said. "Please advise." Of course, they didn't reply. But we were soon to find Wiebler through an unexpected source.

In June, Father B went on an annual retreat in St. Louis, Missouri. He called me as soon as he got back.

"Wiebler left the treatment facility," he said. "I was getting a haircut at the retreat house; the barber was a monk there. Man, was he terrible! He hacked my hair up bad and actually cut me in half a dozen places. I'm scarred for life! I told him to thank God he didn't have to make a living cutting hair.

"I told him I was from the Quad City area, and he said, 'We had a priest from your area, a guy named Wiebler, at the treatment facility near here. He just recently took off. The guy was stupid; he lost his entire benefit package, his retirement check, health insurance, everything. He's living in an apartment building two blocks from a grammar school.'"

Wiebler was still an active predator on the loose. I was outraged.

Later investigation revealed that Wiebler had moved into an apartment building 750 feet from an elementary school and 1,500 feet from a preschool. According to a September 15, 2004 article in the *Missouri Post-Dispatch*, there were always kids running through the back yard of the building.

It was the responsibility of the Davenport diocese to alert people when Wiebler left the facility. But according to attorney Patrick Noaker of St. Paul, Minnesota, who had several clients who claimed to be sexually abused by Wiebler when they were children, "They [the Davenport diocese] didn't tell anybody he'd left. And they made representations to us that he was [still at St. John Vianney Center] while they knew he was gone."

When asked about this, Irene Loftus said she couldn't remember when the diocese found out Wiebler had left the facility, but that the diocese had notified the county prosecutor as soon as they did.

The thought that Wiebler was cruising the school neighborhood for children drove me insane. How could I go to work, eat, talk to people, or act like life was the same while he was fondling kids? I couldn't do it. One morning I snapped and went over the top mentally. I decided to drive to Missouri and kill him. I didn't care what happened to me any more. I wanted to die anyway.

I packed a suitcase and put my .40-caliber Beretta semi-automatic pistol and a box of ammo in it. I'd confront Wiebler in the middle of the street, hold him at gunpoint and shout until I had a crowd watching. I'd yell, "I want you all to see what happens to a child molester!" and then empty the clip into his face, blast it into a featureless mass of red meat. After this I would call the cops and turn myself in. Or shoot myself.

I came very close to doing it. I don't know why I didn't. I believe God stopped me. I was suddenly numb and unable to act, and I walked aimlessly back and forth in my office, glancing occasionally

CHAPTER THIRTY-FIVE

at the suitcase without emotion. I finally sat down, opened it and put the gun away.

For weeks I fantasized about dedicating the rest of my life to killing pedophiles. I was a professional hunter and trapper by trade and knew how to stalk animals; I'd simply change my occupation to that of pedophile hunter. No more long, drawn out abuse trials; I'd just kill the perpetrators. I'd hunt down every one I heard about. Finding them would be easy—people talk about them on TV, and the names of registered pedophiles are accessible to the public online. I'd do it sneaky: come up with a plan to avoid getting caught, shoot from hiding like a sniper, plant bombs. I've got a criminal mind, and I could do it well. I'd do it as long as possible until I got stopped. I knew the police would get me eventually, but I was sure I could kill at least 20 pedophiles first.

It was a sick obsession, and I knew it. I stopped it by deciding that I didn't want my daughter to grow up answering questions about why her father was a serial killer.

In late June we received my interrogatories from Wonio. I was stunned at the number of questions I had to answer; there had to be 100, all demanding information about every possible aspect of my life—where I grew up and went to school, the dates of my marriages and divorces, my work history and health history (including each ailment stretching back into childhood), names of each doctor, the length of treatment, the medications I had taken, and on and on. And, of course, they wanted to know, in intimate detail, about every abuse incident, how it made me feel, and how I thought it affected my life.

I remember looking through the questions and shaking my head, overwhelmed at the sheer amount of detail I had to remember or research and write about. I knew full well that going back through the abuse was going to trigger the feelings that had tortured me since I had first remembered it.

I took it one question at a time. I did paperwork late into the night most nights. When I was done, there sat the interrogatories; a black hole sucking energy. I despised them, but I kept plugging away. The lawsuit had now invaded every corner of my life, entered my home, devoured any spare minute and depleted the last of my energy—and I could see no end. Each legal step, setback and stalling tactic sapped me and drained my hope. I became more and more cynical, and paranoid: the Church no longer just wanted to ignore me until I went away; they now wanted to destroy me and humiliate me publicly because I dared to confront them, and their lawyers were getting rich by deliberately delaying. Meanwhile, as I impotently answered endless personal questions that would in the end be used against me, I could picture Wiebler in St. Louis, greedily fondling children without consequence like he always had. I was on trial, not him. Maybe Dr. O had been right when he'd warned me that the Church would crush me if I took them on.

Back on January 1, the *Quad City Times* had announced that David Schoenthaler, the chief judge of the Iowa judicial district that included the Davenport diocese, had asked for consolidation of all the clergy abuse cases against it. By now there were an astonishing 38 lawsuits against the Davenport diocese. District Judge Charles Pelton was to handle them. Schoenthaler's reasoning was that having one judge over all the cases would make consistent rulings more likely and settle the lawsuits more efficiently because of their similar nature and their having the same defendant. Accordingly, on June 3, Judge Pelton made an official "Motion to Consolidate" all the current cases against the diocese. Attorney Craig Levien, of Betty, Neuman & McMahon, would represent the victims. He was already representing many of them individually.

Carrie and Cindy were notified of the consolidation by letter on July 15. I emphatically did not want my case included. In my opinion, settling a bunch of cases at once would make the diocese look better—as if they'd dealt individually with each victim while actually lumping them all together and dismissing them all at once as a faceless unit. Also, I wanted to keep Carrie and Cindy as my lawyers. Judge Pelton granted our request that my case not be included in the consolidation.

CHAPTER THIRTY-FIVE

There was evidently some pressure to settle the consolidated abuse cases quickly, as the trial date had already been set for October 29 of that year, which was only about three months away. Levien was acting quickly, and he arranged depositions for a number of witnesses in July and August. Franklin and Loftus were among them. Although we weren't officially involved with the other cases, Carrie and Cindy were allowed to attend the depositions of anyone relevant to my case, both to listen and collect information and to ask questions.

Levien wanted to depose Irene Loftus in the case of John Doe vs. Father James Janssen and the Diocese of Davenport, and he and Wonio agreed on the date of July 9. Wonio had to have been aware that Carrie and Cindy were supposed to be in on it and question Loftus regarding my case. I'm sure he did not want them doing that, because the answers were sure to be damaging to the diocese. On July 7, Wonio wrote to Levien and asked if he wanted to go forward with the deposition of Loftus in two days. Then he added, "P.S. We should probably have notified Carrie Coyle. Our oversight."

Oversight. Right.

On July 8, Carrie wrote Wonio, "We were notified just 15 minutes ago of the deposition of Loftus by Levien, tomorrow. The diocese never notified us of the time or date. We will attend, but we won't have time to prepare questions. We still need to depose Loftus ourselves."

My lawyers would fight for more than a year to depose Loftus. Wonio would agree to many dates, but then postpone each one.

Loftus's deposition by Levien took place at the offices of Lane & Waterman. I read the transcript because I wanted to know what a deposition was like. I knew Wonio would depose me at some point.

Levien's questions seemed concerned mostly with what Church procedures were when an abuse case was reported and who was responsible for what action. Doubtless some of it was relevant to my case, but I couldn't see anything that jumped out at me. I had to force myself not to skip over most of it.

Bishop Franklin's deposition was on July 29. Carrie and Cindy were there but asked no questions; they had talked to Levien, and he knew what they all needed to know. I read the transcript because I was curious about what made Franklin tick. Why was this legal battle OK with him? He had seemed friendly and concerned at our original meeting.

Levien asked most of the questions, and Wonio cut in at times with objections. The rest of the lawyers basically listened.

Levien started out by asking questions about Franklin's background: his education, when he was ordained, his assignments, and so on. Then he got to the point. He asked a long series of questions about the Church's beliefs regarding celibacy, regulations regarding sexual abuse, and the history of some of the accused priests. It seemed obvious to me that Levien was trying to get Franklin to admit that the Church knew these priests had previously abused other people and that the Church not only didn't follow its own protocol but actually covered up allegations of abuse.

Levien set the stage well. At one point he said to Franklin, "I'm talking about when you became a priest in the Dubuque Diocese—same in the Davenport Diocese—sexual misconduct by fellow priests was something that was viewed as wrong by all priests that have been ordained, wasn't it?"

"Yes," said Franklin.

"And it's an important concern to all dioceses, isn't it," Levien continued, "to have sexual misconduct by a priest—in particular, sexual misconduct with someone under the age of 18—reported if it occurs?"

"Yes."

"And if it is reported, it should be thoroughly investigated?"

"Yes."

"And if reported and investigated, it should also be thoroughly documented—the allegations and the outcome of any investigations?"

"For all concerned, yes."

More questions followed, and then Levien said, "Certainly any effort to cover up any improper sexual contact between a priest and

CHAPTER THIRTY-FIVE

someone under the age of 18 is wrong in accordance with Church policy, et cetera, correct?"

"Yes," Franklin said. "Yes."

They talked about the emotional and spiritual damage done by clergy abuse, and then Levien brought up Father Tom Doyle, an acknowledged national expert on how the Catholic Church had handled abuse cases. Levien asked, "Did it concern you when you heard that there was public testimony by Father Doyle that Davenport was the third worst diocese out of the 800 allegations he conducted regarding their handling of sexual abuse cases?"

"There was very little I could do about that," Franklin responded.

That answer surprised me. I was to discover that it was very much in character with Franklin.

The questions covered more topics, and then Levien began asking about Franklin's knowledge of specific events. At this point Franklin's answers took a turn; his operative word changed from yes to no. He also began to add the classic politician's comment, "I don't recall."

"Part of what Father Janssen did when he had the boys at the Optimist's cabin was to go down there," Levien said, "and there was a group of boys with no other adult present. Were you aware that that's what happened?"

"No," Franklin said.

"Were you aware ... one of the first things Janssen did after all the adults cleared out was to remove his swimsuit, instruct all the other boys that were there to remove their swimsuits, and jump into the river or backwater that is down there, and go nude swimming?"

"No."

"Did Irene Loftus tell you that one of the complaints that [plaintiff] Greg Schildgen made was that he couldn't believe that a priest would engage in nude swimming with—around boys ... Were you aware of that complaint?"

"I do not recall it, no."

More questions followed, and then Levien asked, "Did you instruct Irene Loftus to advise Greg Schildgen that the priest he was probably with was Father Janssen?"

"I do not recall doing that."

"Did you ever advise Irene Loftus at that time that she should tell him [Schildgen] that Father Janssen—complaints about those activities were in his personnel file dating back to the 1960s?"

"I do not recall that."

Then Levien got specific. "Did you ever have a policy, while you've been Bishop, not to tell victims that have made complaints about specific priests and sexual misconduct under the age of 18—not to tell that victim about other instances of sex abuse by that priest?"

"No, no policy such as that."

When I read that, I couldn't believe it. At our meeting, Franklin had mentioned Wiebler's previous abuse history and said it was in his file. When he said that, I had asked Franklin, "What's in his file? What else is documented about other incidents?" Franklin had replied, "We can't discuss Wiebler's file with you."

If this case went to trial, I wanted that conversation pointed out.

Levien continued. "Do you remember [plaintiff] Don Green or his wife asking you if there had been other victims or other instances of Father Janssen abusing other individuals?"

"Yes."

"Did you tell them?"

"At the time I was talking to them I did not know, but we did go back to the parish to check to see if there were other victims."

"But," Levien asked, "did you get out Father Janssen's personnel file and the secret archives sitting in the safe at the offices of the diocese . . ."

"No," Franklin interjected.

Levien persisted. "... at the chancery office, and tell them that in early 1954 to '56 there were initial complaints, that he had been suspended twice for misconduct with underage individuals in the '60s—in the late '50s, that he had received psychological treatment

CHAPTER THIRTY-FIVE

for it back in the '50s, and that there were a number of complaints that you know now about? Was that ever disclosed to Don or Ann Green?"

"No."

"Why not?

Wonio jumped in at this point. "I'm going to lodge an objection, before the answer comes in," he said. "The question is argumentative. It seeks to impose a legal duty on the diocese and its personnel that does not or did not exist ..."

No kidding! As far as I could see, Levien had just spent the better part of half an hour establishing, based on Franklin's responses, that the Church had a legal duty to inform victims of previous abuse by a priest. Evidently Wonio was doing his best to prevent Franklin from saying anything that might hurt their case. So much for the truth.

Levien was a bulldog, and he had really done his homework. He quizzed Franklin for hours, inexorably building evidence that secrecy had, indeed, been the unspoken policy. Records had been kept hidden, known abusers had repeatedly been reassigned to other locations, and the advice of psychiatrists had been ignored.

At times Franklin seemed confused, even befuddled by the situation, and I came to think, not without sympathy, that he was in way over his head. He was simply unable to deal with the issue. It seemed like he hadn't studied or read much, if any, of the trial material, research or even news about what was indisputably the single most important issue impacting the Catholic Church at the time. His constant "no," "I don't recall," "that I don't know" and "I'd have to go back and check on that" showed a basic ignorance of the situation. His responses indicated an inability to act decisively—or a flat refusal to do so—and at times he made pathetic attempts to be evasive when it dawned on him that Levien had backed him into a corner.

Wonio objected frequently to Levien's questions in order to protect Franklin and block important evidence, but he was essentially ineffective.

This was the first part of the deposition, and it lasted from 9 A.M. to 4:30 P.M. The deposition was continued on August 19 and went from 9 A.M. to 12:10 P.M. It consisted of basically more of the same. The closing statements were also typical.

"What is the name of the facility in St. Louis that Father Wiebler was sent?" Levien asked.

"I would have to get that for you," Franklin said.

"Don Green and others have made complaints specifically about Father Janssen ... why wasn't he sent to a treatment facility like Wiebler?'

"I couldn't answer that."

"Who could from the diocese?"

"I would have to go back and do some checking ..."

"Does someone monitor his [Wiebler's] comings and goings and who he has contact with?"

"I cannot give you a positive yes or no."

"And that [monitoring] has never been done with Father Janssen, correct?"

"No."

"And you don't know why?"

"No. I ..."

The deposition covered a lot more ground than there's room to go into here. But I was smiling when I finally finished the 365-page document. Levien had done a wonderful job, and our case had been strengthened considerably.

Later that month, Carrie gave me the legal schedule leading up to our trial, if there was to be one. There would be a settlement conference on November 10, 2005, and if a settlement couldn't be reached, the trial would be set for December 5th to 16th the same year.

Over a year away. I almost cried. I'd never met Wonio and didn't even know what he looked like, but in my mind he'd become a monster, cynically stalling, playing with me and coldly pushing me to desperation. The case had invaded every area of my life and become the major element in it. Maybe it would be that way for the

CHAPTER THIRTY-FIVE

rest of my life, until I died. I couldn't take much more. I wished I were dead now.

I dimly remembered the stability AA had given me in the past, and in August I started going back to meetings again. I didn't attend many—maybe one every couple of weeks. My AA friends were glad to see me, but they didn't push me or lecture me. AA is a program of attraction, not promotion, and I was grateful that they respected my privacy. I began to feel moments of serenity, flashes of acceptance of my situation. I knew the meetings were a source of these feelings, but I still hung back. God forbid that an alcoholic with an addiction to negativity do what's good for him.

CHAPTER THIRTY-SIX

ONE MORNING FATHER B and I were at IHOP, and I was complaining about the same old thing. I was upset, I was scared of a trial, the whole process was nerve wracking and emotionally draining and hard on me, blah, blah, blah. I was really whining.

Father B finally raised a hand to stop me. "Why don't we go see Bishop Franklin again?" he said. "Maybe if we tell him what's been going on and what his attorneys have been doing, he'll tell them to drop it."

"I'll get in trouble with Carrie," I said. "I'm not supposed to talk to them."

"Maybe I can get Franklin to say it's off the record—that we're just going over there to talk. A social call, sort of. And then if it ever comes up, it never happened."

I agreed, and Father B called Franklin. Franklin said it was no problem and that we should get together. He invited us to come on over.

Franklin received us in his office. He was again dressed casually in black pants and shirt, with a clerical collar. We shook hands and sat.

Calmly and politely, without any attitude or raising my voice, I told the bishop as concisely as possible what was going on and what

CHAPTER THIRTY-SIX

his attorneys were doing. I finished with, "This is totally unnecessary. This is hurting me. All it's doing is recreating the emotional pain. You know what happened. You know Wiebler abused me."

He nodded; he knew what happened. "But it's out of my hands," he said. "It's out of my hands; there's nothing I can do."

I hadn't expected that answer. "What do you mean, it's out of your hands? It's not! You can stop this anytime with a phone call. Those attorneys work for you, bishop!"

"It's out of my hands," he repeated.

"That can't be true! You run the diocese!"

"It's out of my hands." He was no longer looking at me. "We bishops don't have the power we used to have."

I couldn't believe that; couldn't understand it or accept it. "You know," I said, almost pleading, "we could all sit down and in five to ten minutes have this whole thing wrapped up very amicably and very nicely. For what you're paying your attorneys, you could have already paid me and saved money. If you want to look at the financial end of it, it's just unnecessary. You're going to pay double the cost. And you're going to hurt me in the process. Why would you want to continually hurt me? Is that what you really want? Is it so out of your hands that you're willing to let this insanity continue? You know what happened because of the meeting we had with Wiebler. Is there any doubt in your mind?"

Franklin said nothing. He was obviously uncomfortable.

I repeated the question, more emphatically. "Is there any doubt in your mind that Wiebler abused me?"

"No, there isn't," he replied. "There's no doubt in my mind what happened. But it's out of my hands."

An ageless scene came to my mind—a judge, saying to a man's accusers, "This man is innocent. But I turn him over to you. Crucify him if you will. I wash my hands of it. It's out of my hands."

The meeting lasted maybe 15 minutes, and I left more frustrated than ever. Who could I turn to? There didn't seem to be any way to end this insanity. The diocese would continue to waste money on a case they admitted was wrong, and I'd continue to be put through hell.

Father B tried to console me. He said Franklin was a good man and would have done something if he could have, but his hands were tied.

Bishops don't have the power they used to? I thought. *That's ridiculous.*

On August 16, I stopped seeing Dr. O. It wasn't helping, I'd come to believe he was incompetent, and I'd come to dislike him as well. I should have cut it off sooner. I continued to take Adderall, however. If anything, my mood swings got worse.

The legal dance continued, a dirge waltz in molasses. Wonio scheduled depositions for himself and Levien on September 7 that included witnesses we also needed to question. Again, we were not included. When Carrie found out, she wrote to Wonio and said that she realized the consolidation put everyone in a tough scheduling position, but that it was imperative for us to be included. She and Cindy were able to attend.

I was becoming convinced that it would never end. One night in late September, I was at my desk doing paperwork when my mind literally stopped. I sat paralyzed, barely aware of the papers in front of me, my office around me, or the flickering, quietly muttering TV on the wall ahead of me. They seemed distant and of no importance.

I opened the right-hand desk drawer and took out my Beretta pistol. It was dark and heavy in my hand. I took a loaded clip from the drawer, inserted it into the bottom of the gun's handle, and pushed it up until it clicked home. I pulled the slide back, and a bullet popped up into position. I let go of the slide, and it slammed forward, picking up the bullet and seating it in the chamber. The gun was cocked and loaded.

I put the barrel up under my breast bone, closed my eyes, took a last deep breath, let it out, and started to pull the trigger.

Suddenly, the phone rang.

I opened my eyes. The caller ID said it was my mother. I put the gun down and answered the phone.

CHAPTER THIRTY-SIX

I don't remember a word of our conversation. I sat there for some time after I hung up, still dazed. I was frozen, unable to complete the act, unable even to put the gun away. God had once again reached down into my life and stopped me.

I made a decision to do everything in my power one more time to save myself, and on September 29 I entered Trinity Enrichment Center. I decided that if this didn't work, I'd definitely kill myself. It was one last shot at survival.

At Trinity, a psychiatrist named Dr. Saintfort, a tall, slender black man in his early forties, treated me. I also saw a psychologist, Dr. Melissano, an attractive dark-haired Italian woman. Dr. Saintfort was known as an expert on medication for mental and emotional issues. Doctors rarely say anything bad about other doctors, but when Dr. Saintfort heard that Dr. O had me on Adderall, he could barely hide his concern. He was obviously startled, and shook his head, frowning, in apparent disapproval. He started the process of tapering me off it and the other drugs that Dr. O had me on.

After seeing Dr. Saintfort's reaction, I did some research on Adderall. I was amazed to read that the only two approved uses for it were for attention deficit hyperactivity disorder (ADHD) and narcolepsy, the condition where sudden tiredness hits you and sometimes causes you to uncontrollably fall asleep. Adderall is an amphetamine that is closely related to Dexadrine. It's speed, basically—Ritalin on steroids. Why was Dr. O giving it to me for bipolar and PTSD?

I discovered that the side effects to the drug were terrible. The ones that horrified me most were difficulty falling asleep, extreme irritability, severe headaches, muscle and joint pain, extreme mood swings, euphoria and depression (Dr. O had diagnosed me as bipolar, for God's sake!), hyperactivity, delusions and hallucinations. Prolonged use could lead to tolerance, extreme psychological dependence, and severe social disability. I'd been on it for two years. I'd described all these symptoms to Dr. O, but he'd insisted the drug I needed most was Adderall.

The list of meds that were contraindicated with Adderall was huge as well. It included seven major classes of drugs, in particular most antidepressants and anti-psychotics. Doctors also did not advise Adderall for people with pre-existing mental illness or a history of alcohol and drug abuse. I wondered how many adverse drug reactions I'd experienced because of the jumble of meds Dr. O had put me on. What had he been trying to do, kill me? I should have researched these drugs before, but I'd trusted him.

I began seeing Dr. Saintfort and Dr. Melissano weekly. Saintfort started me on Lexapro, an anti-depressant, and we'd spend about 15 minutes talking about my responses to it and my withdrawal from the other drugs. He emphasized that meds were not a cure-all; the patient had to work on therapy too. He encouraged me to go to more AA meetings, and he told me to pray.

"I know you enough now," he said, "to tell you I'm sure you'll get better."

That was tremendously reassuring. I was already calming down from stopping the Adderall and the other drugs.

After I met with Dr. Saintfort, I'd have a 45-minute talk therapy session with Dr. Melissano. She was a quiet woman, compassionate and understanding, with a real understanding of sexual issues. It calmed me to be with her.

This time, the effect of the therapy lasted longer than a few hours. Slowly, I started to stabilize.

On October 4, Wonio made a settlement offer of $100,000. I told Carrie and Cindy there was no way I'd accept that amount. We decided to counter-offer with $300,000. I was willing to negotiate; I wanted this finished.

On October 21, Carrie wrote to Wonio and said, "We met with Bill and discussed your proposed settlement of $100,000. Bill authorized us to settle for $300,000. This offer is confidential, and we still need to resolve all issues with Wiebler. If we receive no response by October 22, we'll assume you're not interested in resolving the case without a trial."

There was, of course, no response. The trial for the consolidated cases was scheduled for October 29, and we waited for it with considerable interest. Then, on the 28th, to avoid going to court,

CHAPTER THIRTY-SIX

the diocese settled 37 claims for $9 million. That came out to about $243,000 for each claimant. The diocese was willing to give that amount to each of the other claimants, but wouldn't negotiate their $100,000 offer with me? I was upset, puzzled, and a little paranoid. Did they *want* to screw with me?

The settlement made a big splash in the national media, to say nothing about the local reaction. It almost overshadowed another interesting revelation in the October 29 *Des Moines Register*. Shirley Ragsdale's article in that issue stated that on January 6 of that year, a national audit of clergy abuse over the past 50 years in all U.S. dioceses had been released. Davenport was listed as the only diocese that did not cooperate with auditors or even send in a report.

CHAPTER THIRTY-SEVEN

A WEEK AFTER the diocese settled the 37 claims, I went to Maine to trap fisher, an exotic, beautifully furred northern predator, with Bob Noonan, the co-author of this book. Bob has been a full-time freelance writer and editor since the '80s. I'd met him in 1994, when I started writing for *Wildlife Control Technology*, a national magazine for people in the wildlife damage management field. Bob was the editor. We'd met a number of times at conventions and hit it off, and when I told him I'd always wanted to trap a fisher, he invited me to Maine for a week.

Bob picked me up at the airport, and on the way to his home we discovered we were both in AA. We started swapping stories, and I opened up about the abuse and the lawsuit.

We spent the next day making fisher sets, with me setting the traps and Bob overseeing. I fell in love with Maine—the thick evergreen pines, hemlocks, spruces, firs, and cedars; the grey and white leafless trunks of the hardwoods; the many streams and lakes; the farmland pastures stretching up into the rolling wooded hills; the blue mountains in the background. We went to an AA meeting that night, and for the first time in months I went to bed at peace.

The next day I met Emmanuel, a boy of 13.

CHAPTER THIRTY-SEVEN

Bob had mentored him, taken him on the trapline, and taught him safety rules, how to shoot and all that—just like Terry Mapes had taught me. Emmanuel's mother had died, and the rest of his family was scattered across the country. He lived nearby with his guardians, a schoolteacher and his wife, and their daughter. Bob asked me if it was OK if this kid came along with us a couple of days to check traps. I was hesitant at first because I'm not really a kid person, but I remembered how Dix and Terry and the other guys used to take me hunting and how much it meant to me. So I said sure.

The next morning we picked Emmanuel up at his guardians' home. He was a bright-eyed, dark-haired, good looking kid, small for his age, like I had been. He immediately reminded me of myself.

We went to the Purple Cow for breakfast. It was a small mom-and-pop restaurant with homemade hash, great pancakes, an extra egg (if you ordered two), and endless refills of coffee. Emmanuel told me that everyone called him E-Man. I got a kick out of that. He was quiet, but he seemed comfortable and at ease with himself.

E-man ordered a pancake with blueberry jam and whipped cream. It was huge. It completely covered the big plate, and it was almost invisible under a three-inch layer of juicy, thick blue syrup and fluffy white whipped cream.

"You'll never finish that," I said. "It's twice as big as your head."

He grinned.

"Got a girlfriend?" I asked.

He blushed, nodded, and grinned wider.

"Ever kiss her?"

He blushed still more, grinned even wider, and shrugged his shoulders.

"I'll take that as a no," I said. "Does she know you like her?"

He nodded happily.

"She likes you too?"

More nodding and grinning.

We had a great breakfast, kidding around and joking. E-man ate the whole pancake and washed it down with two big glasses of chocolate milk. The kid was just plain lovable. I was glad he was with us.

He had his hunting license and was carrying Bob's single-shot .410 shotgun in case we saw any grouse or rabbits. Bob's truck was a club cab, and E-man sat in the back seat, the empty shotgun across his lap, clutched in his hands, barrel pointed down and action open like good safety rules demand. He never let go of the gun. At each stop Bob would hand him a cartridge, and he would load the gun and walk slowly ahead, with us following him, to each trap. I remembered my first times carrying a loaded gun.

At the third stop I had two traps in different directions. Bob and E-man went to check one, and I went alone to the other.

We were using humane lethal traps called Conibears that were set in baited wire cages four feet off the ground in trees. Fisher climbed well, and this high position kept other animals from accessing the trap. As I approached the set, I could see a dark form hanging from the tree. I ran to the set and found one of the most gorgeous animals I'd ever seen. It was a big male fisher, four feet long from its nose to the tip of its long, bushy tail, with thick, glossy, long, dark chestnut-brown fur and a light sprinkling of pure white hairs throughout. It had a palm-sized vivid white patch on its dark chest. The trap had hit it right behind the ears, and the fisher had died so fast that it didn't even move the trap out of its position in the cage.

I whooped and yelled, and Bob and E-man ran up. For ten minutes we high-fived, pounded each other on the back and took pictures. Bob said the fisher was unusually big and in remarkably good condition. I had decided to mount the first fisher I caught, and this was the best specimen I could have hoped for.

Over the next several days I caught two more fisher, and E-man missed a shot at a grouse. He didn't seem to mind; he was just happy to get a shot. We all sniffed the fired shotgun case and agreed it was a great hunting smell. E-man never stopped grinning the whole

CHAPTER THIRTY-SEVEN

time he was with us; he loved every minute of it. It brought back memories of when I used to get taken hunting.

By the end of the trip I'd told Bob every detail of the abuse and the legal ordeal, and I asked him if he thought there was a book in it.

"Maybe eventually," he said, "but not yet. The case isn't settled, so there's no real ending yet. Let's see how it plays out."

The trip to Maine was pivotal for me. I was still a mess when I'd arrived, and I left in much better shape. Bob and I went to AA meetings almost every night. Emmanuel took me out of myself and reminded me of the good times in my youth. Maine was primal and beautiful, and life seemed simpler there. I'd always had a vague plan to live a simpler life closer to nature, and that trip rekindled it.

When I got home I started going to AA meetings regularly again, several times a week. I was welcomed back without criticism or judgment. They were glad to see me.

The legal games continued. On November 10, Wonio wrote Carrie that they'd reviewed my discovery responses, but that my patient authorization to release my medical records was limited to Dr. O, and they needed records from all the therapists mentioned. Carrie responded that full authorization for everyone was already in my answers to their discovery, but she again included authorizations for the other six therapists besides Dr. O. Wonio wrote back that the other doctors wouldn't accept the authorizations we provided. Carrie sent new ones.

On and on it went, ad nauseam. To me it was classic legal nitpicking stalling tactics.

The year 2005 arrived with everything still dragging along. It had now been two and a half years since the original meeting with Wiebler and Franklin.

On January 19, Carrie wrote to Wonio and said, "We reasonably expected by now to have your discovery material. If we receive nothing by February 1, we'll file a Motion to Compel." (A Motion to Compel is a legal action to force the other party to cooperate and produce requested information.) "Also," Carrie continued, "concerning your letter of August 12, 2004, our first response on August 20, 2004 and our second on October 7, 2004, we again note that two documents from Wiebler's personnel file were faded and illegible. We ask again for legible copies. Also, what is your position to our proposal of a $300,000 settlement, sent October 21, 2004?"

On the same day she wrote to Brian Fairfield, Wiebler's attorney, and said, "We had reasonably expected to receive discovery from your client [Wiebler] requested on September 30, 2004. If no response, we will file Motion to Compel on February 1."

Dr. O was no help, either. On January 31, Wonio wrote Carrie, "My legal assistant has made several attempts to get Dr. O's office to send your client's records, without success. We keep getting promises that the records will be sent, but recently they aren't responding to messages.... I wonder if it would help if one of you would contact Dr. O's office and urge them to send the records ..." He concluded with, "With regard to the [Wiebler] documents you requested, I will see if we have better copies, but some of the copies in the original file are none too good."

I suspected we'd never see anything useful.

In February, a Father Robert Gruss became the new chancellor of the Davenport diocese, replacing Irene Loftus. At the time, I was unaware it had even happened. His appointment would be pivotal to my case.

The sparring continued, with Wonio saying he wouldn't provide more information unless I agreed to a deposition, and my lawyers saying I wouldn't be available for a deposition until Wonio provided the interrogatories requested the previous September. Wonio had stalled for five months on this point alone. Of course he was being paid the entire time, and it was costing me, too. It seemed obvious to me that dragging out the lawsuit was a win-win for Wonio; he and his firm made more money, and the more my costs went up the more willing I might be to settle. For less. I wondered at what

CHAPTER THIRTY-SEVEN

point the diocese would have paid more in legal fees fighting the settlement than the settlement itself would have cost. Insanity.

Finally, on March 17, Wonio sent my lawyers the answers to interrogatories. He then scheduled my deposition for April 19.

Cindy responded, "Thank you for your Notice of Videotape Deposition of Plaintiff, which is set for April 19. Unfortunately, you did not find it necessary to contact myself or Carrie Coyle prior to setting this date, and neither of us is available at that time.... It is my hope that upon prior consultation with our calendars, we will reach a mutually agreeable time to set these depositions. Please be advised that our client is unavailable from May 25 through June 2."

Wonio replied, "Had I received the courtesy of a response to my March 17 letter, I would not have simply given notice of the deposition. I will ask my assistant to call around and get mutually available dates."

Courtesy of a response? He'd set the date in the letter itself, without consulting us. And Carrie had responded, in well under three weeks. Wonio routinely took much longer.

After mutual consultation, my deposition was set for May 23.

Correspondence between Wonio and my lawyers about the depositions and other issues continued. By late May, both sides had agreed to extend the deadline for the remaining necessary information. Wonio wanted to depose our expert witnesses, and my lawyers agreed to disclose their names by September 1.

The additional material on Wiebler we'd gotten from the diocese was pretty much unreadable, so Carrie asked for a better copy of Wiebler's dossier. She also requested the depositions of Loftus, Gruss, Franklin and Wiebler, as well as Montgomery, Crowley, Sweeney and Miclot, people involved in the consolidated cases who claimed Wiebler had molested them. On the same day, she sent Dr. O a subpoena to produce audio and/or videotapes of my sessions, and my medical records.

Dr. O never responded.

CHAPTER THIRTY-EIGHT

MY FIRST DEPOSITION was on May 23. We sat around a table in a conference room at Carrie and Cindy's law offices. In addition to Carrie, Cindy and me, there was Wonio, Fairfield, a male shorthand reporter, and a female videographer with a male helper. The room felt packed and claustrophobic. It was the first time I'd met Wonio or Fairfield face to face. The other people were total strangers. I was the center of attention, and I didn't like it one bit.

I had never been to a deposition. My attorneys had told me that Wonio would ask a lot of very detailed questions about my story, including written responses to interrogatories—mine and possibly others. "Wonio is a professional," Carrie said. "He's good. Just stay calm and stick to the facts, and you'll be fine."

"Tell the truth and turn it over to God," Father B had told me. "He'll take care of you."

Wonio wasn't what I expected. He looked to be in his early fifties. He wore a suit coat and dress shirt but no tie—"casual professional." He was about six feet tall, broad-shouldered and stocky; a good-looking man with a full head of graying dark hair. He looked like a retired football player who had kept in shape. He was friendly and asked if I wanted a cup of coffee.

CHAPTER THIRTY-EIGHT

I was sworn in, and Wonio started the questions. At first it was just the usual background information: where did I live, what was my business, and so forth. He definitely wanted specific details: what business training did I have, what did my house look like, what were the dates of my previous two marriages.

Then things got more personal. He leaned forward, looked into my eyes and asked, "Is there anything about your relationship with your daughter that you would describe as anything other than a normal father/daughter relationship?"

What did my relationship with my daughter have to do with the case? And what did he mean by "other than normal"?

"No," I said, "other than she doesn't reside with me." Then I added, I guess as a sort of attempt to describe my relationship with her, "We're going to a family function in Houston this week." I hadn't learned yet not to volunteer extra information.

Wonio immediately focused on it. "What family function are you going to in Houston?"

I explained that my brother lived in Houston and that my mother, daughter, uncles and I went there every Memorial Day. Wonio wanted to know my brother's name and age, and then asked, "Anything else that you do on this annual trip to Houston? Do you just visit, or are there any special activities involved?"

Why did he need to know about any "special activities"? Where was he going with this? There was nothing "other than normal" about my relationship with Brooke or our family get-togethers in Houston. I felt the familiar stirrings of fear.

"No," I said, "we just visit."

Wonio's friendly, relaxed demeanor had evaporated, and in its place was an expressionless but intent manner that was almost predatory in focus. He'd look down at his notes, look up and fix me in a direct gaze, and then ask questions that were clearly prepared to lead somewhere. His enunciation was clear, and he didn't hesitate or search for words. His questions were well prepared; he knew exactly what he was going to say, and he pursued every answer for detail. He was all business now, and definitely in control.

He asked about my family and my relationship with them, my alcoholism and my treatment. Then he leaned forward again. "This is the interrogatory where I ask you to describe each and every act of sexual abuse that's part of this lawsuit. Let me ask you for a little bit more detail about that. As I read this, it doesn't really tell me in complete detail—or perhaps it does."

Or perhaps it does? What did he mean?

I got very specific and spoke about Wiebler's Mustang, my mother's signing our family up at Lourdes, and that sort of thing. I knew that some bogus abuse claims had been made against the Church, and Carrie had told me that part of Wonio's job was to determine if mine was legitimate. Undoubtedly he was simply doing his job, watching to see if I contradicted myself or tripped up some other way. But repeating specific details of the abuse brought it back. I didn't like that much. Besides, Franklin had admitted at the original meeting with Wiebler that I'd been abused. Hadn't he told Wonio? If Wonio was aware the abuse had happened, why did he need to determine that my story was legitimate?

"We're going to take another branch in this discussion," Wonio said. "Please tell me when you called Wiebler, what happened and where he was—everything. Tell me all about it."

I described in detail the first phone calls, the confrontation with Wiebler at the diocese, and the abuse incident at the pool table. "He reached around very slowly to my genital area like that, and then I froze," I said.

"What did he do after that?" Wonio asked.

"He just rubbed on it, on my genital area, and I froze. I don't remember anything else than that on that occasion."

"How long did that episode last?" Wonio asked.

"Just a few seconds."

"And did he touch you over your clothing?"

"Over my clothing."

"Did he say anything to you?"

"No."

"Did you say anything to him?"

"No."

CHAPTER THIRTY-EIGHT

Maybe Wonio was just doing his job, but I was being forced to relive feelings that had made my life hell since they'd resurfaced. Why? They knew the abuse had happened. They knew I wasn't faking anything.

I was also extremely uncomfortable about relating these intimate details in front of strangers, who scrutinized and evaluated every response, silently recorded every word, and filmed every reaction on my face. It was humiliating.

Wonio pressed on. "And then, I take it, he removed his hand. And then what happened? Did you continue to play pool?"

"Yeah. I ... I ... I didn't know what else to do."

"You say you froze. Why did you freeze?"

"I was scared."

"And why were you scared?"

Was he serious? Didn't he understand anything about sex abuse? If he did, the question was demeaning and cruel.

"I think at the time I knew it wasn't right, wasn't normal," I said. "He was a priest, and to me he was more like God himself and I ... I wasn't going to question it, I was just scared. I was frozen with fear about it and I didn't ... didn't do anything. I didn't tell my mom; I didn't say anything to my brother; I didn't do anything. I just acted like it didn't happen."

More questions followed, and then he asked me to describe the second incident, at the river. Again he probed for detail. "So you were standing there on the beach ..."

"We were sitting," I said.

"Or sitting," he said. "You had to take some clothes off to put your trunks on, is that correct?"

"That's correct."

"And then he reached over to help you put your trunks on?"

"That's what he acted like he was doing, I believe."

"Okay," Wonio said. "And without belaboring it too much, how long would you say this touching lasted?"

"A few seconds," I said.

Then he proceeded to belabor it. "You know, again, is it ..."

"Fifteen seconds," I guessed.

"And what did he do specifically when he was touching you?"

Was all this necessary for the trial? I was now acutely aware of the videographer and the shorthand reporter; I couldn't even look in their direction. I had begun to hang my head to avoid seeing anyone's face. Talking about these minute, intimate details in front of all these strangers was degrading. What would the trial be like? Was Wonio letting me know that if the case went to trial I'd be treated the same way in front of the judge, the jury and the press?

I gave Wonio what he wanted. "He grabbed my penis and stroked it."

Wonio pressed on. "How long was it after that first event in the rectory that this second incident happened?"

"I'm not sure," I said.

"After the first incident, why did you go back and have anything to do with him?"

I suspected where this was headed. He wanted to determine if I had willingly participated.

"I have no idea," I said.

"Did you tell anyone about the second event?"

"No."

"Why didn't you tell somebody?"

"I was probably too scared."

He wouldn't let it go. "As you sit here now, why do you think you didn't tell somebody?"

"I was too scared about how it would … how it would make me look. What people would say."

Next came the bowling coach incident. Again he wanted every sordid detail. When I finished, he asked, "Did you tell anybody about what he had done to you?"

"No."

He leaned forward, and a slight, vaguely mocking smile appeared. "My friend," he said, "I've never heard of a 'bowling coach' before. How did this guy become one? Was he associated with the bowling alley, or what was the deal?"

CHAPTER THIRTY-EIGHT

I didn't miss the faintly sarcastic shift in language: "my friend," "what was the deal." He didn't believe me. What was a kid supposed to know about an adult's official position?

"I believe he was associated with the bowling alley," I said. "He was ... he helped us kids."

Wonio pressed on. "How ..."

I was too distraught to continue. "Excuse me."

"Do you want to take a break?" Wonio asked politely. "Any time you want to, just let me know."

After the recess, the humiliation continued.

"Mr. Christman," said Wonio, "going back to this unpleasant memory about the bowling coach, how did you feel about what he was doing to you at the time?"

By now I knew he was going to coldly force me through every degrading fact and emotion. It was obvious from his manner that he couldn't care less how it affected me. Why was this necessary? They knew it had happened.

"I felt it was wrong," I said. "I was again frozen. As a matter of a fact I ... during ... that time I tried to scream but nothing came out."

"What did you do after he completed this act upon you?"

"I didn't move."

"You've said that he ejaculated upon you, is that correct?"

"Yes."

"Was this on the blanket you were wearing?"

"Yes."

"Did it get on you at all?"

"Yeah, 'cause I felt it."

This was beyond embarrassment. What did whether or not I felt the guy's semen have to do with the case? A mental image came unbidden to mind: myself on the witness stand describing the sensation of the bowling coach's semen to a courtroom crowded with prurient, fascinated people. I shriveled inwardly.

After that came the Bill Beck incident. That line of questioning didn't go far; Beck was a registered sexual predator, very active during the time I knew him, and my story of him offering me alcohol jibed with his known method of using alcohol to seduce boys my age. No ammunition for Wonio there.

Then he shifted to the timing of my memory with the breaking national news of the Boston clergy sex abuse scandals. "What information do you remember from this coverage?" he asked. "Attorneys would appear on these shows as well?"

I knew where this was headed. I answered honestly about what I'd seen and heard. He moved on.

Next came my initial call to Loftus. "You mentioned earlier," he said, "that she asked if you were making an allegation of sexual abuse against a priest, and you told her no. Why?"

I told him that I'd had the flashes of memory and wanted to speak to Wiebler before making any allegations.

"It sounds to me," Wonio said, "that at the time you were making these first contacts to Irene Loftus, and then to Wiebler, you weren't even really quite sure whether this had happened, is that right?"

I agreed.

"What is it that allows you to have a more clear memory about it now than when you first thought about it?"

"Wiebler's responses to my questions, and the meeting we had at the diocese."

"Well," he conceded, "that makes sense to me. What were you hoping to accomplish at the meeting?"

"I was hoping to find out from Wiebler's mouth the truth about what he had done to me. I wanted to hear him say it, and I wanted him to apologize."

"Why did you want to tape-record the meeting? Did you want to use the recording for litigation?"

"Not at the time."

"Had the thought ever crossed your mind that you might need it for litigation?"

"Yeah, it had crossed my mind."

I described the meeting in detail again. Wonio asked, "Were you unhappy about how the meeting was handled?"

CHAPTER THIRTY-EIGHT

I told him how Loftus never took the notes she had said she would and how they had never told me where Wiebler was or apologized, as they promised they would.

"I think I was a little naïve," I said, "in thinking that the Catholic Church as a whole really cared, which I know now they don't. They're more concerned about themselves and how they're going to handle these cases as painlessly as they possibly can, without thought for the victims. And though they state in the newspapers and in masses that they're sorry for what has happened to victims of this type of abuse, they ... I think it's obvious to most people that ... I don't know, I speak for myself. It's obvious to me that they don't really care, and to offer me pastoral care is like slapping me in the face. I ... I know you're here to do your job because it's your job and ... but I ... I don't agree with the way it's being handled."

I was angry now. "You know, I'm not happy about the process of having people I don't know sitting in this room hearing every intimate detail about my life. I know it's your job, but that doesn't mean I'm happy about it. I believe this could have been handled a lot differently, and a lot more painlessly for me. But it's not going to go that way; it's going to drag on after today. You know that. And in the end, I don't believe even the Bishop himself will call me directly and say, 'I'm really sorry about that.'"

During my whole outburst, Wonio had sat back and listened with a slight, condescending smile. I'd just vented my frustration, and it seemed like he was smirking at me. It hadn't seemed to bother him at all; in fact, I was beginning to suspect that it pleased him to see me upset. Maybe he was trying to rattle me to increase the chances I'd say something inconsistent—something he could use against me.

I was beginning to intensely dislike the man.

We covered some more general ground: my second, private meeting with Franklin; people I'd talked to about the abuse; that sort of thing. Then Wonio asked, "Were you satisfied with the care that was being provided to you by Dr. O?"

"No," I replied.

"Why not?"

I explained that Dr. O often contradicted himself; he'd say one thing one day and then something different another time. I gave the example of how one time he had said my going to AA was a good thing and I should continue, and then another time he'd mocked AA and said he had patients who quit going and found out they could drink safely again. I explained how he would often talk about himself, how he often seemed irritated at me, and how some of the medicines he had prescribed had made me sick. I noted that another psychiatrist I had seen after I stopped my visits with Dr. O had told me I shouldn't have been on them.

The topic of Dr. O, I was to discover, would surface again. With a vengeance.

We next discussed my injury and operation and my back pain and pain meds. Then came my workers' comp claim.

"Has that been resolved?" Wonio asked.

"Yes."

"Please tell me how."

I explained that I had been paid a settlement of $98,000 for lost wages, on top of my medical bills.

"It was an arbitration?" Wonio asked.

"Yes."

"So you actually had to take this claim to some kind of a hearing in front of an arbitrator. Was there an opposing medical opinion?"

"There was one opposing medical opinion from a doctor in Chicago," I said. "His dispute was not that I needed surgery or anything; it was my being able to work in what capacities after the surgeries and here on out in the future."

"You had some kind of claim or lawsuit against United Airlines. Is that correct?"

I said yes and explained that I was on a plane that caught fire. When the plane landed, the crewmembers were rushing people to get off. The stewardess was literally pushing people down the inflated ramp. I was recently out of surgery and still had staples in my back and bandages on my incisions. I was trying to figure out

CHAPTER THIRTY-EIGHT

how to bend to get on the ramp when the stewardess pushed me directly on my incision. I tumbled down the ramp to the tarmac. I went to a surgeon immediately to see if everything was all right. The claim was to recover the cost of that meeting, about $1,200.

"Did you actually file a lawsuit?" asked Wonio.

"No," I said. "I gave that to my attorney at the time to handle, and he never did anything."

"Did you make any kind of a claim against the attorney to reimburse you for that?"

"No."

"Did the tumble down the walkway, or whatever it was, cause you any long-term problem with your back?"

I told him that nobody had been able to determine where my pain came from and exactly what the cause was.

Wonio followed this up with a series of questions about my surgery, my rehab and my employees. Then he asked, "Has your back condition caused you to not have the earning power you had before your back was injured?"

"Yes," I said.

"What impact has it had on your earnings to have to hire help to replace what you used to do, and to the success of your business?"

I told him that including my employee's salary and the jobs that had to be subcontracted out, it had affected me in the range of a couple hundred thousand dollars annually.

Wonio leaned forward and fixed me with the focused, dispassionate look I now knew announced the beginning of some intense, uncomfortable grilling. "Do you believe that the sexual abuse perpetrated upon you by William Wiebler has injured your earning power?"

I wanted to ask him sweetly, "Is this your first sex abuse case?" but I bit my tongue. He knew the answer. He just wanted to interrogate me about it. I could understand that.

I took a deep breath. "Yeah."

"Please explain," he asked clinically.

"I believe that it has greatly affected my relations with people in general, whether it's personal relations, customer relations, or just relations with the general public. I suffer from a lot of fear most of the time, and although I try to keep it ... keep it at bay, and I try to keep pretty much a business face about everything I do, I'm not as friendly as I could be. You know, I ... I think I could be more friendly and sympathetic, much more caring of a person than I really am. I ... I constantly think ... I'm not the kind of person who thinks that overall most people are good; overall I think most people are bad."

I was sweating, almost stuttering. My mind was in turmoil. Even describing my feelings triggered them.

I struggled on. "I think that ... you know, I was telling somebody the other day that I ... you know, I don't wake up with a ... I don't wake up in the morning thinking, *Wow, another day; it's a great day.* I think, *It's another day that I have to endure.* And with that type of attitude and outlook, it definitely affects every area of my life."

"How does that translate into loss of earning power?" Wonio asked in a detached tone.

Another absurd question, but undoubtedly any inconsistencies or weak points in my response would be used against me. How could I verbalize it properly?

"Well," I said, "I believe that if I was ... if my attitude and outlook on life was much better, I believe it would open up a lot more opportunities for myself, not only in my current business, but maybe other ventures or businesses that I might be able to involve myself in."

"What ventures and business might that be?" He was like a dog with a bone. Evidently he wanted me to analyze the effect of my abuse on specific potential ventures.

I was afraid to say something wrong and struggled to answer coherently. "I don't know in particular. I don't have, like, an example of a business right offhand. I think that ... I think it has affected why I didn't continue with certain things in my life, like college. I ... I don't think it ... or I think it's directly affected my ... certain ambitions that, you know, I don't feel secure in expanding." I

CHAPTER THIRTY-EIGHT

floundered on. "I'll give you an example. I could possibly open up other wildlife services around the country if I wanted to. I think if I had the right frame of mind and outlook, it would be much easier. Whether it would be successful or not, I don't know, but I think ... I just think in general that my relations with the general public and ... whether it be personal or, you know, just in general ... is I have to work at being outgoing and friendly."

I felt like I was wandering and repeating myself. I took a deep breath and tried to clarify the last point.

"I don't mean that I'm, like, mean to people all the time. I just mean that I ... I ... in the past my relations with other people have shown to not be the greatest."

Boy, that sounded lame! I shut up.

Wonio remained impassive. "Why do you relate that to the abuse by William Wiebler?"

Did I have to say it again? This guy was relentless.

"Well, I think I suffer from a lot of fear relating to that. I ... although I've found a decent way of living through Alcoholics Anonymous, I haven't ... and have struggled greatly with my relationship with God. I have not been involved in any organized religion, and I think a good relationship with God would probably affect every area of one's life."

"How do you put dollars and cents to that?" he asked.

I was beaten. "I don't know how you do that."

"Is there some idea you have about how much you would ask a jury for loss of earning power because of the abuse?"

He knew full well what our offer was, and that we had tried to negotiate. Now I was frustrated as well as aggravated. "Honestly," I said, "I would leave that up to my attorneys."

He dropped that approach and asked, "What impact do you think the sexual abuse by the bowling coach has had on you in an earning power sort of way?"

I knew where he was headed. I told him I had no idea how I would have turned out as a man if only Wiebler had abused me.

He switched to questions about my father. "Do you believe that knowing the circumstances of your father's death also contributes to any problems you're having now?"

I agreed it had, especially not having a father figure around.

"But," he pressed, "does it add an additional stress to you knowing and understanding what the circumstances were of his death, rather than just a heart attack or something?"

"Yes, it's disturbing to know that he probably committed suicide."

"And do you feel that knowing that increases some of the troubles you've in your life?"

I admitted it had.

"Significantly so?" he asked.

"I would say so."

"And how," he asked, "would that compare to the stresses caused in your life by being sexually molested by William Wiebler?"

I understood that if he could get me to quantify the effects of these other incidents and show that other factors had also messed me up, he could possibly use the information to diminish the amount of an abuse settlement. I couldn't blame him there; he was doing his job. But I wasn't going to give him any ammunition. Or satisfaction. I said nothing.

Finally, he said, "Can you even make a comparison?"

"I don't know that I can make a comparison," I said, "because I don't know what life would have been like without those things having happened."

He'd failed to pin me down, so he said, "All right, fair enough," and returned to the bowling coach. "When you were molested by the bowling coach at age 11, did you think about when you were molested by Wiebler?"

"No," I said.

"Are you saying that for all of those years until some time in 2002 you had no memory of being molested by Wiebler?"

"That's correct."

"When did you shut out that memory?"

CHAPTER THIRTY-EIGHT

How would I know? It was a trick question. If I could remember when I had blocked it out, it meant that I hadn't blocked it out, and my statement that the memory had returned in 2002 was bogus.

"I must have shut it out whenever I was abused," I said.

"And never thought about it again until 2002?"

"That's correct."

"You didn't think about it when you were molested at age 11?"

"No." He'd just asked that.

"Did you shut out the memory of being abused at age 11 until 2002?"

"No." He knew I hadn't. He was using the same interrogation tactics they teach cops: ask the same questions over and over, in slightly different contexts, until the criminal makes an inconsistent answer, and then accuse him of not telling the truth. Then you can use it as evidence in court that the person is lying.

Wonio bulldozed on. "You thought about that from the time it happened until now?"

"No, I didn't think about it all the time."

"But it was there; it was a memory?"

"It was there, but it wasn't a memory that was predominant every day."

He leaned forward and peered at me over the top of his glasses. "Why do you think you were able to remember the abuse at age 11 but not remember the abuse by Wiebler at age whatever it was—seven or eight or nine?"

"I don't know."

He leaned back in his chair. "Have you talked to any mental health professionals about why you didn't remember the Wiebler abuse until 2002?"

"Yeah," I said. "They've stated that it's not unusual, that it frequently happens to victims of sexual abuse, and that certain things can trigger memories. Those things depend on the circumstances, and a number of different factors will determine whether someone remembers it every day of his life or doesn't remember anything."

"I guess I don't understand how you remember one and not the other," he said. That had to be another tactic; he had to know what repressed memory was. "Has anybody explained to you how that works?"

"I don't think they know how it works," I said. "They just know that it's consistent with other victims of abuse. Maybe it has to do with age. I don't know."

No satisfaction there, so Wonio made another abrupt topic switch. "Are you involved with any other litigation right now, other than this case?"

I told him that I had a case pending on a car paint job. I'd paid up front for it, the painters had messed it up, and I wanted my money back. I also had a car accident case; I'd been rear-ended and wanted to collect the cost of the resulting emergency room visit. Wonio nodded, and the slight smile reappeared. I suspected that along with the workers' comp claim and the aborted United Airlines claim, he was well on his way to proving that I was an ambulance chaser.

I knew enough not to mention the collection cases. My company deals with about 700 customers annually. Of course, not everyone pays their bills, and I usually had a dozen or so collections in small claims court over a year's time. It's a normal business practice, and the amount of cases fit the normal bad debt ratio of about two percent for most service businesses. However, I knew what Wonio would do with the statistic that over the life of my business I'd had well over 100 additional "lawsuits."

Wonio asked a number of different questions about my mental health providers, what I knew about the Church, and other contact I'd had with Church officials. Then he came back to Wiebler.

"Please give me a personal statement," he said, "about how you feel the abuse by William Wiebler has affected your life. I know you've talked about that somewhat, but this is an even more expanded scope. I think we talked about earning capacity before."

You think? I thought he'd beaten that one into the ground.

CHAPTER THIRTY-EIGHT

"Please tell me in your own words," he continued, "how you believe the abuse has affected your life."

How many times did we have to go over this? I made an effort to calm myself. "Probably the biggest thing is ... I mean, we talked about my relations with other people. It has instilled a fear in me that prevents me from trusting and having good healthy relationships. It has prevented me from knowing or showing love. I have a great deal of trouble in the area of affection even with my fiancée, my daughter, my friends and family. I ... I can't even be ... for example, if you were to pat me on the back and say, 'How are you doing, Bill?' I would freeze. I ... I can't allow, especially males, to hug or ... you know, I ... I can't have that type of affection, and I can't ... I don't say I can't, I have a very difficult time showing affection. I ... I'm afraid most of the time."

He smiled. "Well, I don't like hugging other males either. I'm not keen on that kind of contact, and I haven't experienced sexual abuse. Why do you relate that kind of feeling to being sexually abused by Wiebler?"

"Because I jump. Not physically; I jump on the inside."

He asked me if I'd looked at Dr. O's records—mainly his answers to the interrogatories.

"Yes," I said, "and I couldn't read most of it." Dr. O's handwriting was notoriously bad.

We clarified a few points, and then Wonio said, "Under item 5, O says, 'Discussed attempted rape at age nine by bowling coach.' Did you tell him you were nine when that happened?"

"No."

He wanted to know why the doctor had written that, and I told him he did things like that. "He'd say things, and then he'd say he didn't say them. Like the example I gave earlier."

"Is there anything else wrong on this record?"

I read further. "His statement, 'One month regular use of cocaine' is wrong. I used it for six months. And he says I liked marijuana. I did not. It made me crazy, made me tired. I don't think I would have ever said that. And here he says, 'Alcohol, especially whiskey like Jack Daniels, makes me very mean and nasty.' I can't imagine ever making that statement, 'cause I never drank Jack Daniels."

As we went through Dr. O's statements, I found error after error. It was full of remarks I'd never made, as well as serious discrepancies. At first I was just puzzled. But when I read, "Talked about his anger toward former psychiatrist for being quite taken by Michelle," I started to get upset. "No," I said. "My anger toward the first psychiatrist was because he told Michelle that she should leave me because I told him about being attracted to another woman." Where was O coming up with this stuff?

The errors continued. Dr. O stated that one of my AA sponsors named Mick was "the vice president at John Deere." Mick worked at John Deere, but he wasn't vice president. The doc had thrown that in. God knows where he came up with it.

Later, Dr. O stated I had "reestablished [my] relationship with [my] daughter." "I have no idea what he's talking about," I told Wonio. "I've never had to reestablish any relationship with my daughter; I've always had one."

I pointed out more inaccuracies, and then Wonio said, "Let's go to O 35. Tell me if anything about that record of April 30, 2002, is not accurate."

I read it, and shook my head.

"What?" said Wonio.

"Section 2, where he's quoting me as saying, 'I guess I want an apology, but it seems the only way to get them to be humble is to hit them where it hurts them, in their wallet.' He said that, not me."

Wonio said, "Let's go to O 38, dated May 6, 2002. He states this about himself, quote: 'I feel manipulated by Bill, so I think he's milking his diagnoses to get the Catholic Church to give him millions so he won't have to work a day henceforth.' How do you respond to that?"

I was stunned and felt blindsided. "I can't imagine ... it makes me angry that he'd say that about me. Anybody who knows me knows that if there's ever been a hard worker, I'm it. As a matter of fact, I probably work too much. This isn't about getting millions of dollars. I believe there does need to be compensation, but millions

CHAPTER THIRTY-EIGHT

of dollars as the way he worded it ... that's an untrue statement. This is the same guy who when I first discussed this with him, his first comment to me was, 'The only way you're going to get them to realize what they've done is to hit them where it hurts, in the pocketbook.'"

Wonio asked, "Why do you think he changed his records to make that your quote instead of his?"

"I don't know. Maybe he was jealous of me. He's recently filed for bankruptcy, and he also stated ... yeah, down here, he says, 'Bill does not work.' Bill does not work? I've always worked, hurt or unhurt. And here, 'He brags about lavish expenditures.' I've talked with him about my buying things to help myself feel better at times, knowing that it doesn't work ..."

I felt completely betrayed. "I've talked to him about personal, vulnerable things to gain insight and help, and then he turns it around and judges me like that. It's infuriating."

I read Dr. O's next statement: "'And freely waves 50- and 20-dollar bills.'" I had to stop to calm myself. "I've never waved money at anybody in my life, other than to take money out of my pocket to pay a bill."

I remembered now; the doc wasn't part of my health insurance plan, so I had paid him out of my own pocket, usually in cash. "If he calls that waving money around ... the only logical explanation that I have for his betrayal is that he's jealous and he ain't got anything and I do." I was shaking with anger.

Wonio asked, "Anything else incorrect about ..."

I cut him off. "Taking a break."

After the recess, the examination of Dr. O's testimony continued. I pointed out more errors and told Wonio that O's inconsistencies were one of the reasons I stopped seeing him. "He says one thing and then he says another," I said. "He wanted me to 'forgive and forget.' Get over it. OK, well then, I'll just get over it. He would state one day, 'You need to hit 'em where it hurts, in their pocketbook; that's the only way they'll listen.' And then the next day, 'I don't know if you should do this; they'll destroy you, Bill. The Catholic Church is very powerful, and they'll hire very powerful attorneys.'"

"Do you think I'm a powerful attorney?" Wonio asked.

I didn't see that one coming. "Yeah, I do," I said. Was he kidding? I felt absolutely dominated and manhandled.

"Do you think I would destroy you?"

Where was he going with that one? How was I supposed to answer? Safely, I decided.

"No, I don't," I said.

On we went, error after error. Dr. O wrote that my mother and brother had stated that Michelle was anorexic. They would never have said that—and besides, Michelle was a bodybuilder for God's sake!

Many of Dr. O's quotes of what I said were not even in language I used. He quoted me as saying, "I have been so caught up in all these stressors plus this Velcro relationship with Michelle ..." Stressors? Velcro relationship? I never use words like that! I told Wonio, "I think as he's writing reports he thinks of his own things and puts them in. He must."

Wonio continued. "Where the record says, 'In our previous sessions Bill said he was not working, which led to my questioning him about the source of his income because he travels for pleasure a lot. I reminded him that he told me he was fearful that Michelle would expose his IRS shenanigans.' Are you saying that's not accurate?"

I was astonished. "It's completely inaccurate. I never told him I wasn't working, and I don't have any IRS problems."

"Did you ever tell him you were fearful Michelle would expose your IRS shenanigans?"

"No, because I don't have any IRS shenanigans!"

"What do you think he could possibly be talking about here?"

"I have no clue." I never hid a nickel from IRS; I had always reported every penny I made. Everyone knew that I was obsessive about recordkeeping and paperwork. I was proud to be an American,

CHAPTER THIRTY-EIGHT

proud I made a living, and happy to pay taxes to do my share. Dr. O and I had never discussed the IRS. Why would he say this?

Wonio must have been ecstatic when he first read O's testimony; it was a gold mine for a lawyer for the defense. The testimony would be damaging in a trial, even though it was lies. How would my word stand up against that of a licensed psychiatrist? Well, Wonio was going to hear the truth.

On we went, with me correcting or denying Dr. O's observations and my supposed "quotes" when needed. For example, "I never called Michelle's dad a red-necked abusive alcoholic."

Then we came to a joint session I'd had with my mother. Wonio said, "O says that he wants your mother to help him, quote, 'Understand the roots of her son's fragmented selves, one of which is a severely judgmental and moralistic prig, and the other of which is a cunning, sociopathic, lying con artist who is a materialistic and self-centered rage-aholic.'"

Wonio looked up at me. "How would you respond to that?"

Dr. O was right about my rage, but his other judgments were ludicrous and outrageously insulting. I'd never heard anything like this type of diagnosis from any of the other psychiatrists or therapists I'd seen, or from anyone else I knew. He must have despised me from the beginning! We'd had our personality conflicts, but they were mild, and I thought they had developed over the course of our work together. I had no idea he had felt this strongly about me from the beginning. He had certainly hid it well enough.

"He never talked about this or presented it to myself or my mother," I said, "because if he had, it would have been the end of the session. I'm not saying he doesn't believe that; we just didn't talk about it. It's untrue. The guy's nuts, too." I read another quote aloud: "'Mary, in front of Bill, recounted her late husband, with whom she endured nine tortured years of incessant alcoholism and bouts of rage before she divorced him.' She never divorced him; he died! She found him dead in the garage! Get it correct!"

I stopped and looked up at Wonio. He wore that familiar slight, superior smile. My turmoil did not bother him at all.

I read another quote, supposedly by my mother, concerning my father: "'[He] always favored Bill over his brother because Bill was a mean cuss like his father. His father saw his other son as being too gentle. Never missed an opportunity to make that boy furious.'"

My mother and I had probably both told Dr. O that my father liked me because I was rambunctious and into everything, but I know neither of us had ever said that Dad looked down on Jeff, and he never picked on him. The doctor had twisted everything, added his own interpretation and then made it sound as if it was my mother speaking.

"I don't know what he's talking about," I said. "I never heard her say those words. And if you knew my mother, it's just totally out of character. I mean it's just ... oh, believe me, I'll be going over this with her."

"That's probably a good idea," Wonio said, "because I probably will be too, during her deposition."

"Oh," I said, "I'm sure you will."

Neither of us could decipher what Dr. O meant in the next comment. Wonio asked, "What is he saying as far as what you suffered in the way of post-traumatic stress? Do you know?"

I tried to figure it out, but couldn't. The comment made no sense.

"See, that's what infuriates me about this," I said. "During some of these sessions he would talk to me in one manner, and now I'm seeing for the first time some of the things that he's putting down. And you're sitting there like, well, why ... you know, why didn't I get rid of him a long time ago? Well, I would have if I'd have known this."

Wonio started another question. "At the end ..."

I cut him off. "It'll be interesting to see what he tells you during his deposition."

Wonio asked one last question about Dr. O's comment that I thought I was doing considerably better "despite the fiasco with Michelle's family yesterday." I couldn't remember the incident; it probably couldn't compare with today's fiasco anyway.

CHAPTER THIRTY-EIGHT

We adjourned and agreed to meet again on June 13 to finish my deposition. My mother's deposition, and Father B's, were to be on the same day after mine. Dr. O's deposition was scheduled for June 14.

Barring short recesses, we'd been at it for seven hours. I felt exhausted and beaten. Carrie tried to console me. "Wonio's not a bad man, Bill," she said. "He's just doing his job, and he's good at it. He's smart, cunning. He didn't intend to make this easy on you. He knows the abuse happened and that there was emotional damage. But he knows you had other abuse incidents too, so why should the diocese pay for everything? He's right there, you know. He had to ask these questions."

I disagreed with her, vehemently. "He didn't ask me much of anything he didn't already know. He wasn't trying to get the facts; he could have done that in an hour. He didn't want the truth. He wanted to intimidate me and show me what will happen in a trial."

Carrie had to agree with that. "Part of this is to scare people from going to trial and hopefully force a favorable settlement for the diocese. It's his job to protect them."

"Not like that," I said. "He was sarcastic and mocking. He was messing with me, trying to upset me and trip me up so I'd say something he could use against me. He asked me to remember stuff from my childhood that nobody can remember, hoping I'd be inconsistent so he could use it against me. He took things out of context to make them sound bad. He was cold. He acted like the abuse was nothing."

"He couldn't express sympathy, especially verbally," Carrie said. "Legally, that would be tantamount to admitting liability."

I was furious. "No excuse. He went way too far. The more upset I got, the more he smiled. When I gave him grief he smiled. He enjoyed it. He's got to know that making a victim describe all the details of the abuse makes them relive it. It re-victimizes them. These memories have been tormenting me for more than two years now, and Wonio deliberately triggered them and rubbed my nose in them. Who's on trial here, me or Wiebler?"

I was particularly infuriated at Franklin, who doubtless would not want to know how the deposition had been conducted, and who was willing to look the other way and let the lawyers do whatever they felt necessary to protect the diocese. I knew that if I confronted Franklin with what had happened today, he'd say he had no power to stop it. "It's out of my hands." He knew Wiebler had abused me and that I was innocent of any wrongdoing.

I was deeply upset by Dr. O's statements. I had gone to him in a state of complete despair and vulnerability. I had trusted him, and he had betrayed me. He must have wanted to help destroy my case; why else would he have lied so blatantly? His comments that I was a lying, manipulative, sociopathic con artist who wanted to extort millions out of the diocese were exactly what Wonio needed.

"I know what he did," I told my attorneys. "He just taped everything. He must have wet himself when Wonio demanded notes of our sessions, because he never took any. He had the dates of all our visits, though, so he went back and recreated everything from memory, plugged in his own thoughts and made stuff up. I'm sure he's terrified this might go to trial and he might be dragged up on the witness stand, so he assassinated me and gave Wonio great ammunition to force us to give up and settle out of court. Well, by God, he's messing with the wrong person."

I was enraged. I was finished being victimized. Wonio had hoped to intimidate me, but it had backfired. Now I wanted to go to court.

"We have to get Dr. O's tapes," I said. "They'll show he's lying. We can destroy him."

"We sent a letter to him today," Carrie reassured me. "We subpoenaed his audio and videotapes and your medical records, and demanded delivery by June 7, before your next deposition and before his. If this goes to trial, we can take him apart."

"He shouldn't be practicing," I said. "His license should be revoked."

I was shaking, near tears. I badly needed to talk to Father B.

CHAPTER THIRTY-EIGHT

Communication between the lawyers continued. Carrie wanted to depose Franklin because Levien had run Franklin's deposition the year before and she had questions more relevant to our case; Wonio said he'd file a Motion for Protective Order to prevent "retaking" Franklin's deposition. Wonio also asked for what kinds of testimony she wanted from Gruss, Montgomery, Crowley, Sweeney and Miclot, and then mentioned possibly preventing their depositions the same way.

Wonio asked that disclosure of our experts on September 1 also include their full and complete opinions on the case by that date. "Depending on what experts you have and what they say," he wrote, "I may need to have your client examined by a mental health professional."

In late May, Wonio wrote that he intended to use Dr. O's testimony in the trial. "We believe O's opinions and the content of his records put Jack Doe's credibility at issue." Further, although Wiebler had admitted abusing other boys, he denied having any sexual contact with me, because of my age. I was seven at the time, and Wiebler's preferred victims were teenagers. Wonio also said he would use information and records about my bad back. Undoubtedly, that would be useful to him in reducing lost wage claims.

Carrie asked once more for better copies of Wiebler's records. Wonio responded, "I'm sorry, but these [copies] are really the best that I have. The documents were found after Irene Loftus spent many hours going through old files of the Priest Personnel Board. The documents in those files were copies themselves and are no better than what you have. The documents are legible, but I acknowledge that it is certainly a struggle to read them."

A struggle? They were essentially useless. We'd get no satisfaction from that source.

CHAPTER THIRTY-NINE

MY SECOND DEPOSITION was on June 13. The same group sat around the same table in the same arrangement. But this time I was different. *No more victim,* I thought. *No more victim.*

Wonio started the questions, as usual looking for details and fishing for inconsistencies. He asked if I'd mentioned the abuse by Wiebler to my first psychiatrist. No, I told him, I'd stopped seeing him in late 2001, before the memory returned. Remember?

More questions about the psychiatrist continued, and then Wonio asked, "Other than the incident where you believed the doctor violated a confidence, did you have any other complaint with the care he provided to you?"

"He had another woman in his office during every session who would take notes for him," I said, "which was a little unpleasant."

"Why?" Wonio asked.

"Well, just having another woman there. Just like having this woman here. I don't know her. You know, I don't ... I don't like everybody knowing personal, intimate things about me unless I absolutely have to."

"You're referring to the young woman running the video machine?"

"Correct."

CHAPTER THIRTY-NINE

"Does it comfort you at all to know that she's a certified person in this field and is pledged to keep your confidences to herself?"

"No."

"Why?"

"That doesn't mean that people don't talk and say things." Hadn't we just discussed how the doctor himself had violated my confidentiality?

Wonio didn't say, "I'm sorry you feel that way," or anything sympathetic; in fact, he didn't even do me the courtesy of acknowledging my answer. He just resumed questioning, moving from topic to topic. We discussed my back, my business, specific work contracts and what they entailed, property descriptions of the job locations, and information that had no relevance to the case as far as I could see. Then he started in on Wiebler again.

"I got a transcript of your first deposition," he said. "I read through it, and I must not have asked good enough questions, because I'm a little unclear about some of the details, if you don't mind, of the second abuse incident involving Wiebler that happened in Buffalo."

I knew the drill now. He was going to drag me through it again, looking for inconsistencies.

He asked about each small step in the ordeal. Wiebler drove me from Bettendorf to Buffalo, correct? In a green Mustang, correct? Abused you while helping you put on a bathing suit, correct? It happened at this beach, correct? Were you inside or outside the vehicle when he abused you?

"Outside, from what I remember." My breath was coming in short stitches; I was reliving the incident. I had vowed not to lose control, but I was.

"It was necessary for you to change from your street clothes into a bathing suit, correct?" he asked.

"Apparently," I said.

He pounced on that. "You say, 'apparently.'"

"Well, I mean, I don't ... my recollection of it is ... even thinking about it right now ..." I was stammering, and hating myself for it.

"I don't know," I concluded. Wasn't it necessary to change into a bathing suit to swim?

He probed on. "You had gotten out of the vehicle and had moved some distance away from it when this happened?"

How was I supposed to remember how far we were from the car? "I would assume so," I said.

He was on that instantly as well. "Why is that an assumption?"

"Because I can't tell you right now that I can remember exactly getting out the door of the Mustang and walking down the beach." It happened more than 20 years ago!

"Are you confident that it did happen on this beach and not in the Mustang?"

"Yes." Who cares? It happened.

He jumped abruptly to my current mental health care with Dr. Saintfort and Dr. Melissano. How often did I see them? Did I see them at the same location? When was the last time I saw them? Then he asked, "Why is it necessary for you to see Dr. Melissano once a week until, as you say, this is over with?"

"Because it's upsetting," I said.

"What's upsetting?" As if he cared. As far as I could see he'd been trying to upset me, and smiling when he succeeded.

I told him that the entire ordeal—the depositions, the legal wrangling—all bothered me.

"Being involved in litigation is upsetting to you?" he asked innocently. It was like an inquisitor asking, "Does that hurt?"

"Yes." I didn't want to give him any satisfaction.

More therapy session questions followed. "When was the last time you saw Dr. Melissano?"

"Last week."

"What happened during that session?"

"We talked about the first deposition, about the Catholic Church in general . . ."

He jumped on that quickly. "What was your conversation about regarding the first deposition?"

"That I think a lot of the questions asked are ridiculous," I said. "That the process is upsetting, with the ... you know, the cameras

CHAPTER THIRTY-NINE

and microphones, the people I don't know. Nothing personal, I just don't enjoy it."

Apparently, I'd finally hit a nerve. He leaned forward and frowned. "So what's ridiculous about the questions that were asked of you in the …"

Suddenly, I'd had enough. I cut him off. Time for him to hear it from me. "I think you and the Catholic Church and everybody knows exactly what happened," I said. "And I think the repetitive questions regarding exactly what happened and the different questions that you ask are just a bunch of double-talk."

"Why?" he asked. The smirk was back; he'd regained his composure.

"Because the Catholic Church knows what's going on, and they don't care. You know as well as I do that this isn't about justice or getting down to the truth; this is about damage control and how can you keep a decent face on the Church—that's your job. Nothing personal, Mr. Wonio, but I don't believe this is about getting down to the truth or about what really happened. I think it's a bunch of junk."

"What do you mean by damage control?" he asked.

"As you know, the Church has been involved in numerous litigations regarding numerous victims throughout the country, and the Pope and the Catholic Church as a whole could care less about this. We wouldn't even be here if they did. You guys are here to do your job, to represent the child molester/rapist, and you're here to take care of the bishop."

"What do you mean by 'damage control'?" he persisted. "Are you talking about money?"

"No, not necessarily. I'm talking about the Church keeping a good face for the community."

But money was the issue now. He asked, "What are you here about? Are you here about the truth, or are …"

I knew what he was going to ask, and I cut him off before he could. "The truth," I said.

He finished, "… you here about money?"

"I'm here about both."

"And how do they mix?"

Talk about money, and I had a captivated lawyer. I wasn't going to give him the satisfaction of an answer to that one. Two could play at the game of pounding on a subject like a broken record.

"I'm here to provide you with the answers and information that you request, even though I know you already know it, because you've heard it before in your private conferences with the Bishop and Irene Loftus. If this is what we have to do to get down to the bottom of it, then so be it, but if you think I'm going to sit here and tell you it's pleasant, it's not."

"What does it mean to you to 'get down to the bottom of it'?" he asked.

"I want the Church to apologize. I want the Bishop to stand in front of me and apologize. I want him to acknowledge what happened and quit hiding behind his attorneys. And I want Wiebler in jail."

"You accuse Bishop Franklin of hiding behind his attorneys. Do you think he has the right to defend the diocese in these cases?"

"I believe he has a right to a certain extent. But he is quite aware of what happened. I wish, Mr. Wonio, that you had been sitting in the room the day I questioned Wiebler, because then we wouldn't be having this discussion. And this is also about how good of a witness am I going to be. You know, you could care less what happened to me. You're here to do your job, and that's fine; that's your job. I have a job too. But it seems to me that this is unnecessary."

I felt better having dumped this, but it obviously bothered him not at all. He smiled, which was a mistake.

You think you've seen me mad? I thought. *You've seen nothing. Now I knew I wanted to go to trial. You want a fight? You don't know what you're getting into. I'll kick your sorry butt so bad you won't be able to hold your head up in public.*

Wonio continued on, unperturbed. "You said the Bishop has a right to defend the diocese to a certain extent. What did you mean by that?"

"I mean he has to do what he has to do to protect the institution he works for, but at the same time, I believe he doesn't necessarily

CHAPTER THIRTY-NINE

have to make me continually talk about this, especially with people I don't know, and constantly answer the same questions over and over again. He stated to me one time that bishops don't have the power they used to have. Well, I know that's not true. I mean, he has complete power over the diocese."

Wonio disagreed, and then shifted back to my therapy—what care Dr. Melissano gave me, how long the sessions were, was I satisfied with them, and on and on. Then he returned to the point of the lawsuit. I wanted an apology from Franklin, and Wiebler put in jail, correct?

"I want Wiebler to go to jail," I agreed.

"Do you understand that there are statute of limitations problems?" he asked. "You understand that the Catholic Church just can't put him in jail?"

"I'm not that naïve or stupid to think that the Catholic Church can put him in jail," I said. "They're not a law enforcement agency, and they don't have police powers. But they could definitely turn over their information to the authorities in St. Louis and tell them that he lives down the street from a public school. They've never done that."

"How do you know that?" Wonio asked.

"I've never been updated as to that by the Church or my attorneys."

"Are you aware that the diocese informed the county prosecuting attorneys in St. Louis when Wiebler left the treatment facility in that area?"

"No, I wasn't aware of that," I said. "That's good."

"It happened a long time ago," Wonio said, as if I should have known. They'd never even told me that Wiebler had been in the facility to begin with.

"Well, I'm glad I'm just being informed of it."

Wonio then went back to money. What else did I want to accomplish with the lawsuit? I told him I wanted them to pay for my seeing therapists and doctors in the future. This, of course, brought us back to the same old runaround. What percentage of my mental health trouble had the bowling coach caused? Had my father's death caused?

I wasn't biting this time. I told him I wasn't saying the Church was responsible for all my problems, but that Wiebler's abuse was a major factor. "To what degree," I said, "I don't know. I guess that's going to be for experts—a jury, attorneys—to figure out."

Wonio went back to Dr. O. He read a statement that the doctor claimed I had made: "I bought two horses; one for Brooke, and one for me."

Wonio leaned forward. "Apparently, Dr. O, at least, says here in this record, 'How do you think the insurance company you are suing is going to see your riding a horse, Bill?' And it says here, quote, 'That never entered my mind.' Is that an accurate notation by Dr. O about talking to you about buying a horse, and your response that it never entered your mind?"

It was another major Dr. O discrepancy and comment put in my mouth to make me look bad. "The horses I bought were for Brooke and Patty," I said.

"In other words," Wonio said, "what you're saying is that you did not tell him one of the horses was for you."

"Correct."

"Well . . ."

I cut him off. "Did he ever provide the tapes?"

"I don't have the tapes. Did he tape your sessions?"

"Yes."

"Every single one of them is tape-recorded?"

"Yes, I believe so."

"No, I don't have copies."

I stared back at him, confident. "'Cause we can clear a lot of this up real quick."

"Why do you think he has these inaccuracies, according to you, in his records?"

"I think he didn't like me, for one. There's nothing wrong with that. It's irrelevant. And he had some sort of jealousy, I believe. But during the sessions he was far different than what he's writing here. These notes are fairly short, and incomplete. I've looked

CHAPTER THIRTY-NINE

through a lot of this, and for an hour-long session with continual conversation, these notes are fairly short and incomplete. We'd be able to verify that with the tapes. I also believe that these were written some time after the appointment."

Like within the past month, I thought.

"Why do you believe that?" Wonio asked.

"Because I don't remember him ever writing like this during an appointment, so they would have had to have been done at a later time. And we all know that ... at least, I know that if I don't write things down, I'll forget it."

On we went, discussing error after error. Statements put in my mouth that I'd never made in language I never use; his frequent comments that I didn't work; confusion of facts.

"He embellishes," I said. "He expands on comments and puts his own wording in." I pointed out one statement. "Look at his written notes ... the typed notes are completely different."

"Did you tell him you were sleeping better since using the homeopathic cream you got from Wal-Mart?" Wonio asked.

I laughed out loud. "No. No."

"That's totally made up?"

"It must be. I've never had any homeopathic cream from Wal-Mart." I could see Dr. O throwing that in, though, to make it sound modern, New Age.

More discrepancies. After a particularly egregious one about something that didn't even happen I said, "I think this is just another indication of where he sits there and listens, and by the time it goes through his brain and gets interpreted, it comes out on paper different. You're questioning me on all these notes, and I know that some of it's just flatly untrue, and some of it's inaccurate. This seems to be of quite some interest to you, so I'm going to make sure that it's gone through thoroughly."

Wonio responded quickly. "Well, I'm trying to go through it thoroughly also, because when I see a reference in his notes that you're somehow trying to exaggerate or manipulate your diagnosis to get a lot of money from the Church, I think all of these references are important, to get to the truth. Do you agree with that?"

"I think Dr. O doesn't want to have anything to do with this litigation," I said. "That's why he stated that I was the one who said that the only way to get the Church to pay attention was to hit them where it hurts, in the pocketbook. I remember the day he said it; I thought it was odd that he even stated that. And then he puts in his notes that I said it. That's just completely untrue. What would he have to gain from that? I don't know. I don't know what his thinking is."

I was sure by now, though. Dr. O's recordkeeping system was a complete mess and many of his comments fabrications, and if this case ever went to trial, my lawyers and expert witnesses would tear him apart. He'd be ruined professionally. The doctor was deliberately giving Wonio false, damaging information to use against me, to get me to back down and not go to trial.

"I just know what's true and not true," I said. "That's why we subpoenaed his tape recordings. I know he has tape recordings; he recorded sessions on many, many occasions. He's well known for doing that."

Wonio leaned forward. "How do you know he was tape-recording sessions?"

"Because it was almost one of the first things he talked about. He'd ask, 'Do you have your tape recorder?' and if I didn't, he'd use his."

Wonio asked me if I had any tapes of the sessions, and I told him no, I'd erased them or thrown them away because they were irrelevant to me at the time.

"If you're trying to get at whether I got rid of evidence for this proceeding," I said, "no, I did not. If I have anything, it's been provided to you. I have been completely forthcoming about everything you've asked for."

"Why did you make tapes of your sessions with Dr. O in the first place?" Wonio asked.

"He asked me to do so specifically. He always brought it up. The very first thing he'd indicate when I walked into his office was that he wanted these sessions taped so that if there was a discrepancy, we could go back and figure it out. He specifically talked about

CHAPTER THIRTY-NINE

that from the very first time I talked with him. A couple of times he got upset because I didn't have my tape recorder with me. Then he'd use his. So I know he's lying about a couple of things. He's hiding tapes that I know he has, or he's destroyed them. You can probably find out through other patients of his. He has quite an extensive thing he uses to tape the sessions. It's like a big boom box thing with a double recorder. He's got another smaller one on his desk."

"How many sessions did you tape?" Wonio asked.

"A couple. I didn't think about bringing a tape recorder every time I went to see my psychiatrist. He's lying to you guys when he says he doesn't have those tapes."

"Why didn't you keep your tapes if he was so emphatic about the fact that it ..."

"You've got to understand that at the time, recording the sessions wasn't a big deal to me. I was suffering from pain, from a divorce, from a lot of different things. A tape recorder was not at the top of my list. It was irrelevant. Besides, he had two of 'em in his office, and I knew that if I didn't bring mine, the session was going to get recorded anyway. I think it's kind of interesting that now all of a sudden they disappear, because you'd be able to go through them and then you'd be saying, 'Jack Doe is telling the truth.'"

"Well," Wonio said, "I'd like to be able to verify that."

"I'd love for you to verify that, because this is ridiculous."

"What's ridiculous?"

"These ... your ... the accusations that I'm making about his notes not being true. You're pretty much insinuating that I'm the one who's lying, because why would this doctor ... why would he lie, or make inaccurate notes? Why would he do such a thing? I wish I had the tape so you could listen to it and ask him, 'Why would you say that, Dr. O? Why would you say that your patient said that?' I'd love to be sitting in the room. I can't wait until we get to him."

"That will be tomorrow, I believe," Wonio said. He frowned. "Is there something wrong with me reading these records and asking you whether they're accurate or not?"

I tried to explain why I was upset; that my anger was primarily toward the Church, that I didn't deserve being treated this way, that my doctor, who was supposed to help me, was lying about me, and that I had to sit here and go through this.

"It's on my mind all the time," I said. "I leave town every weekend just to get away from it."

I took a deep breath. "I think this would be a good time for a break."

Wonio agreed.

Afterward, Wonio resumed quizzing me about my taping the sessions. How many times had I done it? Less than five, I guessed. Had I tape-recorded any sessions with any other mental health care providers? No. When was the last time I recorded a session with Dr. O? I couldn't remember.

Finally he let it go and shifted to O's tapes. "Did you say you've actually seen a collection of his tapes?" he asked.

"He has a large collection behind his desk," I said. "He has 'em all over. He has some on his desk, some next to the recorder, and a bunch by his boom box and in the computer area behind his desk."

He dropped that line of questioning, and we jumped from topic to topic. Patty, my back pain, Michelle, pain medication, quitting smoking. Dr. O's notes continued to be cryptic, contradictory, and sometimes blatantly untrue or fabricated.

"The doctor apparently quotes himself here," Wonio said. "He says, 'So let's say you get caught with tax evasion and the book gets thrown at you. How would you feel?' And then he has you saying that would be bad. Is that a conversation you had with him on that date?"

"No," I said. "This greatly disturbs me. I don't know why we would talk about tax evasion, because I pay all my taxes. I pay everything. I pay all my employee contributions. I pay quite a bit in taxes."

We went over a few more of Dr. O's comments. None contained accusatory or incriminating statements about me. Wonio's attitude had changed; he seemed finished, almost anxious to wrap things up.

CHAPTER THIRTY-NINE

Then Brian Fairfield, the lawyer who represented Wiebler, took over.

Fairfield was much less aggressive, almost friendly, and his questions were on material already covered. What were my flashbacks like and when did they start; how did I do in school; when did I start drinking alcoholically; who was the attorney for my second divorce; that sort of thing. He skipped around and didn't pursue anything in much detail. It was if he were checking to see if he'd gotten his basic facts straight.

"How did you know Dr. O filed bankruptcy?" he asked.

"I got a phone call from my mom," I said. "She read it in the paper."

"I think that's all I have for now," he said. "Thank you for your time."

The videographer said, "We're off the record at 12:44 P.M."

We'd started at 9:18 A.M. Today's session had lasted a little over three hours. Where the last deposition had traumatized me, today's had actually empowered me. The depositions had had exactly the opposite effect that I believed Wonio had worked so hard to obtain. I felt he wanted to intimidate me so I'd settle and do anything to avoid a trial. But now I wanted one.

My fear had always been that the public would be repulsed and back away from me when they heard the details of my abuse, particularly if Wonio took me apart in the trial like he had tried to do in the depositions. But I'd come to the point where I felt there was nothing more the diocese could do to me. I felt shredded, raped. And I was furious.

Let's lay it all out on the table, I thought. *Let's see what the community says. At least they'll hear the truth. Let's see how it goes over when you blame a seven-year-old kid. And how are you gonna get by that initial meeting with Wiebler, when he admitted to molesting children, and Bishop Franklin admitted the abuse happened, and offered compensation?*

The only ammunition Wonio had was Dr. O's testimony. That made Wonio's case a house of cards, because his testimony was a pack of lies and fabrications.

You can get away with this now, I thought, *cause me pain and rip me up. But the jury will deliberate one hour, and they'll come back and they'll smoke you. So bring it on. Is this all you got?*

CHAPTER FORTY

FATHER B'S DEPOSITION was at 1:30 the same day. It took less than an hour. It was basically a quick fact-checking session, and the facts checked. Wonio was courteous to Father B, and of course Father B was courteous back, even calling Wonio by his first name. "Well, as I said, Rand, we're part of a support group that meets at least weekly …"

Despite his practical awareness of real life, there's an innocence about Father B that seems to defuse antagonism and frustrate manipulation and threats. I think if the devil himself grilled Father B, the priest would take it in stride. I can see him saying, "Hey, Lucifer, lighten up," and I can see the devil sighing and thinking, *I'm not gonna get anywhere with this guy.*

My mother's deposition started at 2:23 P.M. that afternoon. I called her afterward. She was upset, and furious.

"It was one of the worst things I've ever been through," she said. "I was fairly relaxed and comfortable when I went in. I thought it was no big deal. I had nothing to hide, and all I had to do was tell the truth. I thought he'd respect me because I was the mother. "He acts nice, and you think he's your friend, but he's not. He kept asking me the same questions over and over, trying to trip me up.

As the process went on, I got more and more nervous. My heart was thumping. I kept thinking, *They think I'm a liar. They think I'm stupid.* I knew what he was doing, but I couldn't help how I felt. I think he deliberately made me nervous, and that makes me very angry."

I saw the transcript of her deposition a few days later. Wonio had pushed her for details that had little to do with the case and that she'd have little reason to remember, and he'd invaded her feelings. For example, he asked, "Did Bill and Jeff start CCD classes right away after you joined at Lourdes?"

"I don't remember," my mother said. At this point she was already rattled. "I do not remember. I don't know."

"Did you get to know any of their CCD teachers or people involved in the program?"

"Not until later. One woman, and she happened to live in the apartment building also, and ... but I didn't really get to know her. I knew who she was."

"Who was that?"

"Amy Reams."

"Amy Reams?"

"Her name is changed now."

Wonio persisted. "What is it now?"

"She changed it back to her maiden name of Campanelli, or Campanile."

"Campanail?"

"I'm not sure."

"Does she still live around here?"

And so forth. He pried into personal matters, pretending to feel bad about it. He asked her if she remembered when I left the church and hid in her car during my First Communion.

"No, I don't remember that," she said.

"Does that sound like something you would remember if it had happened?" Wonio asked. I felt he was playing her off against my testimony that it had happened, hoping for a contradiction.

"Not necessarily," she said. "It was a time in my life when there were a lot of things going on with me and my family and my own inner problems of being a single parent."

CHAPTER FORTY

He jumped on that. "Well, without prying too much—and I don't mean to get too personal—can you tell me what those things were going on in your life that make you believe you might not necessarily remember an event of that nature?"

Now she had to prove that she had a good reason not to remember an event that he had announced was important. She felt obligated to describe working, and struggling with finances, and raising children alone. My mother is not a complainer, and I know it bothered her to do it.

He very professionally kept her on the defensive. He asked her about problems between Wally and me, about exactly when Wiebler got involved with us boys, about how I told her about the abuse, and so on.

He ended with a flourish of aggression and dominance. He asked, "The last sentence of the first paragraph of that statement you prepared, would you please read that aloud?"

She read, "'They also spent some time individually with Wiebler on different occasions.'"

"What can you tell me about those individual sessions?"

"I can't tell you anything about 'em. I don't ... I don't recall where they went or what they did."

He repeated the same questions.

"Did they, in fact, have individual times with him, as you state here?"

"As far as I can recollect, yes."

"But you can't tell me anything about them, is that right?"

"No, I cannot. I don't know what they did or where they went."

"Sounds like it's something fairly hazy in your memory," Wonio said. "Is that a fair statement?"

"Yes, it is," my mother agreed.

"Has Bill ever told you about being abused by anyone other than Wiebler?

"Not until this came about did I learn of the abuse at the bowling alley."

Wonio jumped instantly on the word "at." He asked, "Did Bill say this actually happened at the bowling alley?"

"He didn't say where." She didn't know where; she'd just said "at" as a manner of speech. But it was an opening, and Wonio attacked. "Well, you just testified that he said he had been abused at the bowling alley. Is that what he told you?"

Of course, she had "testified" that I had "said" no such thing. But he had succeeded in confusing her.

"Well, yes," she said, "then it …"

He cut her off before she could say more and possibly clarify the point; he'd gotten what he wanted. "Thank you. I have no further questions."

He left my mother feeling that she had somehow hurt my case. And feeling humiliated.

I wanted him in court.

CHAPTER FORTY-ONE

DR. O'S DEPOSITION was on June 14 and lasted exactly one hour. When I read the transcript, I laughed aloud at some of his responses. I also cursed mightily at others.

After preliminary questions about dates, reasons for treatment, and so forth, Wonio got to the point.

"Doctor," he asked, "when you meet with your patients, is it your customary practice to tape-record your sessions with them?"

"Not always," Dr. O said.

"Sometimes you do so?"

"I usually ask them to tape the session, or if I record the session, I usually give the tape to the patient. I don't keep my own."

I laughed at that. His office was full of tapes, stacks of them everywhere, all labeled with patient names and session dates.

Wonio continued. "So if you had recorded any sessions with Mr. Christman, would you have given him the tape?"

"Yes, sir. It would be with his permission."

"Is it your customary practice not to keep the session tape but to give it to the patient?"

"It is my customary practice not to keep the session tape unless I tell the patient I'm going to keep one."

"And," Wonio concluded, "did you keep any of your tapes of sessions with Mr. Christman?"

"No, sir."

It was a bald-faced lie, but it handily disposed of the problem of having to produce any tapes. With that Wonio dropped the topic, evidently satisfied with the answer. No intense grilling or attempts to catch Dr. O in a contradiction despite my repeated statements that he had tapes of all my sessions and I had none. Apparently Wonio believed the doctor without question. It was obvious who he didn't believe.

There was some discussion of Dr. O's diagnosis of me, which was that he felt I was bipolar and had post-traumatic stress disorder. Then, while explaining the correlation between these conditions and Wiebler, the doctor said that, "The incidents with Father Wiebler were never mentioned until May of 2002. I did not know he considered it a serious issue, because throughout this time I was seeing him almost every day, because my focus was that he was going to kill himself. Never between April 2 to May did he mention the priest. So when he brought up the name of the priest in May, it came as a total surprise to me."

Of course it had been a surprise to him; it had been to me, too. I hadn't had the memory until late April 2002.

"What do you think is the source of his original affective disorder and post-traumatic stress disorder?" Wonio asked.

"I can confidently say," Dr. O replied, "that my belief system says it is genetic." He went on to explain in some detail the chromosomes associated with these disorders and how my family displayed them.

"If we were to assume that Mr. Christman was, in fact, abused by William Wiebler," Wonio said, "what effect would that have on his affective disorder or post-traumatic stress disorder?"

"This is where I'm very troubled," Dr. O replied, "because while he came in a very urgent way and I saw him every day and encouraged him to call me or e-mail me any time he needed to, never in the first month did he mention Bill Wiebler. If it was

CHAPTER FORTY-ONE

really that intense of causation, it would have been foremost in his discussion. This is why he took me by surprise."

Of course I hadn't mentioned it the first month; I hadn't had the memory yet.

"When did he eventually tell you that he had been abused by Wiebler?" Wonio asked. "Did he say that it was a recovered memory of some kind?"

"I asked him that," Dr. O said. "What led me to ask was because he was talking about the coverage on CNN and FOX about the scandal in Boston. He denied that it was a recovered memory."

I swore loudly. He had told me it was a recovered memory. I had accepted that because he was my psychiatrist.

"For the record," Dr. O continued, "my understanding of recovered memory as it applies to therapy is that a lot of so-called recovered memory is induced by hypnosis and may also be induced by a suggestion on the part of the therapist. Never in my sessions with Mr. Christman did I do hypnosis with him, nor did I suggest that a priest had sexually abused him. In fact, this came as a surprise to me because he was so anti-Church."

When I had told the doctor about my memory of Wiebler, he had told me that suddenly recovered memories of abuse were perfectly normal.

Dr. O went into more detail about bipolar and post-traumatic stress disorder, saying my father's extreme abuse was probably the main cause of my PTSD. Then Wonio asked the big question: "Why do you believe he was milking his diagnosis to get money from the Catholic Church?"

"Because," Dr. O replied, "at the time I really could not believe that the two isolated incidents with Father Wiebler were as severe as what was happening with his ex-wife Michelle and the abuse he received from his father. To me, those were super-ordinate. I thought the Wiebler thing was background noise."

Maybe to him, I thought. I knew Wonio liked that answer.

A question came up about the age at which I'd been abused by the bowling coach. Dr. O claimed that at first I'd said I was nine, and then 12. Wonio asked, "Did you find that unusual that the age was different?"

"Yes, sir," Dr. O said. "He told me he has problems with his memory. That's the reason I told him to tape the sessions; because after the first session he told me I never said something, and I said, 'I mentioned that in our last session.' So I said, 'I suggest you tape and you listen to those tapes.' An example of that was the age."

"Did he tape the sessions?"

"Yeah, he did. He had his own digital tape recorder.

"How frequently did he tape?"

"Every time, until toward the end when he became frustrated with me."

That blatant lie was Dr. O's reason to not produce the tapes that would show his testimony was false.

The rest of the deposition dealt with small details, with Dr. O explaining a couple of therapy techniques. Wonio finished with what I felt was a reasonable question.

"Doctor, do you have any hard feelings, or any feelings, toward Mr. Christman?"

"I have negative feelings toward Mr. Christman," Dr. O said. "The kind of things he said in his deposition with you were very inflammatory and very personal. He was calling me a nut case—he was calling me insane—which I thought was uncalled for."

"I did, in fact, provide you with a copy of the transcript of the first day of his deposition," Wonio said. "And you've read it?"

"Yes, sir. It took me from 7 P.M. to 10:30 P.M. to read that."

Wonio had given Dr. O a copy of my first deposition, knowing what I'd said about him? It was undoubtedly legal, maybe even standard practice; my lawyers had given me the transcripts of Loftus's and Franklin's depositions by Levien the previous summer. But the reason for Wonio's timing seemed obvious—to let Dr. O read my deposition just before his own deposition had the predictable results of prejudicing him against me and giving him time to prepare answers to protect himself. Like his lie that he always gave the tapes to the client.

CHAPTER FORTY-ONE

The questions I'd been asked in my deposition, and my answers, were so intimate and personal that I had naively assumed they'd be kept at least moderately private, at least until the trial. I never even suspected that they'd be immediately turned over to Dr. O; I assumed, naively again, that Wonio wouldn't want to taint a witness. It might have been legal, but it seemed sleazy to me. It seemed obvious to me that Wonio didn't want the truth; if he had he would have questioned Dr. O more closely about my concerns without letting him know their origin. But he evidently accepted everything O said, in his interrogatories and his deposition, without question.

"Doctor, the feelings that you have about Mr. Christman," Wonio continued, "have they had any effect at all on the testimony or opinions you've expressed today?"

"It would be a gross disingenuousness to say it didn't," Dr. O admitted.

Wonio then asked if his conclusions about the causes of my condition were based on his professional background, not on his feelings toward me. Dr. O said his professional opinion, formed before his personal feelings, was still the same: I suffered from bipolar affective disorder and post-traumatic stress disorder.

Brian Fairfield questioned Dr. O very briefly. Interestingly, there was another inconsistency, and to my mind an important one.

"But you believe," Fairfield said, "that the April 30, 2002 appointment was the first time that he was talking about abuse at the hands of a priest?"

Astonishingly, Dr. O said, "I don't think so. I think he mentioned it briefly before that session."

Now he was saying it was late April when I'd told him, not May like he'd said earlier. So much for his statement that he was very troubled by my not mentioning the abuse during our first sessions. I hadn't had the memory until late April; now it seemed obvious that I'd told Dr. O as soon as it happened.

Fairfield didn't seem interested in, or even aware of, the inconsistency. Wonio said nothing, either, but I knew he was too sharp to miss it. He would have been all over me if I'd made a similar mistake.

On June 15, Wonio wrote to Carrie and said, "I'm sure it comes as little surprise to you that I believe the complexion of the case has changed dramatically as result of discovery completed so far. There are numerous inconsistencies in your client's story. Your client's deposition testimony did not help his cause, and the testimony of Dr. O seems fatal to your client's case. Any argument that Dr. O is prejudiced against your client or is somehow not telling the truth will likely not be well received by a jury. After all, Dr. O didn't start to believe that your client was milking his diagnosis recently—that was his opinion on May 6, 2002."

He concluded with, "I wonder if you and your client would consider a cost-of-defense settlement offer. On the basis of the current record, I'm not going to be able to recommend an offer near to the amount you previously discussed with the diocese ... I'm not even sure the insurance company will consider making an offer ..."

My testimony was full of inconsistencies? Wonio had forced me to tell and retell the same incidents, and if he had found any inconsistencies, he would have jumped on them. The letter was a blatant attempt to intimidate and threaten me.

The next day Carrie responded, "Obviously our opinions differ in regard to the discovery so far. We believe the depositions show the profound negative effects the abuse has had on our client. We believe Dr. O's statements were well beyond how you interpret them. Our last offer was for $300,000 ... we would certainly be more than willing to explore any options for settlement."

She concluded with, "Judge Pelton ... strongly encouraged that we sit down and try to settle this. He offered the use of Judge Schoenthaler as a settlement judge, or suggested that we obtain a mediator and submit this case to mediation. We are open to options for resolutions."

Then Carrie set dates for the depositions of Loftus, Franklin and Wiebler. Wonio definitely didn't want that to happen; he knew

CHAPTER FORTY-ONE

full well their testimony would help my case. At least mediation was back on the table, but God forbid that direct action result.

On June 21, Wonio wrote, "I have received your Notice of Depositions.... A major part of the value in agreeing to mediate the claim is to avoid the great expense of performing discoveries of this type." Then came a teaser: "The more money saved on legal expenses might translate into more money available for settlement."

Maybe he *was* interested in negotiating. At the very least it hinted that he knew his case wasn't as strong as he was insisting. He concluded with, "I request that you withdraw the Motion to Compel and hold taking the depositions in abeyance until we have had an opportunity to proceed with mediation."

By then my lawyers had contacted three expert witnesses. One was Dr. Mic Hunter, a psychologist and nationally recognized expert on the effect of sexual abuse on boys. He had written a number of books and articles on the topic and was a frequent expert witness in abuse cases. Another was Dr. Mark Schwartz, a psychologist internationally known for his knowledge of sexual trauma. He'd also written numerous articles, and a book on sexual abuse.

The third was the legendary Father Tom Doyle, a Dominican priest with a doctorate in canon law and five different Master's degrees. In 1984 he had become involved with child sexual abuse by Catholic clergy, and he was now an expert in both the canonical and pastoral dimensions of the issue. Father Doyle worked with victims, their families, accused priests, bishops and other high-ranking Church officials. He had interviewed 2,000 victims of clerical sexual abuse in the U.S. alone and was the only priest to testify in court in more than 200 cases as to the legal liability of the Church. He did lectures and seminars for clergy and lay groups throughout the U.S. and was an international consultant/court expert in clerical abuse cases. The Church, of course, considered him a renegade and had relieved him of his position in Germany as an Air Force chaplain, supposedly because of a minor pastoral disagreement with his archbishop. Basically, they had fired him.

After more legal dancing, mediation was tentatively scheduled for August 25. My lawyers kept the pressure on and scheduled the deposition of Loftus on August 15. Wonio said Loftus couldn't make that date because she'd be on family vacation. Carrie pointed out that the last time we had wanted to depose Loftus she was on vacation, and we needed to take her deposition as soon as possible. Then she subpoenaed Loftus to appear on the 15th.

Wonio responded, "Irene Loftus was served with a subpoena last night ... she will be out of the city next week and cannot attend her deposition ... we'll make her available at a mutually convenient time after her return."

So Loftus's deposition was moved ahead again. Then Wonio asked that mediation be moved ahead to September 28.

"OK," I said, "but that's it. No more stalling. I've had it. If he wants to postpone it again, move it ahead again, no mediation. We go to trial."

Levien was scheduled to depose Wiebler on August 25, and Carrie and Cindy were to depose him the next day. On August 19 Brian Fairfield, Wiebler's lawyer, wrote to Carrie and Levien and said that Wiebler would not be at his scheduled depositions because he claimed his health and "other factors" wouldn't let him travel. "I can do nothing," Fairfield added, "because he has terminated the services of my firm."

Levien responded, "The Iowa Rules of Civil Procedure do not provide that a properly noticed deposition can be cancelled due to unspecified 'health and other factors.' Your Motion to Withdraw does not alter your client's responsibility to attend.... Your letter provided no evidence of any health problems ... I assume by asserting this he is intending to waive any claim of physician/patient privilege, and I enclose a full and complete release of all medical information [because] he apparently now is placing his health directly at issue in this case.

"At this time, I am unwilling to voluntarily cancel his deposition scheduled August 25. I intend to appear with a court reporter and the videographer. If your client does not attend the deposition, sanctions and costs will be sought against him. I must appear at his deposition to preserve the record for obtaining the costs and expenses."

CHAPTER FORTY-ONE

Carrie wrote Fairfield in kind, also saying she'd attend Wiebler's deposition and would seek judgment against him for sanctions and cost if he didn't show up.

The ongoing Irene Loftus deposition dueling and dodging game continued. Wonio offered August 26 as a date. My lawyers obviously couldn't do that date because it conflicted with Wiebler's deposition, so they asked for the 29th, the following Monday. Wonio replied that Loftus was now teaching a university class on Mondays, Wednesdays and Fridays, so she wasn't available those days. He offered five other dates. My lawyers picked one. Alas, said Wonio, Loftus couldn't make that one either. And so on.

The day of Wiebler's depositions arrived, but Wiebler didn't. He blew us off. Why not? He had nothing to gain, and a lot to lose. He was also—unintentionally, I'm sure—helping the diocese. Any admission of guilt, or its blatant reality under good questioning, would have sealed our case.

There was nothing we could do about his being a no-show, and Wiebler knew it. We couldn't go after him financially; he was penniless. I couldn't help wondering if Wonio had known Wiebler had no intention of showing, and in my paranoia I even wondered if the diocese had contacted him and asked him not to come. It was interesting to me that Wonio had made no attempt to block Wiebler's deposition, like he seemed to be doing with Loftus's.

Things were heating up, information was accumulating, and processes were getting finished. The December 5 trial date was only about two months off, and everyone was hustling to wrap things up in case it actually happened.

On August 30, Wonio deposed my fiancé, Patty, my stepfather, Wally, my uncle Roger Mall, and my friend Forrester McCleery. The depositions were brief; a couple only lasted 15 minutes. I read the depositions; there was nothing of use to Wonio in any of them.

Father Doyle was unable to be an expert witness in our case, but Drs. Hunter and Schwartz agreed to be. They'd both examined our information, and Schwartz said we had an "amazingly strong case."

"Don't worry about Dr. O," Carrie told me. "These guys will take him apart."

I was hot to go to court. I wanted the public to hear what Wonio and the diocese had done to me.

As agreed, my lawyers gave Wonio the names of our expert witnesses on September 1. Wonio said he wanted their opinions so he could hire experts to counter what they said and that he should be allowed until November 1st to have me examined by an independent medical doctor. He also wanted to extend the discovery deadline to November 18, even though that was past the mediation date of September 28. Wonio said the diocese would know by November 10th if they wanted to settle or go to trial.

My lawyers said they'd provide our experts' opinions by October 1st.

The wrangling back and forth, of course, continued unabated. My lawyers asked again for the 30 interrogatories they'd requested months before. There was no response, so they threatened filing a second Motion to Compel. They also asked for other material that hadn't been produced. Wonio said they had it already, which, of course, they didn't.

Then Wonio requested that they depose Loftus on October 7. The mediation was scheduled for September 28. Was he maneuvering to move the mediation ahead again? Or, as usual, just making Loftus unavailable?

A little later he told us that the diocese had joined in a "Motion to Replace" the judge who was to rule on our discovery disputes, because the diocese didn't like how he had ruled on previous, similar discovery disputes. Evidently the ruling hadn't been in their favor. Wonio also asked to schedule the depositions of Drs. Schwartz and Hunter.

I was sure there would be no mediation.

CHAPTER FORTY-TWO

IN LATE SEPTEMBER, I got a call from Carrie. The mediation would be held on the 28th, as scheduled. I couldn't believe it would actually happen.

I went to Carrie and Cindy's office on the morning of the mediation meeting. I was frightened; I was sure the meeting would just be another attack. Cindy, Carrie and I argued before we left. They wanted to talk about the possibility of settling, but I wanted to go to court. I was furious, almost yelling. I wanted the diocese exposed, judged and crushed. I wanted Wonio humiliated and his reputation damaged. I wanted Dr. O destroyed and his license revoked so he couldn't damage any more people. I wanted the public to see what the Church did to children. Forgiveness? No way.

I was shaking with rage and fear. "I don't care what they say today," I said. "We're going to court. I've had enough. Get ready, because this is going to be short. This is going nowhere. I'm going in there and telling them all exactly what I think. We're going to court. We've been this far, I've been beat up this much, and I can wait another month." Every intimate detail of the abuse and of most of my entire life had been recorded and filmed in front of numerous people, and the information had been passed around. What more could they do to me?

We all drove together to Lane & Waterman's offices in downtown Davenport. Wonio's secretary met us in the waiting room and took us to a large conference room, where we sat down. My hands were shaking.

About ten minutes passed. Then Wonio, a priest, and another man, who turned out to be the representative for the diocese's insurance company, walked into the room. With them came the judge in charge of the mediation. We all stood.

My face was rigid with fury; I could barely restrain myself.

We all sat down, and the judge talked in general about what the mediation was about. He said he hoped that both sides would keep an open mind and try to come to some resolution.

The priest stood and introduced himself as Father Gruss. He said he'd been chancellor for just a few months. Then he looked directly at me, and spoke.

He said that he had looked at my case thoroughly and wanted to say that on behalf of the Catholic Church, his colleagues and himself, he was extremely sorry for what had happened to me. He wanted me to know that he was sorry for the way my case had been handled and that many mistakes had been made that had actually caused me more harm.

"Ever since I became familiar with your case," he said, "I have prayed for you daily."

I was stunned. It was the last thing I expected. I stared at him, and at that moment God touched me and gave me the grace to see clearly. There was total sincerity in Gruss's face. He meant what he was saying. It wasn't a question of believing him; I saw that he was truthful.

I physically felt my anger and fear drain away.

"I hope and pray that today we could at least in part end your suffering and come to some sort of conclusion," Gruss said. "I'm truly sorry for how you've suffered, and I apologize for the Church, for any harm they've done."

Father Gruss stopped speaking and remained standing. Then Wonio stood.

CHAPTER FORTY-TWO

"Bill," he said, "I apologize for the way your case has been handled. We made some mistakes in the way you were treated."

He explained in detail that he didn't have any experience with abuse cases. I got the impression that he was saying he was sorry if he'd harmed me in any way, but he hoped I understood that he was just trying to do his job. Was he sincere? He seemed to be. But nothing like Father Gruss.

I glanced at Carrie and Cindy. They were both in shock. The apologies had caught us all totally off guard.

I couldn't quite grasp all of what Father Gruss had said. I asked, in disbelief, "Do you really pray for me daily?"

"Yes, I do," he said. "I always will."

The realization that this man, who knew nothing about me except that I had suffered at the hands of a pedophile priest and the Church, would spend the rest of his life including me in his daily prayers staggered me. I believe in prayer; I've seen it work. I felt hope. Maybe I could still leave this all behind me.

My resentment toward the Church evaporated. It had been misdirected all along. It was the organization, the bureaucracy, of the Church that had fought me, savaged me, lashed out at me in fear itself and turned away when I sought help. But two priests had reached their hands out to me to help heal me. Father B, and now this man.

They were the Church.

I had just received the apology I had wanted for so long. Then another revelation came to me: Father B had apologized for the Church from the very beginning. He felt deep sorrow that it had happened. If anyone was a true representative of the Church, he was.

Wonio's apology was less important to me. But I had no resentment left toward him. He was secondary to all this; simply a tool. He would disappear from my life. Franklin? He was a man overwhelmed. I felt sadness for him.

I no longer had any desire to go to court. I felt no need for revenge. I simply wanted this finished.

The judge explained the mediation process. Carrie, Cindy and I would stay in the room. The others would all go into another room and discuss an offer, and the judge would come back in our room and present it to us. We could reject it, accept it or counteroffer. When they left, I told Carrie and Cindy that I would do the negotiating.

A short time later the judge came back and asked if we'd accept $125,000.

"No," I said. "We still want $300,000. They know that."

"This is just the first offer," the judge said. "Don't take offense; this is how these things go. They usually go up in $25,000 increments. I just want you to know how this goes."

"Well," I said, "they're doing better, but it's still unacceptable. Tell them to try for the mid-$200,000s." I'd already decided that $200,000 would be acceptable.

He left, and then returned. "They've gone to $160,000."

I said, "Tell them if they'll accept $180,000, we can all go to lunch."

He left, and in a few minutes they all came out. Wonio remained standing and said, "We accept your offer of $180,000. The only stipulation is that you don't go after Wiebler. We want it all resolved now."

My lawyers and I had previously talked about the possibility of suing Wiebler himself, separate from our lawsuit with the diocese. But I had no stomach for another drawn-out legal action, and Wiebler was penniless anyway. I agreed that we would not attempt to sue him.

I had one more thing to add. "If you're thinking of any confidentiality clause or gag order as a result of this settlement," I said, "you can forget it, or the settlement's off. I may be writing a book about this." They were fine with that.

I felt the chaos of the last three and a half years ebbing. I could breathe. No more legal turmoil, no more agitation, no more resentment against the diocese or Wonio. I'd deal with Wiebler in a different way, in my own mind. Father B would help me.

CHAPTER FORTY-TWO

The settlement was handwritten on one sheet of blank paper. It said simply that the diocese agreed to pay me $180,000 to settle the case, under the conditions that the Catholic Church was no longer liable for damages resulting from sexual abuse by Wiebler, and that we would not pursue compensation from Wiebler.

The atmosphere in the room had lightened considerably. I told Father Gruss, "I was taken back by your comments. I was in shock. I haven't been treated like this during this entire process. I want you to know I believe what you said."

"I meant it," he said. "If you ever need anything, if you ever need to talk, don't hesitate to contact me."

When I shook his hand and looked in his face, I physically felt his compassion.

Everybody relaxed for a bit, and then Father Gruss, Wonio, and the insurance agent, who had never said anything the entire time, excused themselves. The judge asked me, Carrie and Cindy if we wanted to go to lunch. He said he was paying.

While we ate, he said he appreciated my open-mindedness. "I've heard plenty of apologies during mediations," he said, "and they don't usually do much good; in fact, sometimes they just stir up more anger. I was happy and surprised that you accepted theirs."

"They were sincere," I said, "and I'm pretty good about apologies. That's all I wanted from the beginning."

"That was the smoothest mediation I've ever been involved in," he said.

I took the rest of the day off. I called my mom immediately, and then Father B. I told him the whole story.

"I forgave them, Father," I said. "I forgave Wonio. I forgive Franklin, too. He didn't mean any harm, really, he was just in way over his head."

Father B kept telling me how happy he was for me. I could almost hear him thinking, *You still have to forgive Wiebler.* But he knew enough not to say it, and I shoved the thought from my mind and heart.

On October 4, Wonio sent a brief letter to my lawyers, enclosing a check for $90,000 from Kingdom Come, the diocese investment entity, and another check for $90,000 from Travelers Indemnity, the diocese insurance company.

The legal ordeal was over.

A few weeks later I went to Bob Noonan's again to trap. I told him how the case had been settled.

"Sounds like there's a book here now," he said. The following spring we began work on it.

CHAPTER FORTY-THREE

ON SEPTEMBER 19, 2006, the *Quad City Times* reported that a jury trial had awarded Michl Uhde $1.5 million for sexual abuse he had suffered at the hands of Monsignor Thomas Feeney. The article quoted Uhde as saying he didn't care if the jury awarded him one cent; he hoped his lawsuit would push the Davenport diocese to release more information about abusive priests.

"They have done nothing but stonewall us," he said. "It has got to change."

This is crazy, I thought. *It's got to stop.*

I called Father B and told him to meet me at IHOP. I waited until he had a mouthful of pancakes, and then I said, "I want you to take me to Rome to see the Pope."

He didn't choke like I'd hoped, but he did look at me like I was crazy.

"I'm serious," I said. "You've been to Rome twice; you got connections. They dragged this Uhde case out even though they knew his complaint was legit, and it ended up damaging Uhde and the diocese. It happens all the time with these cases. It's a tragedy. I want to tell somebody important in Rome about how my case was handled; maybe it will help change things. Might as well go right to the top. The Pope deserves to hear this one."

Father B called Father Gruss and Bishop Franklin that day. Gruss looked into it immediately and e-mailed back that it could probably be arranged, and that Monsignor Robert Deeley seemed like the man to see. Deeley was an important official with the powerful Congregation for the Doctrine of the Faith (CDF) in the Vatican. The CDF oversees Catholic doctrine, and because of special canonical legislation, that included jurisdiction over clergy sex abuse of minors. Deeley's specific job at the CDF was working on clergy sex abuse.

An audience with Deeley sounded great, but I also wanted to hand-deliver a letter to the Vatican explaining the purpose of my visit and asking for an audience with the Pope. It was a long shot, but worth a try.

In early October, Father Gruss e-mailed me and said that I'd been granted a one-hour audience with Monsignor Deeley at 5 P.M. on November 14. On the morning of November 13, I was to present two letters at the Bronze Doors in the Vatican: one for Archbishop James Harvey, prefect of the Papal household; the other for the Holy Father himself, Pope Benedict XVI. Father B and I were ecstatic.

Father Gruss e-mailed me again a few days later to tell me that Wiebler had died of heart failure at 78. Strangely, I felt absolutely nothing. My only thought was, *Now he can't hurt kids anymore.*

On November 12, accompanied by my mother, Mary, and my brother, Jeff, I met Father B and Bob Noonan at Hotel Nova Domus in Rome. The next morning, the five of us made the 15-minute walk to the Vatican—and entered a world of grace and serendipity.

The massive brown brick walls of the Vatican, lined with windows, rose above us. Visitors, five or six abreast, slowly entered a wide gate on their way into the Vatican museum. We turned left and followed the long line around two complete corners. At its end was the arched entrance into the Piazza.

We walked under triple columns and stepped out into the bright sunlight of St. Peter's Square, a huge, circular open cobblestone area of almost four acres, capable of holding more than 300,000 people.

CHAPTER FORTY-THREE

At least a thousand people were scattered across it, but the crowd seemed thin in the wide space. A tall obelisk stood in the center, and St. Peter's Basilica loomed at the opposite end.

A line of visitors formed a dense procession around the square on our right, against the wall and under a roof supported by rows of tall columns. They were evidently all headed for the Basilica. The Bronze Doors were on the far right end of this colonnade, just before the Basilica, so we had to negotiate the line.

It was barely moving. We threaded our way through, and amazingly, people parted easily to let us pass. We busted that line; we met absolutely no resistance. Everyone was dressed casually, so maybe our suits helped us look like we were on an official errand, but it felt as if something more powerful was at play. Several times we met officials at security checkpoints, X-raying items people carried. I handed them the letters, they X-rayed them, handed them back, nodded and motioned us through.

In 20 minutes we were at the studded, metal panel Bronze Doors, set under a tall arch. They were open. Father B turned to the others and said, "Here's where Bill and I go in. Pray for us."

We went up several steps. The passage was about 20 feet tall and wide enough for at least four people to pass through abreast. A row of Swiss Guards, wearing medieval-looking red and blue striped uniforms and blue berets, and holding tall spears vertically erect, stood silent and motionless on each side of the opening. Two blocked the entrance. I approached one, explained why we were there, and handed him the letters.

To our knowledge, no one but Monsignor Deeley and a few others knew we were coming, or that the letters for Bishop Harvey and the Pope were legitimate. Certainly these guards didn't. The letters were in my standard business envelopes; there was nothing to indicate any official Church business besides the addressees.

The guard examined the letters briefly, paused—and then nodded. He spoke in broken English to the other guard, stepped back, and with his left hand waved us to enter. I was astonished. I had expected the letters would be taken from us at the Bronze

Doors. The guards stomped their feet and saluted as we passed between the two lines, as if we were dignitaries.

"What's with the V.I.P stuff?" I whispered to Father B.

"Beats me," he said, "but I like it." He straightened his back, stuck out his chest, raised his eyebrows, and swaggered slightly for a few steps in mock importance.

Two guards escorted us down a lofty, domed hallway. At the far end, two tall, extravagantly carved wooden doors stood open at the base of a set of wide, shallow, worn marble stairs. A second group of two guards there told us to go up one flight and in a door to the left. There, an official of some sort, in a suit and tie, met us. We explained why we were there. He paused for a moment, and then nodded and said, "Come this way."

We were getting used to the pause and the subsequent cooperation. It seemed to be the action of the day. At our every request there was always a pause, and then we would be allowed to proceed. To me it seemed that as each person considered our appeal, God said silently to them, "Let them pass," and they obeyed.

The man took us into an inner office, where a priest met with us. He seemed very busy, but when I told him why we were there and handed him the letters, he immediately dropped what he was doing and became attentive. Again came the pause, and then his attitude became serious.

"I think I can get it to Archbishop Harvey within the hour," he said. "But I doubt I can get it to the Holy Father before noon." He seemed apologetic.

Father B and I looked at each other, astonished. We'd hoped they'd be delivered during the week we'd be there. Again I had the sense of God arranging things.

I was so surprised by the ease of the whole transaction that I couldn't quite get it through my head that our mission had been accomplished, and I asked the priest twice more if he could make sure they'd be taken to Harvey or the Pope. The priest assured me they would. I was extremely excited that we seemed to be taken seriously. Why were two ordinary visitors being treated as if we were on an errand of importance?

CHAPTER FORTY-THREE

As we went back down the stairs, we were passed by a group of clergy going up. They were extravagantly dressed in formal attire, red caps and crosses.

"German bishops," Father B said. "There's a special delegation here to meet the Pope."

"I'm flabbergasted we were even allowed in here," I said.

He nodded in agreement. He seemed subdued. When we got to the bottom of the stairs and passed through the wooden doors, he stopped. I turned to face him and saw tears in his eyes. I wondered what was wrong.

He took my right hand in both of his, bowed his head, and started to speak in a low tone. I strained to hear and realized he was praying. He asked God that in my heart I forgive Wiebler for what he had done. He asked that I forgive the Church. He asked that any resentment or anger, or anything that would stand in the way of my healing, be removed from me.

As he prayed, I found that there was no strong objection in me to what he was asking. No violent reaction, no anger, no resistance. I participated in his prayer by lowering my head and accepting his words. Briefly, I forgot where I was.

Father B stopped and raised his head to look at me. His tears ran freely. I looked back at him, silent, and calmness filled me.

I looked across a wide battlefield covered with the devastation of a horrific battle that had gone on as far back as I could remember. Now it was utterly still. It was over. I had no sense of being a victor, but relief permeated me. I hadn't been destroyed. I had survived.

I felt cleansed.

I saw movement behind Father B and looked up to see the tall wooden doors at the foot of the marble staircase slowly start to close. Then they slammed shut, with a bang that echoed throughout the hallway.

That sound pierced my soul. It was as if a door had closed on part of my life. It was over and done. I am not a superstitious man, but I cannot dismiss the closing of those doors, at the end of our prayer, as a coincidence. That echoing bang was of great significance to me. A door had closed on a long, tortuous chapter of my life, and I sensed with calm certitude that a new one had begun.

I felt enormous affection for Father B and gratitude for his help, and tears blurred my eyes. I wouldn't have survived without him. He had stayed with me to the bitter end. He had fought for my soul. He was a true priest.

Back outside, my mother, brother and Bob could see in our faces that something had happened, but they didn't pry. We quietly joined the crowd entering St. Peter's Basilica. Inside, hundreds of other pilgrims filled the huge space with the buzz of conversation. Then, above the chatter, someone yelled, "Hey! Father B!"

We turned to see a grinning priest leading a delegation of children our way. Father B introduced him as Father Schowalter. I was blown away to hear that he was from St. Pius X in Rock Island, Illinois. He lived only miles from my home, and he was a classmate, neighbor and friend of Father B's. What were the chances of meeting him at that time in that crowd? Again, the sense of serendipity and benevolent guidance enveloped me.

St. Peter's Basilica was breathtaking. It was enormous in its height and width and vibrant with color. I sensed overwhelming power, and, behind it, antiquity.

Father B wanted us to visit the Chapel of the Blessed Sacrament before we left the Basilica. "It's the most solemn place in the Basilica for people to pray," he said.

The Blessed Sacrament was there at the altar, and there were rows of simple wooden pews in front with a dozen or so people kneeling in prayer. When we entered, Father B stayed back and gestured for me to stay with him. The others knelt in pews up front. Father B and I sat in the back left-hand corner, where we could talk privately.

He closed his eyes, was silent for several seconds, and then turned to me and spoke quietly. "Now is the time, in the presence of the Blessed Sacrament, the Holy Eucharist, to ask our Lord to forgive you and totally free you, Bill Christman, of any lingering doubts or lingering feelings that are negative against Bill Wiebler,

CHAPTER FORTY-THREE

and to ask Him to totally take you into His arms and forgive you and raise you up. Are you ready to do that, Bill Christman?"

I felt no doubt or hesitation. "Yes, I'm ready. I'm willing. I want that."

He took my hand and formally administered the Sacrament of Reconciliation. Then we said a prayer in our Father's name together, and stood up. This time there were no balloons or firecrackers, no slamming doors, no tears. But the calmness and peace returned, and I knew my connection with Wiebler was finished.

The CDF building was in the Vatican, and I wanted to make sure I knew where it was. A policeman gave us directions, and I rang the buzzer by the locked door. A priest let us in, and someone buzzed Deeley. Down the stairs came a tall man dressed in the casual priest's attire of black pants, black shirt and white clerical collar. He stuck his hand out. "I'm Bob Deeley," he said. "Can I help you?"

"I'm Bill Christman," I replied.

"I have a meeting with you tomorrow," he smiled.

"I don't want to bother you, and I won't take any of your time. I just wanted to know where your office was."

We visited for a few minutes. I liked him immediately. I had expected official clothing, a serious face and an air of importance, maybe arrogance. This man was open, relaxed and down-to-earth.

When we left, Deeley gave us directions to the Vatican's famous Scavi Tour of the excavations under St. Peter's Basilica. Father B wanted to see St. Peter's tomb. On the short walk, I said, "You told me this tour has to be booked months in advance. We're not gonna be able to just walk up and get in."

"Maybe somebody cancelled," he said cheerfully.

A priest was at the office gate in the tall stone building. Father B approached him and said, "We're only here for a few days. Is there any chance you can fit us in?"

"Just a minute," the priest said, and went back inside. He was out in seconds. "Can you go right now? It's the end of the tour guide's day, but he says he'll take you. Normally we only do groups of 12, but if you can do it now, he'll do a private tour for just the five of you."

Father B grinned. "God's our tour guide this week," he said.

We hadn't eaten breakfast yet, but we weren't going to pass this up. A young man took us through a low, tight arch and along a dim corridor lined with Christian and pagan burial sites. The passage gradually angled up; we were climbing what had been Vatican Hill 1,900 years ago. The footing was uneven at times as we went along narrow corridors, up stairs, past burial sites of saints and early popes, and then finally to what is thought to be St. Peter's tomb. The sense of antiquity was overwhelming.

As we blinked in the daylight back outside, I asked our guide if he knew of any place to eat nearby.

"You were my last tour," he said. "I'll take you to a great restaurant just outside the Vatican. On the way I can show you some other historical points of interest inside the Vatican and right outside."

Father B elbowed me. I rolled my eyes.

The guide and I chatted on the way to the restaurant. When I told him I worked with wildlife, he got excited and talked about his love for animals, and suddenly we were friends. I was long past being surprised by coincidences on this trip.

We ate outside the restaurant, on the sidewalk under tents. The narrow street was jammed with pedestrians, well over half of them in some sort of clerical garb. I had no idea there were so many different orders and sects.

"This is the spiritual center of the Catholic world," Father B said.

We headed back to the hotel. Bob and I left the others to try a shortcut. Within a few blocks we were completely confused, and the 15-minute walk turned into an hour-long search.

"God is our tour guide," Bob snickered.

"He's punishing you for your cynicism," I said.

Later, the priest who had taken our letters at the Bronze Door called Father B at the hotel to tell him that the letters were in Harvey's hands.

"V.I.P. treatment," Father B said. "Maybe we are important!"

CHAPTER FORTY-THREE

The next morning, we were getting ready to check out shops near the hotel when Father B's phone rang again. During the conversation he kept saying, "Thank you! We appreciate that! Thank you!" and nodding happily.

"That was Archbishop Harvey!" he said when he hung up. "He read your letter, and though the Pope won't have time to see you, he's reading the letter as we speak. Harvey wanted to thank you for bringing it and assure you that it was hand-delivered to the Holy Father."

V.I.P. indeed.

At 5 P.M. I met with Monsignor Deeley at the CDF building. He was again dressed simply, in black pants, black shirt and white clerical collar. The room felt cool after the heat we had been in outside. It had marble floors, ornate woodwork and leather furniture. We started with small talk; my impressions of Rome, his background. He was from Boston. Before Cardinal Ratzinger became Pope in 2005, he had asked Deeley and another canon lawyer from the United States to come to the CDF to deal with clergy sexual abuse. Deeley's original one-and-a-half year assignment had stretched out to five years, and he believed he'd be in Rome on this mission for an unlimited time.

I started my story with the meeting I'd had with Wiebler. When I described the priest's opening comment that I must have been an attractive boy, Deeley shook his head in disbelief. When I told him what Wiebler was wearing, he said, "What?" in astonishment.

"You're one of only a handful of victims who actually sat down with their perpetrators," Deeley said. "It might be helpful for some, but it can be extremely damaging if the priest is not at all remorseful. Wiebler obviously wasn't. His file shows a long history of abuse. That meeting should never have happened."

He was even more disturbed by my description of the long legal ordeal. A number of times he shook his head or put a hand over his face. When I described my depositions, he said, "Oh, no," and several times put his head down into his hands, covering his face completely.

When I finished, Deeley said, "The Church has every right to defend itself and investigate things. But if a priest's file shows that abuse has happened again and again, and the claim is clearly legitimate, there's no need to go through a long, painful, costly legal process like this. We have a lot more work to do. I wish we knew five or six years ago what we know now about the effects of abuse on victims. And we understand now that the disease of pedophilia is irreversible and that it gets worse with age."

I told him about Father B's work with me and how Father Gruss had apologized for the Church and prayed for me daily ever since becoming acquainted with my case in early 2005. I told Deeley I was deeply touched that while I was out working or doing whatever during the day, somewhere across town a man who barely knew me was asking God's help for me.

Deeley was delighted that I had accepted the grace of God. "We don't hear very much good news in this arena," he said.

"Harvey called me this morning to tell me the Pope read your letter," he continued. "I'm not surprised. This is an area of special importance to him. I worked directly with him on this issue before he became Pope, and I can tell you that he takes it very seriously. Fighting clergy sex abuse is one of his personal crusades. I've seen him agonize over victims' stories, how terrible it must be for victims to trust these ultimate authority figures and then be betrayed and abused. He's holding everyone's feet to the fire on this; he wants action. He's speeded up the process of laicizing offending priests, and he demands weekly updates on these cases."

Although he didn't say so, I got the distinct impression that Deeley was a personal friend of the Pope's. Deeley was undoubtedly a powerful man, yet he didn't act it. He was informal, personable and friendly. This was no aloof nobleman paying token lip service to an insignificant supplicant to get rid of him. This was a kind, sympathetic fellow human being who was sharing my pain and anxious to help.

I trusted him.

I had been almost destroyed by a Catholic priest and a Catholic bureaucracy, but in the final accounting I had been saved by Catholic

CHAPTER FORTY-THREE

priests. Real priests. Sincere, personal, down-to-earth and deeply committed men who wanted to be channels for the grace of God. And they were humble. There was no arrogance in any of them. Despite their widely varying rank, from parish pastor to diocese chancellor to a monsignor working directly with the Pope, they were fellow human beings. Without them, I would have died.

Deeley and I stood and shook hands. "I really appreciate your coming," he said, "and I'll definitely share what you said with my colleagues."

"I came to Rome for one reason," I told him. "I wanted to tell the Church that dragging victims through these legal ordeals, when the complaint is legitimate, is the worst thing they can do. It costs the Church much more to go through these lawsuits, and it destroys their credibility and the faith of their followers. It also devastates the victims. It re-victimizes them. In effect, the Church becomes partners with the original perpetrator. I hope my story helps alleviate the suffering of the victims and the Church."

The next day, my brother, Jeff, hired a tour guide named Maria. We got in a little van and Roberto, our smiling young driver, plunged us into utter chaos.

The streets, barely wide enough for two lanes of traffic, wound between vertical stucco walls to flat roofs a couple stories above. The narrow sidewalks were lined with endless doors into apartments and small businesses and crowded with people. Traffic was bumper to bumper both ways, small motor scooters dodged erratically around and between vehicles, and pedestrians darted back and forth across the streets. We moved forward just a bit slower than the foot traffic.

At the first intersection, a bus cut in front of us and stopped, and everything ground to a halt. The air rang with blaring horns. Gridlock.

Roberto and the bus driver got out and had what appeared to be a surprisingly friendly chat, laughing and nodding. The bus backed up what seemed to be one inch, Roberto squeezed through the impossibly tight gap without any screeching metal, and we were on our way again.

And so it went. At some intersections Roberto would stop to let a few vehicles pass, and then push his way through; at others he pushed through first, forcing the intersecting traffic to stop. It was a slow but steady forward ballet, with a multitude of drivers apparently agreeing telepathically on who should let who go by. There seemed to be an attitude of aggression and politeness at work simultaneously. Our van was a blood corpuscle among millions, pushed slowly but inexorably through tight veins and arteries by some distant, powerful pumping force.

We made our way steadily from one historical spot to another, our guide spouting long, detailed personal accounts of ancient citizens as she pointed. Rome was a bustling hive of modern shops, vehicles and sidewalk restaurants and ancient fountains, buildings and monuments. The blood and DNA of ancient Romans flowed visibly in the attractive, confident people who thronged the streets. The Eternal City.

We wound up on a steep one-way lane to a church on a hill and met a big bus coming down. It stopped and backed up until it could pull over to let us squeeze by with at least an inch to spare.

"Does the traffic always move this smoothly?" I asked our guide.

Maria rolled her eyes and lifted her hands in a palms-up gesture of exasperation. "Absolutely not!" she said. "You people must be blessed."

Father B smiled.

That night, Father B celebrated mass for the five of us in his hotel room. I stayed afterward to thank him, and his eyes got moist.

"Hey," I said, "don't get sappy on me."

"Tears of release, and relief," he said. "It happened. All the hopes and expectations of going to Rome have happened. All the suffering and work and prayer have brought us here, to the end. A good end. I always had faith it could."

EPILOGUE

I'VE CHANGED. MY extreme mood swings are gone. My fear has faded; some days I don't feel it at all. I'm much more clearheaded in emotional crises. I don't react violently. My thought processes are more normal and rational. When I get angry, it's for legitimate reasons, and I don't rage. I've quit hating and blaming.

When I came back from Rome, I got involved in a business with a man I thought was a friend. He stole thousands from the business. When I found out, I didn't explode in rage, shake with anxiety and confusion, feel like a failure, or mistrust all people because a single person had betrayed me. I talked the situation over with level-headed friends, thought about it until my mind was clear, and calmly ended the relationship. I accepted the financial loss, forgave the guy, and moved on.

Money isn't the obsession it used to be. During the current recession, my stock market holdings were wiped out, and for a while my business slowed to where I was barely making expenses. My old fear of business failure returned, but this time with a different face. This time I knew it wasn't me that was defective. It was the economy. I knew that if my business failed, I'd survive.

My back continued to bother me, and in December 2007 I had a second operation, an innovative total disc replacement. The result was miraculous; I have no pain at all most days. I had prayed for a cure and the right doctor, and God provided both.

I handle losses differently. My long-time AA sponsor, Ray, died of lung cancer in January 2011, and a week later I came into my office one morning to find my much-loved German Shepherd Fenya dead on the floor. I didn't react with panic, or rage, or a sense of failure. Instead, I sat beside her on the floor and cried for them both.

After researching and writing this book, I understand much more about pedophilia, and I can feel compassion for those afflicted with it. What a horrible curse to be unable to be sexually aroused except by children. I cannot accept the act itself; I can see no excuse for the destruction of children's lives and souls. I can only guess at the internal torment and self-hatred of active pedophiles who understand, however dimly, the destructiveness of their acts and try desperately to rationalize away or deny the consequences. I can respect pedophiles who remain celibate because they refuse to participate in such violation.

Pedophilia is a dangerous burden. I have looked into the eyes of a man who accepted and wallowed in its pleasures, and saw no soul looking back at me.

Although my insane mood swings are gone, at times I still struggle with depression. It may be partly biological in origin, but there are real-life factors to which depression is a normal response. As my head has cleared, it has become more and more obvious to me that the domestic abuse my family suffered at the hands of my father when I was a child had an enormous influence on me. When a therapist with many years' experience working with victims of domestic abuse read the first draft of this book, she said bluntly, "This is Bill's core issue. He won't truly heal until he resolves it." I'm now dealing with that in therapy, and in my prayers. That's my next job, the next part of my life's work, the next piece of the puzzle. I wouldn't have been able to see that—much less deal with it—if the emotional chaos of the sexual abuse hadn't died down.

God gives us burdens for a purpose. For some reason I have been asked to deal with both sexual abuse and domestic abuse in this life. I don't know why that's so, but I accept it. I have faith that good will come out of it. There's a plan for me, as there is for each of us.

This life can be extremely difficult, and some things are breaking points. We can't handle them alone. At those times I say, "God, You have to do something, You know I can't take it. You have the power to do it." I firmly believe that God will step in. I've had it happen too many times.

I am not a failure. I am not defective. Nothing bad will happen that God will not help me with.

I hardly think of Wiebler any more. When I do, I feel nothing. May God have mercy on his soul.

www.ingramcontent.com/pod-product-compliance
Lightning Source LLC
Chambersburg PA
CBHW020358080526
44584CB00014B/1068